S0-BHT-415

Copyright©1972 Libraries Unlimited, Inc.
All Rights Reserved
Printed in the United States of America

Library of Congress Card Number 70-189256
International Standard Book Number 0-87287-045-6

LIBRARIES UNLIMITED, INC.
P.O. Box 263
Littleton, Colorado 80120

TABLE OF CONTENTS

015.73
P748g
1972

INTRODUCTION

A GUIDE TO POPULAR GOVERNMENT PUBLICATIONS: FOR LIBRARIES AND HOME REFERENCE is an annotated bibliography which lists works of current interest published by the United States government. The wide range of subjects (e.g., civil rights, environmental problems, poverty and social conditions, gardening, cooking, the war in Indochina) is indicative of the scope of the publishing effort of the U.S. Government Printing Office.

Most people do not hesitate to consult government publications for information in such areas as atomic energy or space exploration. But few people realize that cookbooks, coloring books, consumer product information, gardening handbooks, or recreation guides fall into the realm of so-called government documents. The value of this bibliography is that it points out the vast array of books, pamphlets, maps, and other materials which are available at a moderate price from the Government Printing Office or, in some cases, free from departments or agencies.

This guide is arranged alphabetically by subject, with a number assigned to each entry. It should be pointed out, however, that although there are 1,394 numbered entries, series titles are assigned only one number; the total number of entries is closer to 1,900. Works published from 1967 to 1971 are emphasized, but important works published earlier are also included if they are still in print.

Most of the publications listed in this bibliography are available from the Superintendent of Documents, Government Printing Office, Washington, D.C. 20402. For these, Superintendent of Documents classification numbers are provided in the entry to facilitate ordering publications or locating them in libraries. Those which are available from specific departments or agencies contain the ordering information in the entry.

A useful feature of this guide is the inclusion of numerous scope notes directly under certain subject headings. These notes briefly explain the coverage of that heading and give titles of bibliographies or addresses of offices which can provide further information.

A detailed subject index facilitates use of this bibliography. Entries in the text are under broad subjects, while entries in the index are by both broad and specific subjects. For example, publications about bees will be found in the text under "insects" with entries in the index for both "bees" and "insects." For those works which may be popularly known by the title, title entries are also made. It should be noted that the numbers in the index refer to entry numbers in the text. But, since all titles in a series are assigned only one entry number, a page reference is also provided for individual works in a series—e.g., Pharmacists, 960 (p. 128).

The rapidity with which government publications go out of print is a significant factor in bibliographical control. Other guides to popular government publications have been published, notably *A Popular Guide to Government Publications* by W. Philip Leidy (3rd ed. Columbia University Press, 1968). However, because of the flux in what constitutes "popular" government publications, Leidy's work is somewhat out of date. There are, for example, no entries for water pollution and only two for air pollution; the entries for the war in Indochina carry 1965 imprints and are listed under the subject heading "Economic and Political Geography" with access only through the index entry "Vietnam" (which also includes travel guides and works of general economic and social interest). Another guide, *Over 2000 Free Publications: Yours for the Asking* by Frederic J. O'Hara (New American Library), also published in 1968, is now out of print.

This guide, with its emphasis on more recent materials, will supplement both Leidy and O'Hara, pointing out the types of publications which are available in a number of important areas of current interest. Thus, the purpose of this guide is to assist even the smallest library in developing a much-needed selection of popular government documents and to offer readers a handy list of currently available publications at relatively low cost.

June 1972   Sally Wynkoop

HOW TO OBTAIN GOVERNMENT PUBLICATIONS

SOURCES

The primary bibliographic tools for locating current government publications are the *Monthly Catalog of United States Government Publications, Selected United States Government Publications, Price Lists* and publications lists of various departments and agencies.

The *Monthly Catalog*, which is the most complete list, includes all works published by the Government Printing Office. Subscriptions may be placed with the Superintendent of Documents for $7.00 per year.

Selected United States Government Publications is a biweekly annotated listing of the more popular government publications. It is available free to anyone who writes to the Superintendent of Documents and asks to be added to the mailing list. Each issue, in pamphlet form, contains an order blank for those who wish to purchase items listed.

Price Lists are also free bibliographies. They are frequently revised booklets each on a different topic, e.g., Home Economics, History, Occupations. There are 47 different *Price Lists* currently available.

Many governmental departments and agencies publish their own catalogs (e.g., *Publications of the Children's Bureau, Library of Congress Publications in Print*), which can be obtained by writing directly to the agency. These often list items not found in any of the other tools listed above.

PROCEDURE

All publications listed in the *Price Lists, Selected United States Government Publications* and those marked with an asterisk in the *Monthly Catalog* are available for purchase from the Superintendent of Documents.

Payment may be made by one of three methods: check or money order for the exact amount accompanying the order, Superintendent of Documents coupons, or charging against an established deposit account. The infrequent patron of GPO will find that payment by check or money order is most convenient. Superintendent of Documents coupons may be purchased from the Government Printing Office in sets of 20 for $1.00. They are especially useful when ordering inexpensive pamphlet-type publications. A deposit account is established by sending a check or money order for $25.00 or more to the Superintendent of Documents. An account number is then assigned and all purchases may be charged to that number.

In addition to the Government Printing Office in Washington, retail outlets have been opened in many cities. These GPO Bookstores, which are open to the public, carry the most popular items published by GPO and will order those not in stock.

Each member of the Senate and House of Representatives is allotted a number of materials published by the Government Printing Office. These publications are available free, upon request, to the constituents of these legislators.

Many publications listed in departmental catalogs are also free. Note of this is made in the catalogs, and requests should be sent directly to the department or agency.

ADDRESSES

Superintendent of Documents
Government Printing Office
Washington, D.C. 20402

BOOKSTORES

Government Printing Office
710 N. Capitol Street
Washington, D.C. 20402

Department of Commerce, Lobby
14th and Constitution Ave., N.W.
Washington, D.C. 20230

USIA Building, 1st Floor
1776 Pennsylvania Ave., N.W.
Washington, D.C. 20547

The Pentagon
Main Concourse, South End
Washington, D.C. 20310

GPO Bookstore
Room 100, Federal Bldg.
Atlanta, Ga. 30303

GPO Bookstore
Room G25, John F. Kennedy
 Federal Bldg.
Sudbury St.
Boston, Mass. 02203

GPO Bookstore
Room 1463—14th Floor
Everett McKinley Dirksen Bldg.
219 S. Dearborn St.
Chicago, Ill. 60604

GPO Bookstore
Room 1C46
Federal Bldg.—U.S. Courthouse
1100 Commerce St.
Dallas, Tex. 75202

GPO Bookstore
Room 1421
Federal Bldg.—U.S. Courthouse
1961 Stout St.
Denver, Colo. 80202

GPO Bookstore
Room 135, Federal Office Bldg.
601 E. 12th St.
Kansas City, Mo. 64106

GPO Bookstore
Room 1015, Federal Office Bldg.
300 N. Los Angeles St.
Los Angeles, Calif. 90012

GPO Bookstore
Room 110
26 Federal Plaza
New York, N.Y. 10007

GPO Bookstore
Room 1023, Federal Office Bldg.
450 Golden Gate Ave.
San Francisco, Calif. 94102

ACCIDENT PREVENTION

See also—First Aid; Safety Measures; Survival; Water Safety.

1. **Accidents and Children.** 1968. 20p. il. $0.15. HE 21.111:48.
Designed to give some idea of the kind of accidents that children suffer and what time during their lives such accidents are most likely to take place. Points out some of the things parents can do to prevent accidents, especially those that take place in the home.

2. **Fire! Look Out! Burns!** 1969. 12p. il. $0.15. FS 17.210:470.
Helps parents make their children aware of how and why fire can hurt them. It discusses fire safety in the home and procedures for getting out of the home in case there is a fire.

3. **Let's Shed Some Light on Pedestrian Safety, Be Safe, Be Seen.** 1970. 4p. il. $0.05. HE 20.1002:P 34. S/N 1713-0030.
Discusses retro-reflective materials as they are used to make the pedestrian visible to the motorist after dark.

4. **Occupational Safety Aids (Series).**
These safety training aids cover a wide variety of topics for accident prevention on the job.

> **Accident Causes.** 1969. 8p. il. $0.10. L 16.49:162/3.
> **Accident Cost Control.** 1970. 10p. il. $0.15. L 16.49:185/2.
> **Conducting a Job Hazard Analysis.** 1967. 8p. il. $0.10. L 16.49:163.
> **Good Housekeeping for a Successful Safety Program.** 1969. 8p. il. $0.10. L 16.49:166/3.
> **How to Investigate Accidents.** 1967. 8p. il. $0.10. L 16.49:169.
> **Preventing Injury from Falls and Falling Objects.** 1969. 4p. il. $0.10. L 16.49:502.
> **Recording Employee Injuries.** 1967. 8p. il. $0.10. L 16.49:174/2.
> **Safe Lifting.** 1969. 8p. il. $0.15. L 16.49:175/2.
> **Safeguarding Machinery.** 1969. 8p. il. $0.10. L 16.49:316.
> **Safety Inspecting for [Detection, Analysis, Correction].** 1969. 8p. il. $0.10. L 16.49:278.
> **Safety Training Techniques in the Classroom.** 1967. 8p. il. $0.10. L 16.49:180.
> **Supervisory Responsibility for Safety.** 1969. 8p. il. $0.10. L 16.49:181/3.
> **Trips, Slips, and Falls.** 1969. 7p. il. $0.10. L 16.49:183.
> **Who Needs Safety Training?** 1969. 7p. il. $0.10. L 16.49:140.

5. **Outdoor Safety Tips.** 1971. 13p. il. $0.15. A 1.68:887/3. S/N 0100-1298.
Provides information on fire safety, travel and survival tips, and first aid.

6. **Preventing Child Entrapment in Household Refrigerators.** 1964. 8p. il. $0.05. FS 2.2:R 25/3.
Prepared by the Public Health Service, this informative pamphlet discusses 10 easy ways to "childproof" a refrigerator. Includes photographs.

AFRO-AMERICANS

See—Negroes.

AGING

Two agencies are exclusively concerned with the subject of aging. For publications lists write directly to these agencies at the following addresses:

> The Administration on Aging
> Dept. of Health, Education and Welfare
> Washington, D. C. 20201

> The President's Council on Aging
> 3618 S. HEW Building
> Washington, D. C. 20201

7. **Basic Concepts of Aging, A Programmed Manual.** 1970. 122p. il. $1.25. HE 17.308:Ag 4.
Users will be able to acquire a broad knowledge of the older population and the processes, problems, and challenges of aging.

8. **Facts on Aging.** 1970. 11p. il. $0.30. HE 17.302:Ag 4/2.
This reprint from the May 1970 issue of "Aging" contains facts and figures on aging with regard to sex, marital status, color, etc.; population of United States and by state; social security facts; income and income sources; and health care.

9. **Food Guide for Older Folks.** 1970. 16p. il. $0.10. A 1.77:17/9.
Tells about older people's food needs and how to meet them.

10. **Foster Grandparent Program, Providing Greater Role for Older Americans, in Service to Their Community.** 1970. 12p. il. $0.20. HE 17. 302:F 81.

11. **Let's End Isolation.** 1971. 46p. $0.30. HE 17.302:Is 7.
Reports upon a number of special community services, each designed to relieve isolation of older people. The brief description of each type of service is followed by a list of publications and sources of further information.

12. **Mental Disorders of the Aging.** 1964. 20p. il. $0.20. FS 2.2:Ag 4/2.

13. **Senior Centers in the United States, A Directory.** 1970. 260p. $2.00. HE 17.302:Se 5/3.
This directory lists senior centers and other organizations working specifically with older persons. Directories are listed by state and city with pertinent data such as hours of operation, address, etc.

14. **Words on Aging, A Bibliography.** 1970. vi + 190p. $0.75. HE 17.311:Ag 4.
This bibliography of selected annotated references was compiled to assist practitioners, teachers, students, and laymen working in the field of aging.

AGRICULTURE

See also—Farms and Farming; House Construction.

Many of the various agencies within the Department of Agriculture issue publications lists which may be secured upon request from the appropriate agency. Please write to Publication Division, Office of Information, U.S. Dept. of Agriculture, Washington, D. C. 20402.

15. **Agricultural Policies In:**

Africa and West Asia. 1968. 74p. $0.70. A 93.27:49.
Europe and the Soviet Union. 1968. 59p. il. $0.50. A 93.27:46.
Far East and Oceania. 1967. 38p. $0.30. A 93.27:37.
Western Hemisphere. 1967. 55p. $0.40. A 93.27:36.

16. **Color Filmstrips and Slide Sets of the United States Department of Agriculture.** 1970. 13p. $0.20. A 1.38:1107/2.

17. **The Yearbook of Agriculture 1970. Rural America and Agriculture in the Jet Age.** 1970. 408p. il. $3.50.
This is an annual publication covering a variety of topics. The most recent issue covers technological developments, poverty in rural areas, bad housing, etc. On the positive side: spectacular gains in farm production efficiency, food programs for the needy in city and country, conservation achievements, the food processing and marketing revolution, U.S. aid to hungry nations. This is a situation report—with hundreds of photographs—for the concerned citizen, student, consumer.

18. **Fact Book of U.S. Agriculture.** 1970. 82p. $0.45. A 1.38:1063/2.
Intended as a general reference for the nonspecialist. Contains selected basic information on agricultural resources, production, finance, marketing, and rural United States.

19. **Official Grain Standards of the United States.** 1970. 66p. il. $0.50. A 88.6/2:G 761/970.
Presents the official United States standards for wheat, corn, barley, oats, rye, grain sorghums, flaxseed, soybeans and mixed grain.

AIR POLLUTION

See—Pollution, Air.

ALCOHOL AND ALCOHOLISM

20. **Alcohol Abuse and Alcoholism Prevention, Treatment and Rehabilitation.** 1970. 181p. $0.70. Y 4.L 11/2:Al 1/3.
Presents hearings held before the Special Subcommittee on Alcoholism and Narcotics. Describes a comprehensive federal program for the prevention and treatment of alcohol abuse and alcoholism.

21. **Alcohol and Alcoholism.** 1967. 73p. $0.50. FS 2.22: Al 1/5.

22. **Alcoholism and the Federal Employee.** 1970. 88p. $0.45. HE 20. 2702:Al 1.
An overview on the governmental awareness of the problem of alcoholism and occupational health.

23. **Alcoholism, Supervisory Guide.** 1966. 22p. $0.25. D 204.6/2: Al 1.

24. **Effects of Moderate Blood Alcohol Levels on Automobile Passing Behavior.** 1971. 21p. $0.25. HE 20.1809:69-4.

25. **Thinking About Drinking.** 1968. 31p. il. $0.20. FS 2.22:D 83.
Prepared for young people as a basis for discussion of attitudes about drinking. Reflects the latest findings in alcohol research. A true-false quiz, with detailed explanations, is provided on the effects of alcohol on the body.

ASTRONOMY

See—Space Sciences.

AUTOMOBILES

See—Motor Vehicles.

AVIATION

The Federal Aviation Administration's useful, annotated guide to publications is available from the U.S. Dept. of Transportation, Washington, D.C. 20590.

26. **Basic Glider Criteria Handbook.** 1968. 139p. il. $1.00. FAA 5.8/2: G 49/962.

27. **Facts of Flight, Practical Information about Operation of Private Aircraft.** 1963. 41p. il. $0.50. FAA 1.8:F 64/2/963.

28. **Flight Instructor's Handbook.** 1969. $1.25. TD 4.408:In 7/3.
Designed for the information and guidance of pilots preparing to apply for
flight instructor certificates and for use as a reference by certified flight in-
structors.

29. **Forming and Operating a Flying Club.** 1969. 60p. $0.35. TD 4.8:
F 67.
Provides preliminary information on forming and operating a flying club,
including what benefits a club can provide its members, different types of
clubs one can form, methods of obtaining equipment, first steps in organizing,
and actual operation.

30. **Glossary of Aeronautical Terms.** Free. FAA.
Explains the standard language used by air traffic control specialists and
pilots in daily communication. Available from Dept. of Transportation,
Distribution Unit, TAD-484-3, Washington, D.C. 20590.

31. **Key to Aviation Weather Reports and Key to Aviation Weather Forecasts.** 1969. 2p. $0.05. C 30.2:Av 5/969.
A self-aid for pilots for interpreting aviation forecasts and reports. Provides
explanations of the symbols used and includes other information pertinent to
aviation forecasts and weather reports.

32. **Medical Facts for Pilots.** Free. AC-140.
Contains important facts pilots should know prior to flying concerning general health, fatigue, alcohol, vertigo, carbon monoxide, vision, panic and
middle ear discomfort. Available from Civil Aeromedical Institute, Aeronautical Center, Oklahoma City, Oklahoma.

33. **Plane Sense.** 1970. Free—FAA. AC 20-5B.
Acquaints the prospective pilot and airplane owner with some fundamentals
of owning and operating a general aircraft airplane. Available from Dept. of
Transportation, Distribution Unit, TAD-484-3, Washington, D.C. 20590.

34. **Realm of Flight, Presenting Practical Information About Weather In
Relation to Piloting of Private Aircraft.** 1963. 42p. il. $0.75. FAA 1.8:F 64/
963.

35. **Student Pilot Guide.** 1970. $0.20. TL 4.8:P 64/3/970.
Presents, in a "how to go about it" fashion, general procedures for obtaining
a student and private pilot certificate. It answers questions on pilot requirements, training, study material, examinations, flight tests, and lists the
addresses of FAA General Aviation District Offices.

BIRDS

See—Fish and Wildlife.

BOATING

See also—Water Safety.

36. **Boating Regulations In the National Park System.** $0.40. I 29.9:B 63/970.
Contains the regulations that pertain to boating in areas administered by the National Park Service. Among the regulations covered are permits, numbering, motorboat classification, equipment required, rules of the road, commercial operations, accidents, and prohibited operations.

37. **International Code of Signals.** 1969. 156p. il. $4.00. D 203.22: 102.
There are 446 signals for distress and emergency; 327 for casualties and damages; 328 for navigation and hydrography; 177 for maneuvers; 137 pertaining to cargo, crew, fishing, pilot, port, and harbor; 169 for meteorology and weather; 13 for international sanitary regulations; and 503 for medical assistance and advice. Answers questions relative to the meaning of various flag hoists, how to signal for assistance, radio telephone procedures, and to facilitate all types of communications that should be part of the equipment of all seagoing yachts. Of special interest to boat owners.

38. **Merchant Vessels of the United States, 1969 (Including Yachts).** 1970. vii + 1590p. $12.50. TD 5.12/2:969. S/N 5012-0019.
For each vessel listed, the official number, signal and radio call letters, rig information, name of vessel, symbols used for signal and radio call letters, classification, gross and net tonnage, dimensions of the vessel in register length, breadth and depth, year of build, place of build, trade or business in which the vessel is engaged, horsepower, name of owner, and home port are provided.

39. **The Nautical Almanac for the Year 1972.** 1971. 276 + xxxvp. il. $4.00. D 213.11:972. S/N 0854-0038.
Provides, in a convenient form, the data required for the practice of astronomical navigation at sea. Index to Selected Stars 1972 is also included.

40. **Official U.S. Coast Guard Recreational Boating Guide.** 1969. 93p. $0.60. T 47.8/3:B 63/966.
This completely revised boating guide is a must for all boatmen. It includes information on boat numbering; minimum equipment requirements; other equipment you should have; operating responsibilities; aids to navigation; hints on safety afloat; under sail, paddles, and oars; emergency procedures; and U.S. Coast Guard Auxiliary services. The texts of the Motorboat Act of 1940 and the Federal Boating Act of 1958 are also provided, plus a new section on safe loading capacity.

41. **Navigation Dictionary.** 1969. 292p. $3.00. D 203.22:220/969.
Defines terms in this subject area as well as in related disciplines, e.g., astronomy, cartography.

42. **Marine Crewman's Handbook.** 1967. 238p. $2.00. D 101.11:55-501/2
Provides information on such topics as shipboard life, small boat and ship handling, piloting, tows and towing, basic construction of small boats and ships, emergency procedures, watches and drills, primary weather indications, communications, rules of the road, marlinspike seamanship, deck machinery and ground tackle, cargo operations, and maintenance.

BOTANY

See also—Plant Pests and Diseases; Poisonous Plants; Weeds.

43. **Grass Makes Its Own Food for Growth.** 1960. 8p. $0.05. A 1.75:223.
Explains how grass makes its own food for growth, for forage, for good land use, and for soil conservation.

44. **Grass Varieties in the United States.** 1965. 102p. AH No. 170.
Available from Forest Service, U.S. Dept. of Agriculture, Washington, D.C. 20250.

45. **Life Processes of the Living Seed.** 1961. Ybk. Sep. No. 3066.
Available from Forest Service, U.S. Dept. of Agriculture, Washington, D.C. 20250.

46. **Underwater and Floating-Leaved Plants of the United States and Canada.** 1967. 124p. il. $0.65. I 49.66:44.

BUSINESS

See—Industry; Labor; Small Business.

CAMBODIA

See—Indochina War.

CANCER

See also—Medicine; Smoking and Health

47. **Brain Tumors and Spinal Cord Tumors, Hope Through Research.** 1970. 24p. il. $0.25. HE 20.3502:B 73.
Describes varieties of tumors, symptoms, prevention and treatment. Also discusses research and progress being made in this area.

48. **Cancer of the Breast.** 1970. 6p. $0.10. HE 20.10:81.
Discusses the detection, diagnosis, treatment, and causes of breast cancer and research in progress.

49. **Cancer of the Larynx.** 1970. 6p. $0.10. HE 20.10:122.
Discusses the symptoms of early laryngeal cancer, stressing the importance of early diagnosis and treatment. Rehabilitation of the laryngectomee and research under way on cancer of the larynx are also included.

50. **Cancer of the Lung.** $0.10. FS 2.50:115.
Discusses smoking and other factors related to lung cancer as well as diagnosis, treatment and prevention of the disease.

51. **Cancer of the Stomach.** 1970. 8p. il. $0.10. HE 20.10:120.
Contains information on the causes, diagnosis and treatment of cancer and on stomach ulcers and stomach cancer research.

52. **Cancer Questions and Answers About Rates and Risks.** 1966. 21p. il. $0.20. FS 2.2:C 16/13.

53. **Cancer Services, Facilities and Programs in the United States.** 1969. 210p. $1.25. FS 2.2:C 16/5/968.
Lists addresses and chief officers of state health departments, advisory groups, members of the cancer committees of state medical societies, cancer teaching coordinators, addresses of state divisions of the American Cancer Society, and other relevant associations.

54. **The Cancer Story, A Brief Look at Science and Cancer.** 1971. 52p. $0.50. HE 20.3152:C 16/970.
Primarily concerned with cancer research, this book also deals with types of cancer, diagnosis and treatment, research on the causation of cancer, cancer-causing viruses, the cell, hormones, nutrition and immunity to cancer.

55. **Childhood Leukemia—A Pamphlet for Parents.** Free. NIH 71-58.
The information presented is divided into four major parts—normal blood and its proper functioning; symptoms, complications, and treatment of leukemia; some of the problems children face during hospitalization and their reaction to their illness; and family and community relations of the parents of leukemic children. Available from National Institutes of Health, Publications and Reports Branch, Room 2B-03, Bldg. 31, Bethesda, Md. 20014 (cite DHEW Publications Catalog, July 1971).

56. **Danger—The Cancer Quacks.** $0.15. FS 2.22:C 16/31.
Discusses various aspects of cancer quackery—how to recognize a quack, how the quack operates, quacks and the law, what the general public can do.

57. **The National Cancer Institute.** 1970. 17p. il. $0.20. HE 20.3152:N 21.
This booklet describes the role of the Institute in the effort to gain and apply the knowledge that will put an end to the problem of malignant disease. Information is given on the research, training, and cancer control programs.

58.   **National Program for the Conquest of Cancer, Report of the National Panel of Consultants on the Conquest of Cancer.** 1971. 376p. $1.50. 92-1:S.doc. 9. S/N 5271-0233.
Includes information on causes and treatment, cure, and elimination, the prospects of success in the cure of cancer, and measures necessary to facilitate it.

59.   **Portfolio of Photographs, A Science Teaching Aid.** 1967. $1.75. FS 2.22:P 83.
Portfolio of 27 visual aids of cancer research to be used for classroom display.

60.   **Treating Cancer.** 1967. 20p. $0.20. FS 2.22:C 16/20/967.
This booklet answers some of the questions often asked about surgery, radiation, and chemotherapy, and their uses in the treatment of patients with cancer.

CAREERS

See—Occupations.

CHILD AND INFANT CARE

See also—Accident Prevention; Child Care Services; Foods.

For further information on child and infant care write
The Children's Bureau, Dept. of Health, Education and Welfare, Washington, D.C. 20201.

61.   **Breast Feeding Your Baby.** 1970. 21p. il. $0.20. HE 21.111:8.
Contains helpful suggestions and hints on proper hygiene and care before and after the baby is born, when and how to nurse the baby, other foods necessary for the baby, proper diet for the mother, and weaning the baby.

62.   **The Care of Your Children's Teeth.** 1966. 12p. il. $0.15. FS 17.210: 439.
This booklet was written to serve as a guide to parents in obtaining good dental health for their children. It describes baby's teeth and the importance of a good diet; tells how to brush the teeth; and explains why regular dental examinations are important.

63.   **Child Health and Human Development: Progress 1963-1970.** 1970. 60p. il. $1.00. HE 20.3352:C 43/963-70. S/N 1746-0004.
The National Institute of Child Health and Human Development is dedicated to conducting and supporting an integrated program of research into the sequential changes characteristic of individual development from the moment of fertilization through old age and death. This report sets forth some of the more significant findings of scientists working on these research programs within its Institute as well as those who receive support from the NICHD.

64. **A Creative Life for Your Children.** 1962. 41p. il. $0.55. HE 21.114:1.
Presents concepts of child development and rearing which can help children grow into creative, constructive adults. The pamphlet discusses the child as a person, his growing understanding of the world, the widening of his life after he goes to school, and the expanding world of the adolescent.

65. **Evaporated Milk, A Good Formula for Babies, Single Bottle Method.** 1969. 4p. il. $0.05. FS 17.202:B 11.
Tells how to make enough formula for one bottle, for either a young or older baby.

66. **The Health of Children—1970.** 1970. 43p. il. $0.50. HE 20.2202:C 43/70. S/N 1701-0376.
Contains charts and tables providing data received from the National Center for Health Statistics, on the health of children in the United States. Some of the topics discussed are infant mortality rates, the impact of illness, health care, and growth and development.

67. **Home Play and Play Equipment for Young Children.** 1968. 23p. il. $0.15. FS 17.210:238.
A guide for supervising the child at play. It tells about his playing alone and with other children; discusses parties and trips; describes toys, books, story-telling, music, and dancing; and shows how to make practical, healthful, and safe outdoor play equipment for the young child.

68. **Infant Care.** 1963. 108p. il. $0.20. HE 21.110:8.
Based on the experience of many doctors, nurses, child development and other experts, this popular book is designed to help parents understand many phases of infant care, such as feeding, clothing, care, growth and development of the baby.

69. **Issues in Human Development.** 1971. 217p. $1.75. HE 20.3352:H 88. S/N 1746-0002.
Presents a synthesis of information and opinions on the aspects of growth and development in the first two decades of life. Through a broad array of view-points many facets of early child development and problems of adolescence are considered. In addition, the final segments of the book deal with environmental influences on the normative developmental process.

70. **Lazy Eye (Amblyopia) Coloring Book.** 1968. 8p. il. $0.10. FS 2.2:L 45.
This coloring book informs parents and children that it is very important that children's eyes be examined before they are six years old.

71. **Mientras Su Bebe Esta En Camino.** 1963. 28p. $0.20. Children's Bureau Publication 391.
Spanish version of **When Your Baby Is on the Way** (entry 77).

72. **Moving Into Adolescence, Your Child in His Preteens.** 1966. 46p. il. $0.25. HE 21.110:431.
This booklet, addressed to parents of youngsters who are early or pre-adolescent, is devoted to the special kinds of concerns of the adolescent stage of development.

73. **Prenatal Care.** 1962. 92p. il. $0.20. HE 21.110:4.
The first edition of this booklet appeared over a third of a century ago and through many revisions it has continued to serve as an excellent guide for expectant parents. While it helps both mothers and fathers prepare for parenthood, it does not, and is not intended to, take the place of a doctor, but supplements his professional advice and guidance.

74. **Prevention of Iron-deficiency Anemia in Infants and Children of Preschool Age.** 1970. 18p. $0.20. HE 20.2752:An 3.

75. **Research Relating to Children.** 1970. 96p. $1.25. HE 21.112:26.
Includes reports of research, in progress or recently completed, on growth and development; personality and adjustment; educational process, exceptional children; the child in the family; socioeconomic and cultural factors; social services; and health services.

76. **When Teenagers Take Care of Children, A Guide for Baby Sitters.** 1964. 60p. il. $0.25. HE 21.110:409.
This guide seeks to provide information that will be valuable to teenagers in meeting their responsibilities in caring for children.

77. **When Your Baby is on the Way.** 1961. 32p. il. $0.15. HE 21.110: 391.
This short picture leaflet on the care of the mother before the baby is born is designed for quick reading and covers the most important points in good maternity care.

78. **World of Children, Films from the 1970 White House Conference on Children.** 1970. v + 18p. $0.40. Y 3.W 58/3—2:2 W 89. S/N 5247-0010.
The films included in this annotated list are resource materials for parents, teachers, doctors, law enforcement officers, and anyone who works with children. They represent some of the best films available, culled from hundreds, on subjects related to children.

79. **Your Baby's First Year.** 1962. 32p. il. $0.15. HE 21.110:400.
Discusses briefly the baby's needs—such as foods, vitamins, sleep, love, play, and clothes; his growth and development; signs of sickness; and other points of similar interest.

80. **Your Child from 1 to 3.** 1964. 24p. il. $0.20. HE 21.110:413.
This short pamphlet covers the most important points parents need to consider as their child leaves babyhood and enters into childhood.

81. **Your Child from 6 to 12.** 1966. 98p. il. $0.55. HE 21.110:324.
It discusses what 6- to 12-year olds are like, what play means in the life of a child, everyday problems, pursuits and hobbies, children and money, keeping your child healthy, and many other topics of interest to parents of children in this age group.

82. **Your Gifted Child.** 1958. 39p. il. $0.25. HE 21.110:371.
The pamphlet answers many of the questions most often asked about the gifted child, and includes suggestions for understanding and helping these children.

83. **Your Premature Baby.** 1969. 13p. il. $0.15. FS 17.215:40.
The purpose of this pamphlet is to let the parents of a premature baby know what is happening to their baby at the hospital until the time when he is ready to be brought home. It discusses the special care needed for a premature baby, and answers many of the questions asked by the parents of premature babies.

CHILD CARE SERVICES

84. **Child Care: Data and Materials.** 1971. 156p. $0.65. Y 4.F 49:C 43/2.
Contains important current statistics, reports, statutory language and regulations on child care.

85. **Child Care Services Provided by Hospitals.** 1970. 34p. il. $0.25.
L 13.3:295.

86. **Day Care Facts.** 1970.
Explains growing need for day care, current and proposed legislation, and innovative programs. Available from Women's Bureau, U.S. Dept. of Labor, Washington, D.C.

87. **Day Care for Other People's Children in Your Home.** 1964. 17p. $0.15. Children's Bureau Publication 412.
Tells women who do not have access to the help of social agencies how to give the best care possible to the boys and girls they take into their homes.

88. **Day Care for Your Child in a Family Home.** 1968. 14p. $0.15. FS 17.210:411.
This pamphlet will assist the mother in knowing what care she should seek for her child while she is away from him.

89. **Day Care Services.** 1968. 44p. $0.25. HE 21.110:420.
Explains why day care services for children are needed; what these services are; where, when, and how they should be developed; and what supplementary and supportive services should be associated with them.

90. **Day Care Services: Industry's Involvement.** 1971. 33p. $0.25. L 13.3:296.
Discusses the need for services for children of working mothers and reports on the past and present contributions of industry.

91. **Good References on Day Care.** 1968. 22p. Children's Bureau, FPEC-1.
Lists books and journal articles on day care center guides and standards, health and nutrition, parental involvement, administration and other aspects of day care center supervision. Single copy free from Children's Bureau, U.S. Dept. of Health, Education and Welfare, Washington, D.C. 20201.

92. **What is Good Day Care?** 1968. 11p. $0.15. FS 17.215:53.

93. **Who Will Take Care of Your Child When You Are in Training or on the Job?** 1969. 12p. il. $0.15. FS 17.210:467.

CHILDREN'S LITERATURE

94. **Children and Poetry, A Selective, Annotated Bibliography.** 1969. 67p. il. $0.75. LC 1.12/2:P 75.
Includes rhyme and more serious poetry, old and new works, works in English and translations. Annotations often include selections from verses in the particular book.

95. **Children's Books, 1970.** 1971. 16p. $0.15. LC 2.11:970. S/N 3001-0039.
Lists under subject headings current books for preschool through junior high school age. Annotated information for each entry includes: author, title, publisher, number of pages, price, grade level, and a brief synopsis of the work.

96. **Serving Those Who Serve Children: A National Reference Library of Children's Books.** 1966. 16p. $0.20. LC 1.17/A:C 437.
Reprint from *The Quarterly Journal of the Library of Congress,* v. 22, October 1965.

97. **Stories Worth Knowing.** 190p. il. $0.70. D 1.10:C 003.

CIVIL DEFENSE

98. **Civil Defense: 1960-67. A Bibliographic Survey on Civil Defense Prepared by the Army Library.** 1967. Free. D.A. Pam. 500-3.
This pamphlet provides references to sources of information and data on civil defense. The bibliography is valuable in learning about and assessing the progress of civil defense in the United States and other countries. Available from state or local office of Civil Defense.

99. **Community Development and Civil Defense.** 1967. 36p. Free. TR-46.
A report illustrating types of newly constructed buildings in various communities, including low rent housing projects, schools, banks, etc., that have included fallout protection. Information on community shelter planning, basic concepts of protection, the professional development program, shielding techniques in design and construction and the professional advisory services are also included. Available from state or local office of Civil Defense.

100. **Fallout Shelters.** 1969. 8p. Free. TR-39.
Technical requirements for fallout shelters with information on slanting techniques, illustrations of Honor Award architecture and other technical materials. Available from state or local office of Civil Defense.

101. **Family Food Stockpile for Survival.** 1966. 16p. $0.10. A 1.77:77/4.
Gives recommendations for two-week food supply, meal planning, cooking equipment and purifying water in family fallout shelters.

102. **Farm Fallout Shelter and Storage, Farm Building Plan No. 5934.**
1962. 2p. il. $0.05. A 1.38:910.

103. **In Time of Emergency: A Citizen's Handbook on Nuclear Attack and Natural Disasters.** 1968. 96p. Free. H-14.
The nuclear attack section contains a checklist of emergency actions; explains the hazards of attack; and gives basic guidance on warning, public and private fallout shelters, improvising fallout protection, shelter supplies and how to manage them, sanitation, fire hazards, and care of the sick and injured. The natural disaster section offers general advice applicable to various types of catastrophes, plus specific guidance on floods and hurricanes, tornadoes, winter storms, and earthquakes. Available from state or local office of Civil Defense.

CIVIL DISORDERS

See also—Political and Social Dissent.

This section on Civil Disorders concerns the violent manifestations of dissent as opposed to the philosophical aspects and their adherents, which are included under the heading Political and Social Dissent.

104. **Bibliography on the Urban Crisis.** 1969. 452p. $3.75. HE 20.2417: Ur 1.
Provides a comprehensive listing of the literature, both academic and popular, on the causes, effects, and responses to urban disorders.

105. **Extent of Subversion in Campus Disorders.**
Presents hearings held before the Subcommittee to Investigate the Administration of the Internal Security Act and other Internal Security Laws of the Senate Committee on the Judiciary, 91st Cong., 1st sess., concerning the

extent of subversion in campus disorders.

Part 1, Testimony of Ernesto E. Blanco, June 19, 1969. 1969. 88p. il. $0.40. Y 4.J 89/2:C 15/pt.1.

Part 2, Testimony of Max Phillip Friedman, August 12, 1969. 1969. p. 89-190. $0.45. Y 4.J 89/2:C 15/pt.2.

Part 3, Testimony of John F. McCormick and William E. Grogan, June 26, 1969. 1969. p. 191-489. il. $1.25. Y 4.J 89/2: C 15/pt. 3.

106. National Commission on the Causes and Prevention of Violence, Staff Reports:

Violence in America, Historical and Comparative Perspectives, vol. 1. 1969. 301p. il. $1.25. Pr 36.8:V 81/H 62/v.1.

Violence in America, Historical and Comparative Perspectives, vol. 2. 1969. p. 303-644. il. $1.50. Pr 36.8:V 81/H 62/v.2.

The Politics of Protest, Violent Aspects of Protest and Confrontation. 1969. 276p. il. $1.25. Pr 36.8:V 81/P 94.

Rights in Concord, the Response to the Counterinaugural Protest Activities in Washington, D.C., Jan. 18-20, 1969. 1969. 141p. il. $1.00. Pr 36.8:V 81/R 44.

Shoot-out in Cleveland, Black Militants and the Police, July 23, 1968. 1969. 100p. il. $0.75. Pr 36.8:V 81/C 59.

Shut it Down, A College in Crisis, San Francisco State College, Oct. 1968-Apr. 1969. 1969. 172p. $1.00. Pr 36.8:V 81/Sa 5f.

Firearms and Violence in American Life. 1969. 268p. il. $1.25. Pr 36.8:V 81/F 51.

Assassination and Political Violence. 1969. 580p. il. $2.50. Pr 36.8:V 81/As 7.

Violence and the Media. 1969. 614p. $2.50. Pr 36.8:V 81/M 38.

Law and Order Reconsidered. 1969. 606p. il. $2.50. Pr 36.8:V 81/L 41.

To Establish Justice, to Insure Domestic Tranquility, Final Report of the National Commission on the Causes and Prevention of Violence. 1969. 338p. $1.50. Pr 36.8:V 81/J 98/2.

107. Youth and Violence. 1970. iv + 91p. $0.55. HE 17.802:Y 8.
This publication is a relatively short, but comprehensive, study of the relationship of young people to violence.

CIVIL RIGHTS

Although the primary source of further information is the Commission on Civil Rights, Washington, D.C. 20425, many other departments and agencies have offices in charge of civil rights,

e.g., Federal Aviation Administration, the Dept. of Health, Education and Welfare and the Civil Rights Division of the Justice Dept.
These offices may be contacted for related information.

108. **A Summary of a Report of the United States Commission on Civil
Rights, For All the People . . . By All the People.** 1969. 28p. il. $0.25.
CR 1.10:18.
This report surveys minority group employment in state and local govern-
ments of seven representative metropolitan areas throughout the country. In-
cludes recommendations for corrective action.

109. **Civil Rights Acts of 1957, 1960, 1964, 1968, Voting Rights Act of
1965 and Voting Rights Act Amendments of 1970.** 1970. 79p. $0.30.
Y 4.J 89/1:C 49/8/970.
Presents a compilation of the Civil Rights Acts since 1957 including the
Voting Rights Act of 1965, and Voting Rights Act Amendments of 1970.

110. **Civil Rights Directory.** 1970. 195p. $0.75. CHP No. 15. CR 1.10:15.
Section A: Federal officials who are responsible for implementation of civil
rights practices; Section B: Federal officials with liaison responsibility for
programs of special interest to Spanish-speaking people; Section C: National
private organizations with civil rights programs; Section D: Official State
agencies with civil rights responsibilities; Section E: Official County and
Municipal agencies with civil rights responsibilities.

111. **For Free Men in a Free World, A Survey of Human Rights in the
United States.** 1969. 250p. $1.25. S 1.2:F 87/2.
Each of the 30 Articles of the Universal Declaration of Human Rights is
quoted. Most of the sections of this publication begin with a summary of the
American tradition, and describe the principal developments during the two
decades since the adoption of the Universal Declaration.

112. **Racism in America.** 1970. 48p. $0.50. CHP No. 20. CR 1.10:20.
Prepared for the Commission on Civil Rights by Anthony Downs, a major
consultant to the Kerner Commission. Includes statements by Commissioners
of the Commission.

113. **"What Students Perceive." Report of the U.S. Commission on Civil
Rights.** 1970. 80p. il. $0.75. CR 1.10:24. S/N 0500-0054.
This report of the U.S. Commission on Civil Rights, contains the results of
interviews of students from 17 cities. The selection process was based on
criteria that would assure adequate racial and ethnic representation, geographical distribution, and full representation of various views and attitudes.
Questions asked dealt with such topics as: education overviews, administration, teachers, curriculum, and perception of others.

114. Who Will Listen If You Have a Civil Rights Complaint? 1969. 16p. $0.20. CR 1.10:13.
This pamphlet explains how to make a formal complaint about the occurrence of racial discrimination and where to send it.

CLIMATOLOGY AND WEATHER

115. The Climate of Cities: A Survey of Recent Literature. 1970. 48p. il. $0.55. HE 20.1309:59.
The climate of a city differs from that of the rural areas surrounding it, and an increasing amount of scientific research is devoted to comparative studies of urban and rural climates. This report is a survey of the literature on city climatology, with emphasis on that written since 1962. Those meteorological aspects of urban climate that have been most frequently investigated are discussed herein; they are temperature, humidity, visibility, radiation, wind, and precipitation.

116. Climates of the World. 1969. 28p. il. $0.35. C 52.2:C 61/3.
Discusses the principal features of climates of all continents, with maps illustrating temperatures and precipitation.

117. Climatic Atlas of the United States. 1968. 80p. $4.25. C 52.2:C 61/2.
Depicts the climate of the United States in terms of the distribution and variation of constituent climatic elements.

118. Clouds. 1969. 8p. $0.25. C 52:2:C 62.
Presents important cloud forms in a full-color identification chart, with brief descriptions of the type, time of year, and the cloud type's meteorological symbol. This publication also describes how cloud types foretell coming weather, and how they are analyzed by weather forecasters.

119. Monthly Weather Review. Subscription price, $7.50/yr; $0.65/copy. C 30.14:vols.
Contains articles describing original research results in meteorology and related sciences, with particular emphasis on numerical weather prediction, satellite meteorology, severe storms, general circulation of the atmosphere's stratospheric meteorology, atmospheric turbulence and diffusion, air pollution, physical meteorology and air-sea interactions. In each issue is an article describing the Northern Hemisphere weather and circulation for the third month preceding the month of issue.

120. Radar Sees the Weather. Free. FAA.
Explains the principles under which radar works and how it is used in observing and forecasting aviation weather. Available from Dept. of Transportation, Distribution Unit, TAD-484-3, Washington, D.C. 20590.

121. **Selective Guide to Climatic Data Sources.** 1969. 90p. il. $1.00.
C 30.66/2:4.11/2.
Provides potential users of climatological data with a list including the availability of such data in published and unpublished form.

122. **Weather in Motion.** 1970. 7p. il. $0.50. NAS 1.19:79. S/N 3300-0310.
The weather over about half the earth changes before the observer's eyes as he moves the three-dimensional cover display (called an Xograph) of this booklet. A spectacular spiral cloud band moves off the northwest coast of Africa in a counterclockwise rotation indicating a severe cyclonic disturbance. The display card is developed from 9 individual pictures taken an hour apart by the ATS-3 NASA satellite. The booklet that accompanies the Xograph describes the ATS satellite and explains its research program for meteorologists.

CLIMATOLOGY AND WEATHER—STORMS

123. **Floods and Flood Warnings.** 1967. 6p. $0.10. C 52:2:F 65.
Discusses floods, flood warnings, and flash flood warnings. Included in the publication is a chart giving safety rules to follow before, during and after a flood.

124. **The Greatest Storm on Earth, Hurricane.** 1969. 38p. il. $0.65.
C 52.2:H 94/969.

125. **Lightning.** 1971. 6p. il. $0.15. C 55.102:L 62.

126. **Thunderstorms.** 1971. 6p. il. $0.20. C 55.2:T 42.
Describes what thunderstorms are, how they form and how they die. An explanation of the unique, destructive offspring of thunderstorms—lightning, thunder, hail and tornadoes—and life-saving safety rules to follow during these phenomena are provided.

127. **Tornado.** 1971. 16p. il. $0.30. C 55.102:T 63/2.
Describes what tornadoes are, when and where they occur, how they produce their destructive effects, what they look like, and what to do when threatened by tornadoes.

128. **Weather Bureau Spotter's Guide for Identifying and Reporting Severe Local Storms.** 1971. 15p. il. $0.30. C 55.108:St 7.
Presents descriptions of thunderstorms and certain associated cloud systems, lightning, hail, heavy rain, and tornadoes. Included are photographs of infant and mature tornadoes, an 8-photo life cycle of a tornado, and photographs of such tornado-like phenomena as waterspouts, virga, thundershowers, and some frontal clouds.

129. **Winter Storms.** 1967. 8p. il. $0.15. C 52.2:St 7.
Describes the phenomenon of winter storms and the threat to life and property posed by these large systems. Safety rules to follow for home, auto, blizzard survival, and livestock protection are also included.

COMMUNISM

For publications dealing with specific communist countries, e.g., Communist China and the Soviet Union, *see International Relations* and *Travel—Handbooks and Guides.*

130. **Communism in Action, Documented Study and Analysis of Communism in Operation in Soviet Union.** 1946. 141p. $0.45. 79-2:H.doc. 754.

131. **Ideas in Conflict, Liberty and Communism.** 1967. 147p. $0.75. D 2.14:Gen-27.

132. **Problems of Communism.** (Bimonthly.) Subscription price, $3.00/yr.; $0.50/copy. IA 1.8:vols.
Provides analyses and significant background information on various aspects of world communism today.

133. **World Communism, 1967-1969: Soviet Efforts to Reestablish Control.** 1970. xiv + 319p. il. $1.25. Y 4.J 89/2:C 73/50. S/N 5270-0924.
This study is a serious, scholarly historical analysis of three years of world communism. It shows the changes that have occurred within the movement; indicates how the Soviets have tried to cope with these changes; and points out certain elements of weakness and forces of strength and cohesion in the Soviet effort to maintain—or, in the alternative view, to reestablish—its world communist hegemony.

134. **World Communist Movement, Selective Chronology 1818—1957:** Y 4.Un 1/2:C 73/114 (vol.).

> **Vol. 1. 1818—1945.** 1960. 232p. $0.65.
> **Vol. 2. 1946—50.** 1963. p. 233-486. $0.75.
> **Vol. 3. 1951—53.** 1964. p. 487-776.
> **Vol. 4. 1954—55.** 1965. p. 777-1001. $0.60.

135. **World Strength of the Communist Party Organizations.** 1971. 248p. $1.75. S 1.111:971.
This 23rd annual world survey of communist parties includes a brief analysis of each party in its domestic environment, and information on party membership and voting and parliamentary strength.

COMPUTERS

136. **ADP Glossary.** 1971. 106p. $1.25. D 201.2:Au 8. S/N 0840-0051.
This glossary, an aid to defining and describing words and terms used in the field of automatic data processing, provides a convenient source for arriving at some common understanding of terminology used by those who are conversant in the use of computers, their applications, and their related products and operations.

137. **Computer Literature Bibliography:**

        1946–63. 464p. $3.75. C 13.10:266.
        1964–67. 381p. $5.00. C 13.10:309.

A very comprehensive bibliography which will be useful to those people making a retrospective search of the literature.

138. **Computer Program for Calculating Capital and Operating Costs.** 1969. 110p. $1.00. I 28.27:8426.

139. **Computers in Higher Education, Report of the President's Science Advisory Committee.** 1967. 79p. il. $0.35. Pr 35.8:Sci 2/C 73.

140. **Economy in Government: Automatic Data Processing Equipment, Report of the Subcommittee of Priorities and Economy in Government of the Joint Economic Committee, Together with Supplemental Views.** 1971. 18p. $0.15. Y 4.Ec 7:Ec 7/26.

Discusses the phenomenal growth in the use of automatic data processing equipment and the adequacy of existing policies for the efficient procurement and management of these resources.

141. **Inventory of Automatic Data Processing Equipment in the United States Government, Fiscal Year:**

        1968. 241p. il. $1.75. GS 2.15:968.
        1969. 263p. il. $2.00. GS 2.15:969
        1970. 394p. il. $2.75. GS 2.15:970

CONSERVATION

See—Ecology and the Environment.

CONSUMER INFORMATION

See also—Family Finances and Budgeting; Foods; Home Economics.

Publications of interest to consumers are listed in the following four subheadings: Credit Information, Education, Product Information, and Rights. For more information write directly to Consumer Product Information, General Services Administration, Washington, D.C. 20407; or to the Office of Consumer Affairs, New Executive Office Building, Washington, D.C. 20506. The Consumer Information Price List No. 86 is available free from the Superintendent of Documents, Washington, D.C. 20402.

CONSUMER INFORMATION—CREDIT INFORMATION

142. **Be Wise, Consumer's Quick Credit Guide.** 1964. 2p. il. $0.05. A 1.11/3:C 86. **—Spanish Edition.** 1965. 2p. il. $0.05. A 1.11/3:C 86/Span.

This folder describes in capsule form such topics as typical credit charges, buying on installment and borrowing money. A working example of how to figure dollar cost of credit is also given. This publication is also available in Spanish.

143. **Credit, Master or Servant, Air Force Pamphlet 190-1-22.** 1966. 52p. il. $0.25. D 2.14:PA-10.
Contains information about sellers and lenders, credit, finance charges and rates, and contracts. Also provides practical advice on debts, saving money, etc. A quick annual rate guide and a table for computing approximate annual percentage rate for monthly payment plans are also included.

144. **Money Worries? A Credit Union Can Help.** 1969. 10p. il. $0.10. HE 3.302:M 74/969.
Tells what a Federal Credit Union is and how it is run; what it can do for you and for others; and how you may lead the way in getting Federal Credit Union services.

145. **What You Should Know About Truth in Lending.** 1970. 6p. Free. 7700-011.
Tips to help the consumer understand and use credit; summary of the provisions of the Truth in Lending Law. Available from Consumer Product Information, Washington, D.C. 20407.

CONSUMER INFORMATION—EDUCATION

146. **Consumer Education, Bibliography.** 1969. 170p. $0.65. Pr 36.8:C 76/B 47.
A listing of over 2,000 books, booklets, pamphlets, films and filmstrips in the field of consumer interests and education.

147. **Consumer Education, What It is and What It is Not.** 1969. 8p. $0.10. PR 36.8:C 76/C 76/3.

148. **Suggested Guidelines for Consumer Education Grades K—12.** 1970. vii + 58p. il. $0.65. Pr 36.8:C 76/Ed 8.

CONSUMER INFORMATION—PRODUCT INFORMATION

149. **Advice on the Purchase and Sale of a Home and Lease of Dwellings by Military Personnel.** 1969. 167p. il. $0.70. D 302.9:11/1.
Explains the nature and extent of assistance and services you may require such as: types of listings; financing; purchase of homes under construction; new homes and home sites; tax considerations; forms; closing (also called settlement); and assistance available. Contains advice on leasing; comments on sample lease; and information on applications for leases. A number of sample forms are also given.

150. **Be a Good Shopper.** 1965. 8p. il. $0.05. A 43.2:Sh 7.
This booklet briefly tells you how to plan first before you start your shopping trip, and how to compare price and quality; discusses the various kinds of sales; and describes the protective agencies and organizations that help us get what we pay for.

151. **Brakes: A Comparison of Braking Performance for 1971 Passenger Cars.** 1970. 31p. $0.40. 5003-0025.
Available from Consumer Product Information, Washington, D.C. 20407.

152. **Cost of Operating an Automobile.** 1970. 11p. Free. 7700-004.
Costs of maintenance, accessories, parts, tires, gas, oil, insurance, etc., for a moderately priced sedan. Available from Consumer Product Information, Washington, D.C. 20407.

153. **Fibers and Fabrics.** 1970. iv + 28p. il. $0.65. C 13.53:1.

154. **Hearing Aids.** 1970. iv + 24p. il. $0.35. C 13.44:117. S/N 0303-0751.
Contains information, useful to the hard of hearing, on several topics relating to hearing and hearing aids, and gives tips on general properties of hearing aids, how to judge a hearing aid, and guidance in choosing and care of a hearing aid.

155. **Performance Data for New 1971 Passenger Cars and Motorcycles.** 1970. 256p. $2.00. 5003-0024.
Includes acceleration performance data plus all information contained in the separate publications: **Brakes: A Comparison of Braking Performance for 1971 Passenger Cars** and **Tires: A Comparison of Tire Reserve Load for 1971 Passenger Cars.** Available from Consumer Product Information, Washington, D.C. 20407.

156. **Safe Toys for Your Child—How to Select Them—How to Use Them Safely.** 1971. 8p. $0.20. Children's Bureau Publication 473.
Tells parents how to select safe toys for their child. Includes information on the care of their child's toys and on safety legislation.

157. **Selecting Automobile Safety Restraints for Small Children.** 1970. 6p. il. $0.10. HE 20.1802:Au 8.
The purpose of this pamphlet is to point out the risks involved in allowing children to ride in cars without proper restraints, and to help parents select good protective devices for their small children.

158. **Speak Up! When You Buy a Car.** 1970. 4p. il. $0.10. Pr 36.8:C 76/ Sp 3.

159. **Tires: Their Selection and Care.** 1970. 28p. $0.65. 0303-0681.
Available from Consumer Product Information, Washington, D.C. 20407.

160. **Washing Machines, Selection and Use.** 1964. 22p. il. $0.15. A 1.77:32/4.

CONSUMER INFORMATION—RIGHTS

161. **Health Education vs. Medical Quackery.** 1966. 6p. $0.10. FS 13.22: 13.
Discusses medical quackery and presents examples of some of the most common types of medical frauds and swindles to be on the lookout for.

162. **Informed Consent.** 1968. 4p. $0.05. FS 13.128/a:In 3.
Discussion of FDA's requirement that a physician obtain the *informed* consent of his patient before he uses an investigational drug.

163. **Landlord-Tenant Relationships, A Selected Bibliography.** 1971. 53p. $0.60. HH 1.23:L 23.
An annotated bibliography of selected materials of special interest to landlords and tenants.

164. **Mail Fraud Laws.** 1971. 32p. Free. 7700-048.
Common mail fraud situations; how the consumer may protect himself. Procedure for reporting fraud to the Postal Service. Available from Consumer Product Information, Washington, D.C. 20407.

165. **Pitfalls to Watch for in Mail Order Insurance Policies.** 1969. 5p. $0.10. FT 1.3/2:1.

166. **Summary of Information for Shippers of Household Goods.** 1970. 17p. Free. 7700-023.
Selecting a mover, making a physical inventory record, estimates and actual costs, preparing articles for shipment, mover's liability for loss or damage, and filing claims. Available from Consumer Product Information, Washington, D.C. 20407.

167. **Householder's Guide to Accurate Weights.** 1971. 6p. Free. 7700-045.
Useful addition to **Summary of Information for Shippers of Household Goods.** Guidelines for determining the accuracy of the mover's weight estimate of goods to be shipped. Available from Consumer Product Information, Washington, D.C. 20407.

168. **Unordered Merchandise, Shipper's Obligations and Consumer's Rights.** 1969. 3p. $0.10. FT 1.3/2:2.
Advises the consumer receiving unordered merchandise that he has no obligation either to return the merchandise or to pay for it under the Federal Trade Act.

CRIME AND CRIME PREVENTION

169. **Crime in America.** Presents hearings held before the House Select Committee on Crime, 91st Cong., 2nd sess., to conduct studies and investigations of crime in the United States.

Youth Gang Warfare, July 16-17, 1970, Philadelphia, Pa. 1970. iv + 270p. il. $1.00. Y 4.C 86/3:C 86/12. S/N 5270-0942.

The Heroin Paraphernalia Trade, October 5-6, 1970, Washington, D.C. 1970. iv + 314p. il. $1.25. Y 4.C 86/3:C 86/14. S/N 5270-0955.

170. **Crime in the United States, Uniform Crime Reports 1970.** 1971. 208p. il. $1.75. J 1.14/7:970.
A nationwide view of crime based on police statistics. The first section is for those interested in the general crime picture for the United States. The volume trend and rate of crime related to current populations are discussed in context with the crime index offenses. Subsequent sections contain technical data of interest to police, social scientists, and other students.

171. **The Criminal Offender—What Should be Done? The Report of the President's Task Force on Prisoner Rehabilitation.** 1970. 24p. $0.25. Pr 37.8: P 93/R 29.

172. **Field Surveys, A Report of a Research Study Submitted to the President's Commission on Law Enforcement and Administration of Justice: No. 3, Studies in Crime and Law Enforcement in Major Metropolitan Areas.** 1967. 2v. il. $3.50/set. Pr 36.8:L 41/C 86/4 v. 1,2.

173. **Firearms Identification for Law Enforcement Officers.** 1970. 32p. il. $0.25. T 22.19/2:F 51/2/970.

174. **The Functions of the Police in Modern Society.** 1970. v + 122p. $0.55. HE 20.2420/2P 75.
Analyzes the basic character of police work as related to the courts and community. Also considers the future of police work such as upgrading police practice, streamlining police organization, and improving the recruitment and training of police.

175. **The Nature, Impact and Prosecution of White-Collar Crime.** 1970. 77p. $0.40. J 1.36/2:70-1.
Seeks to define white-collar crime, to determine the common elements of its operative structure, and to examine how it is detected, investigated, and prosecuted. Its aim is to find measures which will both deter such crimes and provide an extra measure of relief for victims.

176. **1970 National Jail Census, A Report on the Nation's Local Jails and Type of Inmates.** 1971. vii + 19p. $0.35. J 1.37/2:1. S/N 2700-0061.
Discusses the state of the nation's jails and their inmates; the number of jails; the number and type of inmates; the number of jail employees; operating costs, and other pertinent data.

177. **Questions and Answers, Gun Control Act of 1968.** 1971. 32p. $0.20. T 22.2:G 95/971. S/N 4804-0393.
Gives answers to questions most frequently asked about the Gun Control Act of 1968.

178. **Rehabilitative Planning Services for the Criminal Defense.** 1970. xiv + 210p. il. $1.00. J 1.36:70-3. S/N 2700-0060.
Presents an evaluation of the Offender Rehabilitation Project, a program which is designed to aid defense attorneys working with indigent defendants in dealing with social and rehabilitative processes.

179. **The Role of Federal Agencies in the Crime and Delinquency Field, A Compilation of Federal Support Programs.** 1970. 156p. $1.25. HE 20. 2402:C 86.

180. **Who Will Wear the Badge?** 1971. 33p. il. $0.30. CR 1.10:25. S/N 0500-0062.
Examines the barriers to minority recruitment by police and fire departments throughout the United States, and explores a variety of local efforts to surmount these barriers.

CUSTOMS

See—Travel.

DATA PROCESSING

See—Computers.

DAY CARE

See—Child Care Services.

DENTAL HEALTH

See—Flouridation.

THE DRAFT

See—U.S. Selective Service System.

DRUGS

181. **Aspirin (FDA Fact Sheet).** 1970. 2p. Free. 7700-022.
Composition, quality controls, and safe use. Available from Consumer Product Information, Washington, D.C. 20407.

182. **Before Your Kid Tries Drugs.** 1969. 12p. il. $0.25. FS 2.22:D 84/10.
This pamphlet presents factual information for parents on drug abuse.

183. **Caffeine (FDA Fact Sheet).** 1970. 1p. Free. 7700-014.
What it is, amounts in common beverages and drugs, and use as a stimulant. Available from Consumer Product Information, Washington, D.C. 20407.

184. **Directory of Narcotic Addiction Treatment Agencies in the United States, 1968–1969.** 1970. 162p. $1.25. HE 20.2402:N 16/3/968-69.
This directory is limited to programs focused specifically on the treatment of narcotic addiction. It is a report of a study that has examined treatment in depth, and contains information on approximately 250 treatment programs.

185. **Drug Abuse Prevention, A Community Program Guide.** 1970. 24p. il. $0.20. J 24.8:D 84/2.
This brochure is designed to show how to plan a coordinated education program from the planning stage to the actual presentation of the program.

186. **Drug-Taking in Youth, An Overview of Social, Psychological, and Educational Aspects.** 1971. vi + 48p. $0.40. J 24.2:Y 8. S/N 2704-0014.
Discusses the social and psychological aspects of youthful drug-taking; the extent of use; places and social categories where drug users are concentrated; describes the particular setting in which young people find themselves today and the youthful modes in which drugs are important. Relates facts known about the psychology of drug use, motivation and vulnerable personality types. Discusses educational aspects and approaches for effective long-range programs for the development of new attitudes toward drug use in youth.

187. **Drug Treatment in Psychiatry.** 1970. 35p. $0.40. VA 1.22:11-2.

188. **First Facts About Drugs.** 1970. 9p. $0.15. HE 20.4015:21. S/N 1712-0112.
Contains basic facts everyone should know about drugs, giving some important do's and don'ts.

189. **Katy's Coloring Book About Drugs and Health.** 1970. 18p. il. $0.35. J 24.2:K 15. S/N 2704-0011.
This coloring book is intended to provide a basis for discussion of the place of medicine and drugs in children's lives. Fourteen pages of illustrations to be colored are followed by the text which the parent or teacher can use in discussing the topic of each illustration.

190. **LSD, Some Questions and Answers.** 1969. 8p. il. $0.05. FS 2.22:L 99/969.
General factual information about the drug, its psychological and physical effects and its medical uses.

191. **LSD, The False Illusion:**
> **Pt. 1.** 1967. 10p. il. $0.15. FS 13.128/a:L 959.
> Discusses the value and philosophy of the "hippie set," factors underlying the use of LSD, and effects of the drug.
> **Pt. 2.** 1967. 8p. il. $0.10. FS 13.128/a:L 959/pt. 2.
> Tells the LSD story through the experience of the Food and Drug Administration's criminal investigators.

192. **LSD–25: A Factual Account, Layman's Guide to the Pharmacology, Physiology, Psychology and Sociology of LSD.** 1970. 44p. il. $0.30. J 24. 8:L 99/rep.
Factual information on the problems of LSD.

193. **Marihuana and Health, A Report to the Congress from the Secretary, Department of Health, Education, and Welfare, January 31, 1971.** 1971. 176p. $1.50. HE 20.2402:M 33/3. S/N 1740-0314.
Discusses the current status of our knowledge of the health consequences of marihuana use, including the effects of the drug on the individual's physical and psychological health and the effects of use on the society.

194. **Marihuana Fables and Facts.** 1970. 4p. il. $0.05. HE 20.2402:M 33.
Discusses some of the facts and fables surrounding the use of marihuana.

195. **Marihuana, Some Questions and Answers.** 1968. 10p. il. $0.05. FS 2.22:M 33.
General factual information about the drug, its psychological and physical effects and its medical uses.

196. **Narcotics, Some Questions and Answers.** 1968. 8p. il. $0.05. FS 2.22:N 16/2.

197. **Sedatives–Some Questions and Answers.** 1970. 8p. Free. 7700-041.
General factual information about these drugs, their psychological and physical effects, legal controls, prevention and treatment, and research being done. Available from Consumer Product Information, Washington, D.C. 20407.

198. **Selected Drug Education Curricula.**
Selected curricula for drug education and the prevention of drug abuse developed by state and local school systems have been reprinted by the National Clearinghouse for Drug Abuse Information as resources to assist schools in initiating or improving programs. Recently issued publications are:

> **Drug Abuse Education, 1968–Grades 6, 9, 12, Baltimore County Board of Education, Towson, Maryland.** 1970. 108p. il. $1.00. PrEx 13.8:Ed 8.
> **Narcotic and Drug Education–Grades K–12, Flagstaff Public Schools, Flagstaff, Arizona.** 1970. 59p. il. $0.65. PrEx 13.8:Ed 8/2.
> **Strand II: Sociological Health Problems–Grades 4, 5, 6, New York State Education Department, Albany, New York.** 1970. 58p. il. $0.65. PrEx 13.8:Ed 8/3.
> **Drug Abuse Education Unit–Grades K–12, South Bay Union School District, Imperial Beach, California.** 1970. 68p. il. $1.25. PrEx 13.8:Ed 8/4.
> **An Educational Program Dealing with Drug Abuse–Grades K–12, Rhode Island State Department of Education, Providence, Rhode Island.** 1970. 145p. il. $1.25. PrEx 13.8:Ed 8/5.

     **Curriculum Guide for Drug Education—Grades 6—12, Tacoma
Public Schools, Tacoma, Washington.** 1970. 61p. il. $0.60.
PrEx 13.8:Ed 8/6.
     **Drugs and Hazardous Substances—Grades K—12, San Francisco
Unified School District, San Francisco, California.** 1970.
209p. $1.75. PrEx 13.8:Ed 8/7.
     **Tobacco, Drug, and Alcohol Unit—Grade 6, Great Falls School
District No. 1, Great Falls, Montana.** 1970. 133p. il. $1.25.
PrEx 13.8:Ed 8/8.

199. **Some Questions and Answers About Medicines (FDA Fact Sheet).**
1970. 2p. Free. 7700-025.
Quality of over-the-counter drugs, amounts to buy, and storage information.
Effectiveness of weight reduction pills. Available from Consumer Product
Information, Washington, D.C. 20407.

200. **Stimulants—Some Questions and Answers.** 1970. 10p. Free. 7700-
042.
General factual information about these drugs, their psychological and physical effects, and their medical uses.

201. **Up and Down Drugs, Amphetamines and Barbiturates.** 1969. 8p. il.
$0.05. FS 2.22:Am 7/969.

202. **The Use and Misuse of Drugs.** 1968. 15p. $0.15. FS 13.111:46/2.
Describes the use and misuse of prescription and over-the-counter drugs, especially the stimulants and depressants. Outlines the power FDA has to protect society from the abuse of these dangerous drugs.

203. **Youthful Drug Use.** 1970. 39p. $0.30. HE 17.802:D 84.
Discusses a series of projects sponsored by the Office of Juvenile Delinquency
and Youth Development to develop models of rehabilitative and educational
programs as alternatives to control through criminal sanctions. The first section deals with four projects for drug users, and the second with six projects
for professionals working with drug users.

DRUGS—ABUSE

204. **The Control and Treatment of Narcotic Use.** 1968. 41p. $0.20.
FS 17.16:N 16.
Prepared as a resource for parole officials concerned with the treatment of
juvenile offenders.

205. **Drug Dependence and Abuse, A Selected Bibliography.** 1971.
vi + 51p. $0.60. PrEx 13.10:D 84. S/N 4110-0010.
Contains selected listing of references designed to provide an introduction to
the scientific, as well as to the more substantive popular drug abuse literature.

206. **Drug Dependence—Slavery '69.** 1970. 44p. il. $0.50. HE 20.2416:2.
The purpose of this publication is to facilitate the dissemination and exchange of information in the field of drug dependence and abuse and to provide abstracts of current literature in that general field. A major objective is to present recent annotated bibliographic materials in a readable style, together with a number of original articles by professionals in the field.

207. **Drugs of Abuse.** 1970. 15p. il. $0.40. J 24.2:D 84.
Colorfully illustrated, this booklet presents an identification of the most commonly abused drugs, and includes information on narcotics, marihuana, stimulants, depressants and hallucinogens, a description of the drug, how it is taken, through injection, inhalation, etc. and its effects; also the many forms it may take, such as capsule, powder, or tablet. A page of illustrations showing these various forms, and characteristics of each drug, is included. Also presents a detailed chart listing the many slang terms used for each drug, symptoms of abuse, symptoms of withdrawal, dangers of abuse, and manner in which each drug is taken.

208. **Guidelines for Drug Abuse Prevention Education.** 1971. 77p. $0.75. J 24.8:D 84/4. S/N 2704-0016.
This guide presents the educational approaches to drug abuse prevention and offers sample courses of study from kindergarten to grade 12 and beyond, to be incorporated as part of the regular school curriculum, as content in science, health, physical education, biology, and the social sciences as well. Includes an appendix which lists many helpful references and visual aids.

209. **Is It Possible . . . That Someone You Care About Has Changed for No Apparent Reason?** 1970. 10p. il. $0.15. J 24.2:Is 1.
Designed to serve also as a poster, this folder contains very descriptive pictures on some of the effects of drugs.

210. **Mental Health Matters, Drug Abuse.** 1970. 12p. $0.10. HE 20.2402: D 84/9.
Presents brief articles highlighting events and facts that matter to everyone's emotional and mental health. Articles presented are: Drug Dependence; Research Probing Marihuana; Does LSD Cause Mental Illness?; The "Up and Down" Drugs; About "Hard" Narcotics; Teenage Drug Use Research; Hope for Narcotic Addicts; and Intensive Drug Education.

211. **Reports by the Select Committee on Crime.**
Since drug addiction and the related crimes caused by drug abuse are national as well as international in scope and effect, long-range planning is absolutely necessary. Reports, presenting the conclusions and recommendations made by the Select Committee on Crime, dealing with these problems are:

> **Amphetamines.** 1971. v + 44p. $0.25. 91—2:H.rp.1807. S/N 5271-0207.
> **Heroin and Heroin Paraphernalia.** 1971. v + 83p. il. $0.40. 91—2:H.rp.1808. S/N 5271-0209.

212. **Selected Drug Abuse Education Films.** 1970. 10p. $0.10. PrEx 13.8:F 48.

213. **The Terms and Symptoms of Drug Abuse.** 1970. 4p. il. $0.35.
J 24.2:D 84/3. S/N 2704-0015.
A chart indicating the most common symptoms of drug abuse. Indicates the effects of listed drugs, gives slang terms, symptoms of abuse, symptoms of withdrawal, dangers of abuse, and method of use. Furnishes a list of offices on back cover, for contact to report any information regarding illegal use or possession of dangerous drugs.

DUCKS

See—Fish and Wildlife.

ECOLOGY AND THE ENVIRONMENT

See also—Pollution—Air; Pollution—Water; Population and the Environment.

214. **America the Beautiful, A Collection of the Nation's Trashiest Humor.**
1970. 31p. il. $0.35. HE 20.1402:Am 3.
In an effort to alert the public that a crisis in solid waste management exists, this booklet is published in the hope that it will serve as a reminder to bring about that realization. Its approach is lighthearted but its objective is serious.

215. **The American Outdoors. Management for Beauty and Use.** 1965.
76p. Misc. Pub. No. 1000.
Offers a wealth of practical information based on 60 years of research and resource-managing experience that can be used to combine utility and beauty on range, woodland, farm, and suburb, and all places where man's hand has altered the appearance of the landscape. Some of the subjects covered include the selection of plants for specific purposes, planting tips, and the application of esthetics to resource management, road location and design, trails, forest structures, signs, and recreation areas. Also lists sources of information and assistance help. Available from Forest Service, U.S. Department of Agriculture, 12th & Independence Ave., S.W., Washington, D.C. 20252.

216. **Community Action for Environmental Quality.** 1970. 42p. $0.60.
Pr 37.8:En 8/C 73.

217. **Effects of Surface Mining on the Fish and Wildlife Resources of the United States.** 1969. 51p. il. $0.60. I 49.66:68.

218. **Electric Power and the Environment.** 1970. xi + 71p. $0.75. PrEx
8.2:El 2. S/N 4106-0024.
This report proposes a program for resolving the apparent conflict between power needs and environmental protection.

219.   **Energy Model for the United States, Featuring Energy Balances for the Years 1947 to 1965 and Projections and Forecasts to the Years 1980 and 2000.** 1968. 127p. il. $0.70. I 28.27:8384.

220.   **Environmental Quality, The First Annual Report of The Council on Environmental Quality, Transmitted to the Congress, August 1970.** 1970. 351p. il. $1.75. PrEx 14.1:970.
Discusses the growing awareness and understanding by the American people of the nature of the threat to the environment and the interrelationship of environmental problems; various forms of pollution and local antipollution programs; control of land use; the expansion of population; waste of resources; international cooperation; the need for better, stronger institutions, improved measurement of the environment and comprehensive policies and strategies.

221.   **Guide to Natural Beauty.** 1967. 32p. il. $0.55. A 1.38:1056.
Suggests ways and means to beautify the home, community and countryside, and contains practical hints for maintaining and achieving natural beauty. Illustrated with many color photographs.

222.   **It's Your World.** 1969. 96p. il. $2.00. I 1.95:5.
A Department of Interior's Conservation Yearbook. Tells of the new grassroots movement in the U.S. in which people, individually and in groups, have taken positive action in improving their environment.

223.   **Let's Grow! Community Benefits from Watershed Projects.** 1970. 16p. il. $0.40. A 1.75:337.

224.   **Man, An Endangered Species?** 1968. 100p. il. $2.00. I 1.95:4.
This fully illustrated Conservation Yearbook takes up a new theme in which man, through unbridled technology and population pressures, has made himself a threatened species.

225.   **New Communities, A Bibliography.** 1970. 84p. $0.75. HH 1.23:C 73/969.
This annotated bibliography includes books, chapters of books, articles, conference proceedings, and reports published in the English language throughout the world. Its major purpose is to contribute to the understanding and improvement of new community building by providing reference sources on the current status of knowledge and experience on the subject.

226.   **Nuclear Power and the Environment.** 1969. 30p. il. $0.50. Y 3.At 7:54 En 8.
This report concentrates on the radiological and thermal aspects of the environmental effects of nuclear powerplants, procedures followed by the AEC to minimize the impact of nuclear plants on man and his environment; and on the research conducted by AEC.

227. **Outdoors USA, The Yearbook of Agriculture, 1967.** 1967. 408p. il.
$2.75. A 1.10:967.
A handbook of conservation, consumer's guide to outdoor recreation, and
primer on beautification. Short, readable chapters, 43 color photographs, and
some 200 other photos.

228. **People, Cities and Trees.** 1970. 16p. il. $0.10. A 1.68:958. S/N
0100-1109.
Trees in the city are being increasingly recognized as a vital asset in soil and
water conservation and in upgrading the quality of an urban environment.
This pamphlet is published to acquaint the general public with how the Forest
Service is attuned to the needs and desires of urban dwellers.

229. **Potential Applications for Nuclear Explosives in a Shale-Oil Industry.**
1969. 37p. il. $0.50. I 28.27:8425.
Presents the results of an investigation of the feasibility of using nuclear
energy as an aid in the development of a shale-oil industry, and a brief evaluation of large-scale conventional mining methods.

230. **Quest for Quality, U.S. Department of the Interior Conservation Yearbook.** 1965. 96p. il. $1.00. I 1.2:Q 3.
This big, colorfully illustrated Conservation Yearbook outlines the challenges
and problems created by a rapidly growing America.

231. **Surface Mining and Our Environment.** 124p. il. $2.00. I 1.2:M 66/3.
A factual report on how all forms of surface mining have altered the face of
America. Tells what has been done to restore the land, what has not been
done, and what can be done to minimize the future damage.

232. **The Third Wave, America's New Conservation, U.S. Department of
the Interior Conservation Yearbook.** 1966. 128p. il. $2.00. I 1.95:3.
Discusses efforts to restore our land and water, to protect our fish and wildlife, to conserve our fuel and mineral reserves. Three color photo essays and
full-color illustrations throughout.

ECONOMICS

233. **Dictionary of Economic and Statistical Terms.** 1969. 73p. il. $1.25.
C 1.2:Ec 7/7.
This dictionary will serve both as a convenient reference source for those
already familiar with the concepts and terms and as an introductory manual
for those with limited background. Deals primarily with terms used in publications of the Census Bureau and the Office of Business Economics of the
Department of Commerce.

234. **Do You Know Your Economic ABC's?, A Simplified Explanation of
Gross National Product and How It Mirrors Our Economy.** 1966. 40p. il.
$0.20. C 1.2:Ec 7/3/966.

235. **Do You Know Your Economic ABC's?, International Trade, Gateway to Growth, A Simplified Explanation of the Role of Imports and Exports in Our Economy.** 1968. 47p. il. $0.25. C 1.2:In 8/4.

236. **Do You Know Your Economic ABC's?, The Marketing Story, A Simplified Explanation of the Role of Marketing in Our Economy.** 1968. 47p. il. $0.30. C 1.2:M 34/4.

237. **Do You Know Your Economic ABC's?, Profits and the American Economy, A Simplified Explanation of Profit Incentive and How it Stimulates Economic Growth.** 1965. 47p. il. $0.25. C 1.2:P 94/2.

238. **Do You Know Your Economic ABC's?, Science and Technology for Mankind's Progress, A Simplified Explanation of Science and Technology and How They are Applied to Further Economic Growth.** 1967. 46p. il. $0.25. C 1.2:Sci 2/3.

239. **U.S. Balance of Payments. Do You Know Your Economic ABC's?** 1971. 43p. il. $0.35. C 1.2:P 29/970.
This booklet offers a simplified explanation of the U.S. balance of payments, the methods of measurement, the role of the dollar in international monetary affairs, the relationship between the dollar, gold and other currencies, and some of the measures which the United States and other countries have taken to remedy imbalances in their international transactions.

240. **U.S. Economic Growth. Do You Know Your Economic ABC's?** 1970. 47p. il. $0.30. C 1.2:Ec 7/4/970.
A simplified explanation of input and output factors promoting American economic growth. This booklet tells how expansion of natural resources, capital, and manpower has accelerated the American economy.

EDUCATION—GENERAL

In contrast to the standard alphabetical arrangement of subject headings and subheadings in this guide, the number and variety of materials in the field of education necessitated an arrangement of publications not strictly alphabetical.

Two prime sources of literature on this vital topic are the Office of Education catalog, available from the Dept. of Health, Education and Welfare, Washington, D.C. 20201; and Price List 31, available free from the Superintendent of Documents, Washington, D.C. 20402.

241. **American Education.** (Monthly except August-September and January-February which are combined issues.) Subscription price, $4.50/yr.; $0.50/copy. FS 5.75:vols.
This publication covers preschool to adult education, new research and demonstration projects, major education legislation, school and college bound data, grants, loans, contracts, and fellowships.

242. **The Best of American Education, Learning.** 1970. 60p. il. $1.00. HE 5.210:10069.
Contains 17 articles reprinted from *American Education*. These articles cover aspects of education that have been advanced through Federal Government support of research, development, practice, or innovation.

243. **Do Teachers Make a Difference? A Report on Recent Research on Pupil Achievement.** 1970. 181p. il. $0.75. HE 5.258:58042.

244. **Education for the 1970's, Renewal and Reform.** 1970. 34p. $0.30. Pr 37.2:Ed 8.

245. **Education, Literature of the Profession.** 1970. v + 41p. $0.50. HE 5.210:10060-A. S/N 1780-0079.
Contains a bibliography based on the acquisitions of the Educational Materials Center from January 1, 1969, through June 30, 1970. Entries are grouped according to subject under "Books and Monographs" or by format, including indexes, periodicals, and newsletters.

246. **Educational Research and Development in the United States.** 1970. 200p. il. $2.00. HE 5.212:12049.
Explores the development, the present status, and possible lines of future growth of educational research and development.

247. **Goodbye to the Birds and Bees, What's Happening.** 1967. 8p. il. $0.15. FS 5.233:33046.
Reprinted from *American Education*, November 1966, this pamphlet discusses sex education in schools.

248. **Progress of Public Education in the United States of America, 1968-1969, Report for the Thirty-second International Conference on Public Education, Sponsored by the United Nations Educational, Scientific and Cultural Organization, International Bureau of Education.** 1970. 49p. il. $0.55. HE 5.210:10005-69A. —**Spanish Edition.** 1970. 54p. il. $0.60. HE 5.210:10005-69-D.
Reports significant achievements at the elementary, secondary, and higher education levels and discusses the professional development of teachers as a major achievement and innovative movement.

249. **Publications of the Office of Education, 1970.** 1970. vi + 77p. $0.40. HE 5.211:11000-70.
Includes all Office of Education publications currently available for purchase from the Superintendent of Documents, Government Printing Office, Washington, D.C. 20402, and a few additional ones that are available on request from the Office of Education.

250. **Race and Place,A Legal History of the Neighborhood School.** 1968. 103p. $0.45. FS 5.238:38005.

251. **Research in Education, Annual Index, January—December 1970.**
1970. 913p. $6.00. HE 5.77:970-2/ind. S/N 1780-0742.
Cumulates the indexes that appeared in the monthly issues of *Research in Education* from January through December 1970. This cumulation is intended to be a companion volume to the individual issues of *Research in Education*. The four indexes are arranged as follows: Subject; Author; Institution; Clearinghouse Accession Number/ED Number Cross Reference.

252. **Standard Terminology for Curriculum and Instruction in Local and State School Systems.** 1970. x + 319p. il. $3.00. HE 5.223:23052. S/N 1780-0721.
Presents a guide for local and state school systems for items of information used in keeping records and making reports about curriculum and instruction. Concerned with the terminology for describing curriculum and instruction in elementary schools, middle schools, secondary schools, junior colleges, and adult schools or other adult education organizational arrangements.

EDUCATION—DIRECTORIES

253. **Directory of Educational Information Centers.** 1969. 118p. $1.25. FS 5.212:12042.
A listing of information centers offering services to educators in communities throughout the United States. Indexed by subject.

254. **Directory, Public Elementary and Secondary Day Schools, Elementary and Secondary Education:**

> **Vol. I, North Atlantic Region, 1968-69.** 1970. 232p. $2.00. HE 5.220:20126/v.1.
> **Vol. II, Great Lakes and Plains Region, 1968-69.** 1970. 358p. $3.25. HE 5.220:20126/v.2
> **Vol. III, Southeast Region.** 1970. 264p. $2.50. HE 5.220:20126/v.3.
> **Vol. IV, West and Southwest.** 1970. $2.50. HE 5.220:20126/v.4.

This is the first comprehensive listing of every elementary and secondary school in the United States.

255. **Educational Directory, 1970-71.**

> **State Governments 1969-70.** 1970. 163p. $1.00. HE 5.25:969-70/pt. 1.
> Lists principal officials of each state as well as the outlying area governments' departments of education and library extension agencies.
> **Public School System.** 1971. 298p. $2.25. HE 5.25:970-71/pt. 2. S/N 1780-0757.
> Lists the local elementary and secondary school systems, by state, showing name of unit, superintendent's locations, ZIP Code, county name, grade-span and enrollment.

Higher Education. 1971. 515p. $3.75. HE 5.25:970-71/pt. 3. S/N 1780-0648.
Lists institutions of higher education offering at least a 2-year program of college-level or occupational studies beyond grade 12, in residence.

Education Associations 1968-69. 1970. FS 5.25:968-69/pt. 4.
Includes national and regional associations, college professional fraternities, honor societies, and recognition societies (national), state education associations, foundations, religious education associations, and international education associations.

256. **Opportunities Abroad for Teachers, 1971-72.** 1970. 28p. $0.20.
HE 5.214:14047-72.
Opportunities are available under the International Educational and Cultural Exchange Program for qualified American teachers either to teach for an academic year in elementary and secondary schools abroad or to attend summer seminars abroad. This bulletin describes the U.S. government grants to be offered to American teachers for participation in the program during 1971-72.

257. **Research and Training Opportunities Abroad, 1971-72, Higher Education Programs in Foreign Language and Area Studies.** [4] + 28p. $0.25.
HE 5.214:14134-72.
Discusses opportunities for American educators at all levels and graduate and undergraduate students in foreign languages, area studies, and world affairs to participate in research activities and training programs abroad.

EDUCATION—STATISTICS

258. **Digest of Educational Statistics, 1969.** 1970. 128p. il. $1.50. HE 5.210:10024-69.
An abstract of statistical information covering the entire field of American education from kindergarten through the graduate school. Contains data broken down by state on the number of schools and colleges, enrollments, teachers, graduates, educational attainment, finances, federal funds for education, libraries, international education, and research and development.

259. **Financial Statistics of Institutions of Higher Education: Federal Funds, 1965-66 and 1966-67.** 1970. 177p. il. $1.50. HE 5.252:52013-67.

260. **Projections of Educational Statistics to 1979-80, 1970 Edition.** 1971. 174p. il. $1.75. HE 5.210:10030-70. S/N 1780-0769.
Provides projections of statistics for elementary and secondary schools and institutions of higher education, including enrollments, graduates, teachers, and expenditures.

261. **Selected Statistics on Educational Personnel.** 1970. 59p. $0.65.
HE 5.258:58041.

An appraisal of the nation's existing and future personnel needs in the field of education, including preschool programs, elementary and secondary education, vocational and technical education, adult and higher education, and the adequacy of the nation's efforts to meet these needs.

262. **Statistics of Public Schools, Fall 1970.** 1971. viii + 44p. $0.50. HE 5.220:20007-70. S/N 1780-0770.

Presents data obtained from the latest basic statistical survey on public elementary and secondary education in the United States. Collected information includes number of local school districts, enrollment by grade, high school graduates, teachers, buildings, and estimated expenditures.

EDUCATION—PRE-SCHOOL

263. **Head Start—A Child Development Program.** Free. OCD 70-5.

To inform the general public of the aims of the Head Start program, its comprehensiveness and its accomplishments. Available from Office of Child Development, Room 1528, HEW North Bldg., 330 Independence Avenue, S.W., Washington, D.C. 20201. (Cite DHEW Catalog of Publications, July 1971.)

264. **Learning to Talk, Speech, Hearing and Language Problems in the Pre-School Child.** 1969. 48p. il. $0.45. HE 20.3502:T 14.

265. **Preprimary Enrollment of Children Under Six.** Roy C. Nehrt and Gordon E. Hurd. 1969. 17p. $0.30. OE-20079-68.

Shows the number of children 3 to 5 years of age and their enrollment rates by age, as related to family income, occupation of family head, and residence as of October 1968.

EDUCATION—ELEMENTARY AND SECONDARY

Publications in the subheading Education—Elementary and Secondary cover many disciplines from humanities to the sciences and include curriculum guides, classroom projects, and statistics. Student and teacher viewpoints are represented.

266. **Aeronautical Science Course of Study.** 1969. $2.25. TD 4.8:Ae 8.

A two-semester aeronautical course outline providing material for aviation and space programs in high school science classes.

267. **Aerospace Curriculum Resource Guide.** 197p. $1.75.

Published in cooperation with the Massachusetts Department of Education, as a resource guide for grades K-12.

268. **Book Selection Aids for Children and Teachers in Elementary and Secondary Schools.** 1966. 16p. $0.15. FS 5.230:30019.

Describes some of the more useful reading lists now available to elementary and secondary school teachers, librarians, curriculum workers and students themselves.

269. **Books Related to English Language and Literature in Elementary and Secondary Schools, A Bibliography Based on the Acquisitions of the Educational Materials Center, October 1969.** 1970. 24p. $0.35. HE 5.230:30024.
Compiled to answer questions from educators concerning new books related to English language and literature programs in elementary and secondary schools. Includes trade and textbooks involving these areas.

270. **Books Related to the Social Studies in Elementary and Secondary Schools, A Bibliography Based on the Acquisitions of the Educational Materials Center.** 1969. 27p. $0.35. FS 5.231:31011.
List of trade books and textbooks received in the Educational Materials Center between January 1968 and May 1969. Prepared to answer requests from educators about the nature and availability of new books related to social studies programs in elementary and secondary schools.

271. **Classroom Demonstrations of Wood Properties.** 1969. 41p. il. $0.60. A 1.68:900.

272. **Crayons and Related Art Materials for School Use (Types, Sizes, Packaging, and Colors), Simplified Practice Recommendations R 192-63.** 1963. 11p. $0.10. C 41.20:192-63.

273. **Current Expenditures by Local Education Agencies for Free Public Elementary and Secondary Education.** 1970. [4] p. il. $0.10. HE 5.222: 22026-69. S/N 1780-0556.
Reports the current expenditures for free public elementary and secondary education, the average daily attendance, current expenditures per pupil, and percent increase, by region and state for the school year 1968-69.

274. **FDA's Science Project Series:**

> **Analysis for Spoilage Indicators in Butter.** Oct. 1968. 8p. $0.10. FS 13.111:55/2.
> **Identity of Artificial Color on Oranges.** Oct. 1968. 8p. $0.10. FS 13.111:54/2.
> **Identity of Synthetic Colors in Foods.** Oct. 1968. 8p. il. $0.10. FS 13.111:57/2.
> **Rapid Identity of Margarine and Butter.** Oct. 1968. 8p. $0.10. FS 13.111:56/2.
> **Qualitative Analysis of APC Tablets.** Oct. 1968. 8p. $0.10. HE 20.4015:53.
> **Toxicity Studies with Chicken Embryo.** Oct. 1968. 8p. il. $0.10. FS 13.111:58/2.

These projects, suitable for high school biology or chemistry classrooms, include experiments and procedures, subjects for classroom discussion, and sources of additional information.

275. **Gifted Student, Research Projects Concerning Elementary and Secondary School Students.** 1960. 83p. $0.35. FS 5.233:35016.

276. **A Guide for Teaching Poison Prevention in Kindergartens and Primary Grades.** 1965. 95p. il. $0.55. FS 2.6/2:P 75.
Describes learning experiences and activities designed to help pupils learn ways to help parents protect younger brothers and sisters from poisoning in the home; what general types of materials encountered in the home, school, and community environment may be potentially poisonous; how to recognize them; and how to avoid any chance of poisoning by contact with them.

277. **High School and the Cultural Illiterate.** 1967. 7p. il. $0.15. FS 5.233:33044.
Reprinted from *American Education*, November 1966, this publication discusses in detail the necessity for more humanities and arts courses in the nation's secondary schools.

278. **Introducing Children to Space.** 168p. $1.25. EP-36.
A space handbook for teachers, grades K to 6 (featuring maturity levels 5 through 11 years old), developed by the Lincoln, Nebraska, Public Schools. Projects and illustrations are described at each age level.

279. **Junior High School Science Teaching in the Public Junior High School.** 1967. 59p. il. $0.45. FS 5.229:29067.

280. **Language Ability, Grades 7-9.** 1966. 94p. il. $0.50. FS 5.230:30018.

281. **Making Posters, Flashcards and Charts for Extension Teaching.** 1968. 18p. il. $0.15. A 1.38:796.

282. **Miniature Environments, An Environmental Education Guidebook.** 1971. 20p. il. $0.25. I 66.8:En 8. S/N 2416-0040.
Presents examples of teaching tools to be used in the classroom for teaching the processes of nature, emphasizing the environmental and ecological principles which govern life on this planet.

283. **The Planetarium: An Elementary-School Teaching Resource.** 60p. $0.40. EP-42.
A report by the University of Bridgeport on projects for elementary school classes in the Bridgeport Planetarium.

284. **Science and Mathematics Books for Elementary and Secondary Schools, A Bibliography Based on the Acquisitions of the Educational Materials Center, February 1970.** 1970. 19p. $0.30. HE 5.229:29071.
Concerns the science and mathematics textbooks and juvenile trade books received in the Educational Materials Center between January 1969 and February 1970. Prepared as a means of answering questions from educators about the nature and availability of new books of possible use in science and mathematics education programs in elementary and secondary schools in the United States.

285. **Space Resources for Teachers: Biology, Including Suggestions for Classroom Activities and Laboratory Experiments.** 1969. 236p. il. $2.75. NAS 1.19:50.

Developed to supplement biology curricula by incorporating current investigations in the space life sciences.

286. **Space Resources for Teachers: Chemistry.** 228p. $2.50. EP-87.
This curriculum supplement, developed at Ball State University, is designed to enrich chemistry instruction with recent discoveries emanating from the U.S. space program. Monographs presenting background information are followed by detailed suggestions for activities including experiments, demonstrations, projects and ideas for discussion.

287. **Space Resources for Teachers: Space Science.** 144p. $2.00. EP-64.
A book prepared to enrich science curricula with information gained from recent achievements in the space sciences.

288. **Space Resources for the High School: Industrial Arts Resources Units.** 178p. $2.25. EP-44. NAS 1.19:44.
Supplementary material relating space concepts to the industrial arts curriculum. Prepared for NASA by industrial arts teachers, with direction by the Industrial Arts Department of Western Michigan University, for use by teachers at the secondary level.

289. **Teacher's Guide and Key to Exercise Books for Pre-High School Subjects, Introductory Social Studies, A 058, English as a Communication Skill, A 018, Introductory Science, A 068.** 219p. il. $1.25. D 1.10:A 058.4, A 018.4, A 068.4.

290. **Water Intake by Soil, Experiments for High School Students.** 1963. 10p. il. $0.10. A 1.38:925.
Primarily intended for students, this publication presents, in simple terms and with the use of analogy, basic concepts about water intake as related to water delivery, soil properties, floods, and conservation measures.

EDUCATION–ELEMENTARY AND SECONDARY–READING SKILLS

291. **Communicating by Language, The Reading Process.** 1968. 228p. il. $1.75. FS 2.22:C 73/2.

292. **Developmental Reading:**

> **On Your Mark!** 1968. 143p. il. $0.75. D 1.10:A 011.
> **Get Set!** 1968. 217p. il. $1.25. D 1.10:A 012.

293. **Looking Deep into the Reading Process.** 1970. [4] p. il. $0.10. HE 5.230:30027.
Reprinted from *American Education*, March 1970.

294. **Speed and Power of Reading in High School.** 1966. 183p. il. $0.70. FS 5.230:30016.

295. **Teaching Young Children to Read.** $0.55. HE 5.230:30014.
Based upon a conference on beginning reading instruction, containing reports from Canada and England as well as from the United States.

296. **Treating Reading Difficulties, The Role of the Principal, Teacher, Specialist, Administrator.** 1970. 132p. il. $1.50. HE 5.230:30026.

EDUCATION—HIGHER EDUCATION

297. **Aspirations, Enrollments, and Resources, The Challenge to Higher Education in the Seventies.** 1970. 151p. il. $1.25. HE 5.250:50058.

298. **College Volunteers, A Guide to Action: Helping Students to Help Others.** 1969. 73p. il. $0.40. PrEx 10.8:C 68.
This manual's aim is to help advisers convert the enthusiasm and skills of college students into worthwhile social programs. It explores a number of approaches that a school might take to support student volunteers.

299. **Higher Education Administration, An Annotated Bibliography of Research Reports Funded by the Cooperative Research Act, 1956-1970.** 1971. 12p. $0.30. HE 5.212:12054. S/N 1780-0791.
Lists research reports in higher education administration, including studies on communication facilities, financing, institutional management, instructional programs and students.

300. **Higher Education Salaries, 1967-68.** 1970. 57p. il. $0.60. HE 5.253:53015-68.
Presents data on salaries of academic staffs with particular emphasis on the salaries and other characteristics of administrators and faculty. Salary data are tabulated in terms of various institutional characteristics, such as: legal control, level of institution, enrollment size, and geographical location.

301. **How the Office of Education Assists College Students and Colleges.** 1970. 67p. $0.70. HE 5.255:55051-70.

302. **Opening Fall Enrollment in Higher Education, 1970, Report on Preliminary Survey.** 1971. 84p. il. $1.00. HE 5.254:54003.
Presents basic data on total enrollment in institutions of higher education, including total resident and extension enrollment and first-time resident and extension enrollment, tabulated by sex and attendance status.

303. **Report on Higher Education.** 1971. xi + 130p. $0.75. HE 5.250:50065. S/N 1780-0765.
Examines the growth of higher education in the postwar period, discusses present problems in higher education and general directions to be taken.

304. **Urban Universities: Rhetoric, Reality, and Conflict.** 1970. 65p. $0.65. HE 5.250:50062.
Reports findings of a study and a conference concerning "urban crisis" conducted by the Organization for Social and Technical Innovation under the Office of Education sponsorship.

EDUCATION—HIGHER EDUCATION—FINANCIAL AIDS

305. **A Guide to Student Assistance.** 1970. 129p. $0.60. 91-2:H.doc. 221.
Lists and describes major federal programs to financially assist students.
Selected federal graduate fellowship programs, and other selected programs
available to undergraduates are discussed, along with other major non-federal
undergraduate scholarships and loans.

306. **Economics and Financing of Higher Education in the United States,
A Compendium of Papers.** 1969. 683p. il. $3.00. Y 4.Ec 7:Ed 8/4.

307. **Educational Scholarships, Loans, and Financial Aids.** 1969. 84p.
$1.00. D 101.22:352-1.
Lists financial aids available to college students and is designed primarily to
be a guide for dependents of retired, active or deceased Army personnel.

308. **Federal and State Student Aid Programs.** 1970. 82p. $0.40. 91-2:
S. doc. 73.
Presents a list of federal programs grouped according to the level of study of
the recipient and further subdivided by area of study; a selected listing of
career and training opportunities available through various federal agencies;
descriptions of state programs of student assistance; a brief listing of other
sources of information on colleges, career opportunities, and private programs
of student financial aid.

309. **How to Get Money for College.** 1967. 4p. il. $0.10. FS 5.255:55050.
The Guaranteed Loan Program which enables college students to borrow from
banks, credit unions, savings and loan associations, and other commercial
lenders is explained in this pamphlet. There is also a brief discussion on how
to get help from grants, student employment programs, and other loan
arrangements.

EDUCATION—ADULT EDUCATION

310. **Adult Basic Education: The State of the Art.** 1970. 236p. $2.00.
HE 5.2:Ad 9/7. S/N 1780-0699.
Reviews the present state of the art in adult basic education teacher training,
presenting in one document the central research base which undergirds the
adult basic education teacher training programs in institutions of higher
education.

311. **Adult Education, Adult Basic Education Program Statistics, Students
and Staff Data, July 1, 1968—June 30, 1969.** 1970. 37p. $0.50. HE 5.213:
13037.
Provides statistical information on the Adult Basic Education program including enrollments, student characteristics, completions, teachers, and
school facilities.

312. **Arithmetic for Everyday Life: Text.** 1951. 71p. il. $0.35. D 1.10: MA 030.
Prepared especially for servicemen by the United States Armed Forces Institute, the instructional content of this text corresponds to that usually offered in grades one through four.

> **Arithmetic for Everyday Life, Pt. 4: Text.** 1955. 123p. il. $0.60. D 1.10:A 031. **—Workbook.** 1955. 94p. $0.50. D 1.10:A 031.2.
> The instructional content of this text corresponds to that usually offered in the fourth grade.

> **Arithmetic for Everyday Life, Pt. 5: Text.** 133p. il. $1.00. D 1.10:B 032. **—Workbook.** 94p. il. $1.00. D 1.10:B 032.2.
> The instructional content of this text corresponds to that usually offered in the fifth grade.

> **Arithmetic for Everyday Life, Pt. 6: Text.** 1957. 135p. il. $1.00. D 1.10:B 033.
> The instructional content of this text corresponds to that usually offered in the sixth grade.

313. **Books Related to Adult Basic Education and Teaching English to Speakers of Other Languages, A Bibliography Based on the Acquisitions of the Educational Materials Center as of May 1, 1970.** 1970. iii + 18p. $0.30. HE 5.213:13039. S/N 1780-0708.
This bibliography reports on publications received by the Educational Materials Center for teaching adults the first essential skills of reading, writing, arithmetic, community living, and citizenship.

314. **Educationally Deficient Adults: Their Education and Training Needs.** 1965. 60p. $0.40. FS 5.213:13029.
Findings of a study of educational and training needs of educationally deficient adults.

EDUCATION–VOCATIONAL

315. **Agricultural Equipment Technology, A Suggested 2-Year Post High School Curriculum.** 1970. 112p. il. $1.25. HE 5.281:81015.

316. **Career Opportunities in Service to the Disadvantaged and Handicapped, Sponsored by HEW.** 1969. 39p. $0.30. HE 5.237:37059.
Describes various personnel training programs designed to meet the critical shortages of trained personnel motivated and capable of working with handicapped or disadvantaged children and adults. This pamphlet is intended to encourage persons, including returning veterans, to take advantage of the training possibilities offered by the federal government.

317. **Chemical Technology, A Suggested 2-Year Post High School Curriculum.** 1964. 119p. il. $0.75. FS 5.280:80031.

318. **Child Care and Guidance, A Suggested Post High School Curriculum.** 1970. 50p. il. $0.55. HE 5.287:87021-A.

319. **Civil Technology, Highway and Structural Options, A Suggested 2-Year Post High School Curriculum.** 1966. 107p. il. $0.60. FS 5.280:80041.

320. **Diesel Servicing, A Suggested 2-Year Post High School Curriculum.** 1969. 118p. il. $1.25. FS 5.287:87045.

321. **Electronic Data Processing 1, A Suggested 2-Year Post High School Curriculum for Computer Programers and Business Application Analysts.** 1963. 49p. il. $0.40. FS 5.280:80024.

322. **Electronic Technology, A Suggested 2-Year Post High School Curriculum.** 1969. 104p. il. $1.25. FS 5.280:80009A.

323. **Farm Crop Production Technology, Field and Forage Crop and Fruit and Vine Production Options, A Suggested 2-Year Post High School Curriculum.** 1970. 179p. il. $1.50. HE 5.281:81016.

324. **Food Processing Technology, A Suggested Two-Year Post High School Curriculum.** 1967. 97p. il. $0.50. FS 5.282:82016.

325. **Forest Technology, A Suggested 2-Year Post High School Curriculum.** 1968. 142p. il. $1.25. FS 5.280:80054.

326. **Grain, Feed, Seed, and Farm Supply Technology, Suggested 2-Year Post High School Curriculum.** 1969. 185p. il. $1.50. FS 5.281:81014.

327. **Mechanical Technology Design and Production, A Suggested 2-Year Post High School Curriculum.** 1969. 103p. il. $1.00. HE 5.280:80019.

328. **Metallurgical Technology, A Suggested 2-Year Post High School Curriculum.** 1968. 113p. il. $1.25. FS 5.281:81012.

329. **Ornamental Horticulture Technology, A Suggested 2-Year Post High School Curriculum.** 1970. ix + 206p. il. $1.75. HE 5.281:81017. S/N 1780-0738.
Offers suggested curricula for five options: floriculture, landscape development, nursery operation, turfgrass management, and arboriculture. It also includes suggested course outlines with examples of texts and references; a sequence of technical education procedures; laboratory layouts with equipment and costs; a discussion of the library and its use, faculty and student services, and land requirements; and a selected list of scientific, trade, and technical societies concerned with the technology.

330. **Recreation Program Leadership, A Suggested 2-Year Post High School Curriculum.** 1969. 87p. il. $1.00. FS 5.287:87042.

331. Scientific Data Processing Technology, A Suggested 2-Year Post High School Curriculum. 1970. viii + 99p. il. $1.00. HE 5.280:80068. S/N 1780-0740.
Provides a suggested curriculum plan; course outlines with examples of texts and references; a suggested sequence of technical education procedure; laboratory layouts with equipment and costs; a discussion of remote computation and time sharing, library and its use, faculty, and student services; and selected scientific, trade, and technical societies concerned with technology.

332. Suggested Guides for Training Courses.
These guides present the essential characteristics of a program designed to provide basic education and skills required for entry into jobs in a particular field of work. The outlines, course content, class and study time allocation, teaching techniques, and suggested supplemental instructional material are discussed and analyzed.

> **Automotive Body Repairman.** 1969. 17p. il. $0.30. FS 5.287:87035.
> **Automotive Mechanic Entry.** 1969. 21p. il. $0.35. FS 5.287:87041.
> **Automotive Service Station Attendant (Driveway Salesman).** 1968. 18p. il. $0.30. FS 5.287:87026.
> **Building Custodian.** 1969. 25p. $0.35. FS 5.287:87038.
> **Clothing Maintenance Specialist.** 1964. 13p. $0.20. FS 5.287:87005.
> **Companion to Elderly Person.** 1964. 13p. $0.20. FS 5.287:87006.
> **Draftsman, Entry.** 1968. 19p. il. $0.30. FS 5.287:87037.
> **Electrical Appliance Serviceman.** 1969. 14p. il. $0.30. FS 5.287:87039.
> **Electronics Assembler.** 1969. 13p. $0.30. FS 5.287:87032.
> **Electronics Mechanic, Entry.** 1969. 15p. il. $0.30. FS 5.287:87040.
> **Forestry Aide.** 1964. 21p. $0.25. FS 5.287:87011.
> **Heavy Construction Equipment Mechanic.** 1969. 44p. il. $0.50. HE 5.287:87044.
> **Maintenance Man, Building.** 1969. 26p. il. $0.35. FS 5.287:87043.
> **Medical Laboratory Assistant.** 1966. 115p. il. $0.60. FS 5.287:87017.
> **Refrigeration Mechanic.** 1968. 10p. il. $0.25. FS 5.287:87034.
> **Small Engine Repair.** 1969. 71p. il. $0.70. FS 4.287:87036.
> **Supervised Food Service Worker.** 1964. 13p. $0.20. FS 5.287:87004.

Vending Machine Repairman. 1968. 16p. il. $0.30. FS 5.287: 87033.

Waiter-Waitress. 1969. 52p. il. $0.55. FS 5.287:87046.

EDUCATION—SPECIAL AREAS—DISADVANTAGED

333. **Books Related to Compensatory Education.** 1969. 46p. $0.50. FS 5.237:37045.
This bibliography includes elementary and secondary school textbooks, juvenile literature and professional resources which are in the collection of the Educational Materials Center.

334. **Breakthrough for Disadvantaged Youth.** 1969. 256p. $2.00. L 1.2:D 63. —Reprints from above:

> **Basic Education.** 1970. [20] p. $0.30. L 1.2/a:Ed 83.
> **Impact on the Community.** 1970. [35] p. $0.35. L 1.2/a:C 737.
> **Job Placement, Creation, and Development.** 1970. [34] p. $0.40. L 1.2/a:J 575.
> **Prevocational and Vocational Training Programs.** 1970. [41] p. $0.50. L 1.2/a:P 929.
> **Recruitment and Community Penetration.** 1970. [22] p. $0.30. L 1.2/a:R 245.
> **Testing, Counseling, and Supportive Services.** 1970. [59] p. $0.60. L 1.2/a:T 286.
> **Using the Nonprofessional.** 1970. [20] p. $0.30. L 1.2/a:N 733.

336. **Children at the Crossroad.** 1970. 48p. il. $0.65. HE 5.237:37062. S/N 1780-0711.
This booklet is a report on state programs for the education of disadvantaged children.

336. **The Education Professions, 1969-70.** 1970. iv + 84p. il. $1.00. HE 5.258:58032-70. S/N 1780-0722.
This report is concerned with the problem of educating students from low-income families and with the attempt to sharpen understanding of the issues involved.

337. **Federal Research and Demonstration Programs Benefiting the Dis-Advantaged and Handicapped.** 1968. 53p. $0.40. FS 5.235:35092.

338. **It Works Series, Summaries of Selected Compensatory Education Projects.** 1970. v + 33p. $0.35. HE 5.237:37069.
Summarizes the 31 booklets published by the U.S. Office of Education concerning compensatory education projects across the country, and enables the reader to select the booklets which cover the projects he is most interested in studying in detail.

339. **Literature for Disadvantaged Children.** 1968. 16p. $0.20. HE 5.237:37019.
Lists new books received by the Educational Material Center. Prepared to inform teachers, librarians, and others concerned and responsible for the education of disadvantaged children.

340. **Upward Bound, Ideas and Techniques. A Reference Manual.** 1970. 116p. $1.75. HE 5.250:50061.
This manual is designed to provide project staffs with a quick reference to ideas and source materials used in Upward Bound programs throughout the country.

EDUCATION—SPECIAL AREAS—MINORITIES

341. **Education of the Culturally Different, A Multi-Cultural Approach, A Handbook for Educators.** 1969. 64p. $0.35. FS 5.6/2:C 89.
Increasing attention is currently being devoted to the problems of culturally different minority populations as they relate to formal educational processes. One purpose of this essay is to distinguish the concept of the culturally different pupil from that of the "culturally disadvantaged" and to discuss the multi-cultural orientation of schools in the United States.

342. **Ethnic Origin and Educational Attainment: November 1969.** 1971. 8p. $0.15. C 3.186:P 20/220.
This report presents data on years of school completed by persons 25 years and over, by age and selected ethnic origin (English, German, Irish, Italian, Polish, Russian, Spanish, other). The data are for the United States, November 1969. Explanatory text and text tables are included.

343. **Higher Education Aid for Minority Business, A Directory of Assistance Available to Minorities by Selected Collegiate Schools of Business.** 1970. 103p. $1.00. C 1.2:M 66/4.
This directory is a compilation of the opportunities open to minorities in business schools across the country. Contained in this publication are schools offering: financial aid to minority students, special programs to aid minority business, and aid to minorities according to State.

344. **Indian Education: A National Tragedy, A National Challenge.** 1969. 220p. il. $1.00. 91-1:S. rep. 501.
Report of the Senate Committee on Labor and Public Welfare made by the Special Subcommittee on Indian Education pursuant to Senate Resolution 80 (91st Congress, 1st Session). This resolution authorized an investigation into the problems of education for American Indians.

345. **Mexican American Education Study, Report 1: Ethnic Isolation of Mexican Americans in the Public Schools of the Southwest.** 1971. 102p. il. $1.00. CR 1.2:M 57/3/rp.1. S/N 0500-0059.
This report deals with the extent to which Mexican American students in the

States of Arizona, California, New Mexico, Colorado, and Texas attend school in isolation from Anglo students, and describes the participation of Mexican Americans in the education process as principals, teachers, and in other official school capacities.

346. **School Desegregation, "A Free and Open Society," Policy Statement by Richard Nixon, President of the United States, March 24, 1970.** 1970. 30p. $0.25. Pr 37.2:Sch 6.

347. **Se Habla Espanol, Help for Spanish-Speaking Youngsters.** 1967. 4p. il. $0.10. FS 5.230:30020.
Reprinted from *American Education*, May 1967, this pamphlet discusses the education of Spanish-speaking youngsters in the United States.

EDUCATION—SPECIAL AREAS—SPECIAL EDUCATION

348. **Breakthrough in Early Education of Handicapped Children.** 1970. 3p. il. $0.10. HE 5.235:35093.
Reprinted from *American Education*, January-February 1970.

349. **Something for the Special Child.** 1965. 11p. il. $0.20. FS 5.235: 35078.
Suggests improvements for the design of school buildings so that mentally and physically handicapped children could attend regular classes.

350. **Visually Handicapped Child at Home and School.** 1969. 45p. il. $0.35. FS 5.235:35045-68.
Summarizes recent developments in the field of education of visually handicapped children and resources available to assist educators in their efforts to initiate, extend, and improve educational programs for these children.

EDUCATION—INTERNATIONAL

351. **The Brazilian Education System, A Summary.** 1970. vi + 26p. il. $0.25. HE 5.214:14150.
A brief description of Brazilian education since 1966, outlining the administrative structure, summarizing the system, and presenting 1968 enrollment data for each level, elementary, middle and higher. Also it discusses enrollment increases since 1961 and major changes now taking place, particularly at the higher education level.

352. **Education in a Changing Mexico.** 1969. 127p. il. $0.70. FS 5.214: 14139.
This report on educational developments in Mexico discusses Mexico's educational achievements during the past decade against a background of relevant geographic, historical, political, economic, and social factors. Among the factors considered are the government's Eleven-Year Plan (1959-70) to expand and improve elementary education throughout the entire country, its widespread literacy program, and its many cultural activities.

353. **Education in Mao's China.** 1966. [8] p. il. $0.15. FS 5.214:14134. Reprinted from *American Education*, October 1966.

354. **Education in Spain.** 1966. 36p. il. $0.20. FS 5.214:14034-79.

355. **Education in the Hungarian People's Republic.** 1970. 227p. il. $1.25. HE 5.214:14140.

356. **Education in the Province of Quebec.** 1969. 81p. il. $0.45. FS 5.214:14138.

357. **The Education of National Minorities in Communist China.** 1970. vi + 30p. $0.25. HE 5.214:14146.
Describes the education of Communist China's 54 national minorities against the background of that country's internal politics. It shows how the regime's attempt to integrate minority groups into the mainstream of Chinese national life has affected its educational policies in minority areas.

358. **Educational Reform in Brazil, Law of 1961.** 1968. 50p. $0.55. FS 5.214:14135.

359. **The Educational System of Iran.** 1970. 10p. il. $0.15. HE 5.214:14148. S/N 1780-0715.
Describes the educational system of Iran and its current reform. Compares the old system of general and academic education with the new. Discusses such topics as language, grading system, academic calendar, and others.

360. **Educational System of Yugoslavia.** 1970. 10p. il. $0.15. HE 5.214:14147.

361. **Final Examinations in the Russian Ten-Year School.** 1966. 20p. $0.15. FS 5.214:14126.

362. **Higher and Professional Education in India.** 1970. 181p. il. $1.00. HE 5.214:14141.

363. **Studies in Comparative Education:**

> **Development of Education in Nepal.** 1965. 78p. il. $0.30. FS 5.214:14110.
>
> **Eastern Europe Education; A Bibliography of English-Language Materials.** 1966. 35p. $0.20. FS 5.214:14121.
>
> **Overseas Chinese Education in Indonesia, Minority Group Schooling in Asian Context.** 1965. 56p. $0.25. FS 5.214:14114.

ELECTRICITY AND ELECTRONICS

364. **Basic Electricity.** 1970. 490p. il. $4.25. D 208.11:El 2/3/969.

365. **Basic Electronics.** 1968. 538p. il. $3.00. D 208.11:El 2/10/968.

366. **Interior Wiring.** 1971. 119p. il. $1.25. D 101.11:5-760/3.
Provides practical information about the design, layout, installation, and maintenance of electrical wiring systems. Also includes information relating to methods of repairing, remodeling, and extending domestic and foreign wiring systems; troubleshooting; and necessary safety precautions in electrical installations.

367. **Introduction to Electronics.** 1963. 149p. il. $0.75. D 208.11:El 2/16.

368. **Introduction to Sonar.** 1968. 181p. il. $1.50. D 208:11:So 5/2/968.
Presents basic information about sonar equipment, the electronic devices which use sound energy to locate submerged objects.

369. **Typical Electric Bills, 1970.** 1971. 145p. il. $1.50. FP 1.10:76.
S/N 1500-0188.
Provides comprehensive coverage of the cost to consumers for representative amounts of electricity used per month for residential, commercial, and industrial service in all sections of the nation.

ESKIMOS

See—North American Indians.

FALLOUT SHELTERS

See—Civil Defense.

FAMILY FINANCES AND BUDGETING

See also—Consumer Information; Foods.

370. **Family Food Budgeting for Good Meals and Good Nutrition.** 1969.
16p. il. $0.15. A 1.77:94/3.
Contains up-to-date guides for family food budgeting at different cost levels. These food plans were prepared by nutritionists to help the homemaker choose the right foods in the right amount at an affordable cost.

371. **Family Food Buying, Guide for Calculating Amounts to Buy, Comparing Costs.** 1969. 60p. $0.35. A 1.87:37.

372. **A Guide to Budgeting for the Family.** 1970. 14p. il. $0.10.
A 1.77:108/3.
Tells how to develop and carry out a budget for the family, and discusses steps to take in preparing the budget and procedures for making the budget work. Helpful information on the use of consumer credit is also provided.

373. **Managing Your Money, A Family Plan.** 1964. 11p. il. $0.10. A 43.
16/2:M 74.

Gives helpful hints on managing your money; tells how to list how much money is coming in; describes how to make a spending plan; and gives other related information.

374. **Your Money's Worth in Foods.** 1970. 25p. il. $0.25. A 1.77:183. S/N 0100-1170.
Gives information on meal planning and food shopping for consumers interested in economizing on food. Estimates of family food costs, guides for planning meals, and tools for comparing costs of foods are also included.

FARMS AND FARMING

Included in this section are works dealing with farming in general, farm management, farmers' cooperatives, and research. For more specific information, see the subheadings following this section. For related information, see also: *Agriculture; House Construction.*

375. **Facts for Prospective Farmers.** 1970. 22p. il. $0.15. A 1.9:2221/2.

376. **Family-Farm Records 1968.** Free. F 2167.
Available from U.S. Department of Agriculture, Office of Information, Washington, D.C. 20250.

377. **Farm Index.** (Monthly) Subscription price: $2.00/year; $0.25/copy. A 93.33:vols.
Contains articles based largely on research of the Economic Research Service and on material developed in cooperation with state agricultural experiment stations.

378. **Farmer Cooperatives . . . Farm Business Tools.** 1970. 74p. il. $0.45. A 1.75:275/2.
This publication provides general information on the way farmers use cooperatives to improve their farming enterprises. It describes, through specific examples, how they do business, gives some of the values farmers receive by doing business cooperatively, and provides some brief historical and statistical information.

379. **Farmers' Handbook of Financial Calculations and Physical Measurements.** 1966. 54p. il. $0.35. A 1.76:230/966.

380. **Father-Son Agreements for Operating Farms.** 1970. 18p. il. $0.15. A 1.9:2179/3.
Deals with farm-operating agreements only. It explains kinds of agreements; how to plan for the success of such an agreement; decisions to be made; drawing up the agreement; and tax considerations.

381. **How to Start a Cooperative.** 1965. 18p. il. $0.15. A 89.4/2:18.

382. **Insurance Facts for Farmers.** 1967. 23p. il. $0.15. A 1.9:2137/5.

383. **Legal Phases of Farmer Cooperatives.** 1967. 376p. $1.25. A 89.3:10.

384. **Lightning Protection for the Farm.** 1968. 18p. il. $0.15. A 1.9: 2136/3.

385. **Safe Use and Storage of Flammable Liquids and Gases on the Farm.** 1968. 12p. il. $0.10. A 1.9:2156/3.

386. **Simple Plumbing Repairs for the Home and Farmstead.** 1970. 14p. il. $0.10. A 1.9:2202/3.
Briefly discusses simple plumbing repairs that can be made by the farmer or rural homeowner. The booklet also includes measures that can be taken to prevent plumbing troubles such as protecting water pipes from freezing, repairing water closets, clearing clogged drains, and other simple repairs.

387. **Use of Concrete on the Farm.** 1970. 30p. il. $0.20. A 1.9:2203/2.

388. **What Young Farm Families Should Know about Credit.** 1965. 20p. il. $0.10. A 1.9:2135/2.

389. **Where and How to Get a Farm: Some Questions and Answers.** 1967. Free. L 432.
Available from U.S. Department of Agriculture, Office of Information, Washington, D. C. 20250.

FARMS AND FARMING—BUILDINGS AND STRUCTURES

390. **Cattle Dipping Vat and Inspection Facility, Farm Building Plan No. 5940.** 1966. [2] p. il. $0.05. A 1.38:1035.

391. **Cattle Feeders, Farm Building Plan No. 6066.** 1970. [2] p. il. $0.05. A 1.38:1158.

392. **Corral with Curved Chute for Beef Cattle, Farm Building Plan No. 6049.** 1969. [2] p. il. $0.05. A 1.38:1136.

393. **Farm Fences.** 1961. 24p. il. $0.15. A 1.9:2173.

394. **Farm Lighting.** 1969. 16p. il. $0.10. A 1.9:2243.

395. **Farmstead Water Supply System, Farm Building Plan No. 5963.** 1968. [2] p. il. $0.05. A 1.38:1100.

396. **Farrowing and Growing Building for Hogs, Farm Building Plan No. 6032.** 1969. [2] p. il. $0.05. A 1.38:1134.

397. **4- and 5-Room Tobacco Barns, Farm Building Plans No. 6016 and No. 6017.** 1968. [2] p. il. $0.05. A 1.38:1101.

398. **Foundations for Farm Buildings.** 1970. 32p. il. $0.20. A 1.9: 1869/5.

399. **Grain Storage Building, Tilt-Up Concrete Construction, Farm Building Plan No. 6059.** 1969. [2] p. il. $0.05. A 1.38:1152.

400. **Houses and Equipment for Laying Hens, for Loose Housing.** 1967. 30p. il. $0.25. A 1.38:726/3.

401. **Laying House for Poultry, Farm Building Plan No. 6062.** 1970. [2] p. il. $0.05. A 1.38:1161.

402. **Lighting Poultry Houses.** 1968. 12p. il. $0.10. A 1.9:2229/2.

403. **Locating, Designing, and Building Country Grain Elevators.** 1966. 30p. il. $0.25. A 1.75:310.

404. **Machinery Storage and Shop, Plan No. 5849.** 1959. Free. M 785. Available from U.S. Department of Agriculture, Office of Information, Washington, D.C. 20250.

405. **Plastic Covered Greenhouse, Coldframe, Farm Building Plan No. 5941.** 1969. [2] p. il. $0.05. A 1.38:1111.

406. **Preservative Treatment of Fence Posts and Farm Timbers.** 1967. 33p. il. $0.15. A 1.9:2049/3.

407. **Roofing Farm Buildings.** 1969. 28p. il. $0.25. A 1.9:2170/3.

408. **Shed for Drying Hay, Farm Building Plan No. 6070.** 1970. [2] p. il. $0.05. A 1.38:1171.

FARMS AND FARMING—FARM PRODUCTS

409. **Classification of Cotton.** 1965. 53p. il. $0.30. A 1.38:310/3.

410. **Establishing and Managing Young Apple Orchards.** 1967. 22p. il. $0.15. A 1.9:1897/6.

411. **Facts About Pasteurization of Milk.** 1967. [6] p. il. $0.05. A 1.35:408/2.

412. **Growing Summer Cover Crops.** 1967. 16p. il. $0.10. A 1.9:2182/3. Discusses the cultural practices—inoculation, fertilizer, scarification, seeding, and turning under—of summer crops, and gives information on the adaptation, uses, and management of the most commonly used crops.

413. **Story of Cotton.** 1967. [24] p. il. $0.25. A 1.95:37.

414. **USDA Standards for Food and Farm Products.** 1970. 16p. $0.20. A 1.76:341/970.

415. **Varieties of Alfalfa.** 1968. 12p. il. $0.15. A 1.9:2231/2.

FARMS AND FARMING—LIVESTOCK

416. **Beef Cattle Breeding.** 1969. 55p. il. $0.35. A 1.75:286/2.

417. **Beef Cattle Breeds.** 1968. 28p. il. $0.15. A 1.9:2228.

418. **Beef Cattle, Dehorning, Castrating, Branding, and Marking.** 1970. 16p. il. $0.10. A 1.9:2141/3. Describes methods and techniques for dehorning, castrating and spaying, branding, and marking beef cattle and tells why these operations are desirable or necessary.

419. **Breeds of Swine.** 1966. 10p. il. $0.10. A 1.9:1263/12.

420. **Docking, Castrating and Ear Tagging Lambs.** 1969. 8p. il. $0.10. A 1.35:551.

421. **Feeding Dairy Cattle.** 1968. 32p. il. $0.20. A 1.9:2153/4.

422. **Raising Livestock on Small Farms.** 1966. Free. F 2224.
Available from U.S. Department of Agriculture, Office of Information, Washington, D.C. 20250.

423. **Slaughtering, Cutting, and Processing Beef on the Farm.** 1969. 32p. il. $0.25. A 1.9:2209/3.

424. **Slaughtering, Cutting, and Processing Pork on the Farm.** 1967. 48p. il. $0.20. A 1.9:2138/3.

FARMS AND FARMING—MACHINERY AND EQUIPMENT

425. **Automatic Feeding Equipment for Livestock and Poultry.** 1967. Free. F 2198.
Available from U.S. Department of Agriculture, Office of Information, Washington, D.C. 20250.

426. **Electric Water Pumps on the Farm.** 1966. Free. L 436.
Available from U.S. Department of Agriculture, Office of Information, Washington, D.C. 20250.

427. **Equipment for Applying Soil Pesticides.** 1966. 37p. il. $0.20. A 1.76:297.

428. **Equipment for Clearing Brush from Land.** 1970. Free. F 2180.
Available from U.S. Department of Agriculture, Office of Information, Washington, D.C. 20250.

429. **Planning Farm Machinery Replacements.** 1966. Free. L 427.
Available from U.S. Department of Agriculture, Office of Information, Washington, D.C. 20250.

430. **Sprinkler Irrigation.** $0.15. A 1.35:476/3.
Gives information on choosing, designs, buying, operation, and maintenance of sprinkler irrigation systems.

FARMS AND FARMING—SOIL MANAGEMENT

431. **Gardening on the Contour.** 1970. Free. G 179.
Available from U.S. Department of Agriculture, Office of Information, Washington, D.C. 20250.

432. **How to Control a Gully.** 1961. Free. F 2171.
Available from U.S. Department of Agriculture, Office of Information, Washington, D.C. 20250.

433. **Know Your Soil.** 1970. 16p. il. $0.20. A 1.75:267/3.
Briefly discusses the importance of a soil survey, how one is conducted, and how the results can be utilized.

434. **Soil Conservation.** (Monthly) Subscription price: $2.00/year; $0.25/copy. A 57.9: vols.
Official organ of the Soil Conservation Service. Contains articles on new developments and happenings in the field of soil conservation.

FINE ARTS

This section includes art, music, and general studies of culture and civilization. Although the National Gallery of Art and the Library of Congress are the primary sources of information on the fine arts, additional publications may be requested directly from the National Foundation on the Arts, and the National Foundation on the Humanities, both at 806 15th Street N.W., Washington, D.C. 20506.

435. **Art Treasures of the World.** 1968. 207p. il. $12.50. Available from Describes 100 masterpieces of painting, sculpture, and architecture with full-color reproductions of each. Available from National Gallery of Art, Washington, D.C.

436. **The Bite of the Print.** 1964. 272p. il. $12.50.
This book, by Frank and Dorothy Getlein, traces the use of the print as a means of social comment. An explanation is given of the physical processes of printmaking. Includes 290 black and white illustrations. Available from National Gallery of Art, Washington, D.C.

437. **Civilisation.** 1970. 359p. il. $15.00.
A book by Kenneth Clark which explores our history and culture through the diverse creative works of Western man. 286 illustrations, 48 in color. Available from National Gallery of Art, Washington, D.C.

438. **Creative Intuition in Art and Poetry.** By Jacques Maritain. 1964. 424p. il. $3.95.
Nine essays about the creative process of art and prose. Available from National Gallery of Art, Washington, D.C.

439. **Famous Paintings.** $5.00.
Contains 20 color reproductions accompanied by descriptive text, illustrating a general history of painting from the Italian Renaissance to the present. Valuable teaching aid in the general field of art history. Available from the National Gallery of Art, Washington, D.C.

> Angelico, Fra. *The Madonna of Humility*
> Antonello da Messina. *The Madonna and Child*
> Botticelli. *The Adoration of the Magi*

Cézanne. *Still Life*
David, Gerard. *The Rest on the Flight into Egypt*
David, Jacques-Louis. *Madame Hamelin*
Degas. *Achille de Gas in the Uniform of a Cadet*
Dyck, van. *Philip, Lord Wharton*
Giorgione. *The Adoration of the Shepherds*
Goya. *Señora Sebasa García*
Hals. *Balthasar Coymans*
Manet. *The Old Musician*
Raphael. *The Alba Madonna*
Rembrandt. *Self-Portrait (Mellon Collection)*
Renoir. *A Girl with a Watering Can*
Reynolds. *Lady Caroline Howard*
Stuart, Gilbert. *Mrs. Richard Yates*
Titian. *Venus and Adonis*
Velázquez. *Portrait of a Young Man*
Vermeer. *The Girl with a Red Hat*

440. **Favorite Subjects in Western Art.** 1968. 244p. il. $2.25.
A compilation by A. L. Todd and Dorothy B. Weisland of the most widely depicted subjects in painting and sculpture. Available from National Gallery of Art, Washington, D.C.

441. **Folk Music, A Catalog of Folk Songs, Ballads, Dances, Instrumental Pieces, and Folk Tales of the United States and Latin America on Phonograph Records.** 1964. 107p. $0.40. LC 12.2:F 71/3/964.

442. **Masterpieces of Sculpture from the National Gallery of Art.** 1949. 184p. il. $7.50.
A book with 142 full-page black and white illustrations of 56 important sculptures executed by 41 Western artists during the period from 1200 to 1900 A.D. Available from National Gallery of Art, Washington, D.C.

443. **National Gallery of Art: American Paintings and Sculpture: An Illustrated Catalogue.** 1970. 192p. il. $5.00.
A complete checklist with accompanying reproductions of all the American paintings and sculpture. Includes an index of donors and over 500 black and white illustrations. Available from National Gallery of Art, Washington, D.C.

444. **National Gallery of Art; European Paintings and Sculpture: Illustrations.** 1967. 171p. il. $3.75.
This book is a companion to the *Summary Catalogue of European Painting and Sculpture* published in 1965. It reproduces the works of art listed in the Summary Catalogue as well as the new acquisitions of the past two years. Includes an index of donors and 1,228 black and white illustrations. Available from the National Gallery of Art, Washington, D.C.

445. **National Gallery of Art; Summary Catalogue of European Paintings and Sculpture.** 1966. 192p. $2.85.
A complete checklist in one volume. Available from National Gallery of Art, Washington, D.C.

446. **National Gallery of Art: Ten Schools of Painting Series.** 1960. $0.35 each. Set of 10 in slipcase, $3.00.
A series of 10 booklets covering the major schools of painting in the National Gallery with text written by the staff. Each book contains 16 color plates, an historical introductory essay, a page of text about each illustration, and an index. Available from National Gallery of Art, Washington, D.C.

> **No. 1. American Painting in the National Gallery of Art.** By Margaret Bouton. 8-14A-59.
> **No. 2. French Painting of the 19th Century in the National Gallery of Art.** By Grose Evans. 8-14B-59.
> **No. 3. Early Italian Painting in the National Gallery of Art.** By Fern Rusk Shapley. 8-14C-59.
> **No. 4. French Painting of the 16th—18th Centuries in the National Gallery of Art.** By Hereward Lester Cooke. 8-14D-59.
> **No. 5. Flemish Painting in the National Gallery of Art.** By Hugh T. Broadley. 8-14E-59.
> **No. 6. Later Italian Painting in the National Gallery of Art.** By Fern Rusk Shapley. 8-14F-59.
> **No. 7. Dutch Painting in the National Gallery of Art.** By Thomas P. Baird. 8-14G-59.
> **No. 8. British Painting in the National Gallery of Art.** By Hereward Lester Cooke. 8-14H-59.
> **No. 9. German Painting in the National Gallery of Art.** By Hugh T. Broadley. 8-14I-59.
> **No. 10. Spanish Painting in the National Gallery of Art.** By Grose Evans. 8-14J-59.

447. **The Nude: A Study in Ideal Form.** By Kenneth Clark. 1956, Clothbound, $7.50. 1964, Paperback, $2.45. 480p. il.
A survey of the nude from the Greeks through the present. Includes 298 black and white illustrations. Available from National Gallery of Art, Washington, D.C.

448. **Sousa Band, A Discography.** 1970. 123p. il. $1.50. LC 12.2:So 8.
Lists all known recordings of the Sousa Band in the United States and abroad. Thoroughly indexed.

449. **The History of Western Art.** 1959. 320p. il. $1.50.
A comprehensive history of art from the primitive cave painters to the abstract expressionists. Includes 400 black and white illustrations. Available from National Gallery of Art, Washington, D.C.

450. The National Gallery of Art also has available 11'' x 14'' color reproductions of art works in its collection, at $0.35 each. Among reproductions available are Audobon's *Columbia Jay,* Botticelli's *Adoration of the Magi,* Degas' *Ballet Scene,* Picasso's *Still Life,* Toulouse-Lautrec's *Quadrille at the Moulin Rouge,* and Whistler's *The White Girl.*

FIRST AID

See also—Accident Prevention; Safety Measures; Survival; Water Safety.

451. **First Aid, For the Mineral and Allied Industries.** 1971. 191p. il. $1.25. I 28.16:F 51/2/970. S/N 2404—0883.
Provides features, treatments, and techniques in first aid which are widely used and accepted, and which will be useful under the unique conditions encountered in the mineral extractive industries.

452. **First Aid Instruction Course.** 1970. 276p. il. $3.50. I 28.2:F 51/2.
Covers the six fundamental areas in first aid: 1) artificial respiration; 2) control of bleeding; 3) physical shock; 4) open and closed wounds and burns; 5) fractures and dislocations; and 6) transportation of the wounded. The important topics to be covered in each area are given in a logical order of presentation, along with suggested comments, supporting visual aids, demonstrations, and student exercises.

453. **Rescue Breathing.** 1966. $0.05. FS 2.6/2:B 74.
This wallet-sized card (3.7 in. x 2.3 in.) describes the correct procedure for administering mouth-to-mouth resuscitation. One side illustrates the procedure for infants and small children; the other side, adults and children five years and older.

454. **Standard First Aid Training Course.** 1965. 112p. il. $0.70. D 208.11: F 51/3/965.

FISH AND WILDLIFE

455. **America's Upland Game Birds.** 1971. 6p. il. $0.10. I 49.36/2:4/2.
Discusses species of upland game birds: quail, grouse, wild turkey, and chachalaca. Describes each bird, its habitat, and its characteristics, with a sketch of each.

456. **Bald Eagle.** 1969. 6p. il. $0.10. I 49.36/2:20.
Briefly describes the history of the bald eagle in America; tells how it has come to be threatened with extinction; and gives details on the physical characteristics and life habits.

457. **Birds in Our Lives.** 1966. 576p. il. $9.00. I 49.2:B 53/3.
Describes the intensive search for knowledge of how birds migrate over long
distances with great precision, tells of laws and treaties to protect birdlife in
North America, and discusses organizations that are working to assure the
preservation of birdlife.

458. **Desert Bighorn Sheep.** 8p. il. $0.10. I 49.36/2:19.
Describes this extremely rare animal, its migrations, competitors and enemies,
and areas established for its protection.

459. **Diving Ducks, A Wildlife Services Leaflet.** 1971. 16p. il. $0.15.
I 49.13/3:D 85.
Describes diving ducks, including redhead, canvasback, scaup, bufflehead,
ring-necked and related bay or sea ducks. Discusses their autumn migration
and wintering, spring migration, breeding and courtship, and the need for
better care of our nation's wetlands for the preservation of waterfowl.

460. **Dolphins and Porpoises.** 1965. 8p. il. $0.05. I 49.28/2:1.

461. **Ducks at a Distance, A Waterfowl Identification Guide.** 1963. 20p. il.
$0.35. I 49.6/2:D 85/2. **—Spanish Edition.** $0.30. I 49.6/2:D 85/2.
This is a guide for the identification of ducks and geese in their fall migration plumages. Includes full-color illustrations.

462. **Exotic Fishes and Other Aquatic Organisms Introduced into North
America.** 1970. 29p. il. $0.45. SI 1.27:59.
Discusses the extent of introductions of exotic (foreign) life, especially
fishes, into the aquatic environment of North America and comments on the
effects of these releases on the environment and man's economy. The kinds
of exotic fishes are summarized with respect to their place of origin, the mode
of transport, the area of release, and the use of the species.

463. **Foreign Game.**
These pamphlets, issued by the Division of Wildlife Research, contain a
description of the foreign game, its habitat, climate in which it lives, its
food, behavior and general habits, abundance, interbreeding, its relation to
agriculture, sporting characteristics, and its introductions and propagation.
Recently issued pamphlets are listed below.

> **The Bearded Partridges.** 1970. 4p. il. $0.10. I 49.74:7.
> **The Black Francolins.** 1970. 4p. il. $0.10. I 49.74:1.
> **The Black Grouse.** 1970. 4p. il. $0.10. I 49.74:5.
> **The Copper Pheasants.** 1970. 4p. il. $0.10. I 49.74:12.
> **The Coturnix or Old World Quails.** 1970. 4p. il. $0.10.
> I 49.74:10
> **The Eastern Gray Partridges.** 1970. 4p. il. $0.10. I 49.74:8.
> **The Gray Francolins.** 1970. 4p. il. $0.10. I 49.74:2.
> **The Green Pheasants.** 1970. 4p. il. $0.10. I 49.74:13.
> S/N 2410-0206.

The Manchurian Ring-Necked Pheasant. 1970. 4p. il. $0.10.
I 49.74:9.
The Red Junglefowls. 1970. 4p. il. $0.10. I 49.74:6.
The Redwing Francolins. 1970. 4p. il. $0.10. I 49.74:3.
S/N 2410-0196.
The Reeves Pheasant. 1970. 4p. il. $0.10. I 49.74:14.
The South African Graywing Francolins. 1970. 4p. il. $0.10.
I 49.74:4.
The South Korean Ring-Necked Pheasant. 1970. 4p. il. $0.10.
I 49.74:15.
The Yellow-Necked Spurfowl. 1970. 4p. il. $0.10. I 49.74:11.

464. Homes for Birds. 1969. 18p. il. $0.20. I 1.72:14/2.

465. National Wildlife Refuges, 1969. 1970. 8p. il. $0.15. I 49.66:82.

466. Poisonous Snakes of the World. 1970. 212p. il. $3.25. D 206.6/
3:Sn 1.
A training aid and identification guide to the most widely distributed
species of dangerously venomous snakes. Geographic distribution of all
currently recognized species of venomous snakes is presented in tabular
form and information on habitat and biology of important snake species is
provided. First aid procedures in case of snakebite, suggestions for the
definitive medical management of the snakebite victim, and a table of world
sources of antivenins are also given.

467. Puddle Ducks. 1970. 16p. il. $0.15. I 49.2:D 85/2.
Gives a description of puddle ducks, their habits and characteristics, where
they live. Also discusses mating and nesting habits. Illustrations accompany
the text.

468. Rare and Endangered Fish and Wildlife of the United States. 1969.
274p. $3.00. I 49.66:34/2.

469. The Right to Exist, A Report on Our Endangered Wildlife. 1969.
12p. il. $0.25. I 49.66:69.

470. Waterfowl Tomorrow. 1964. 770p. il. map. $4.00. I 49.2:W 29/5.
Details simply but fully the many natural processes and the numerous
activities of man which have affected these birds from glacial times to the
present day. Deals with progress and recommendations for assuring the future
of these wildfowl. It is well illustrated with more than 150 photographs of
waterfowl and dozens of waterfowl drawings by the well-known wildlife
artist, Bob Hines.

471. Whooping Cranes. 1969. 16p. il. $0.10. I 49.66:75.

472. Wildlife on the Public Lands. 1964. 36p. il. $0.35. I 53.2:W 64.
This booklet on wildlife of the public lands of the U.S. contains more than 50
full-color photos and illustrations of Western wildlife, with habitat data.

473. **Wildlife Portrait Series No. 1.** 1969. $2.00/set. I 49.71:1.
Printed in natural color, this set of 10 pictures (each 14 in. x 17 in.) depicts many different species of wildlife.

474. **Wolves of Isle Royale.** 1966. 210p. il. $1.00. I 29.13:7.
Based on a three-year investigation of the wolf-moose relationships in Isle Royale National Park—a 210-square-mile island in northwestern Lake Superior—this book, which includes numerous photographs, gives an account of the great wild dog of North America and its largest antlered prey. An appendix giving descriptions of all observed moose hunts by the wolves is also included.

FLUORIDATION

475. **Better Water Is in the Works.** 1970. 4p. il. $0.05. HE 20.3102:W 29.
Describes the relationship of water fluoridation and healthier teeth for children.

476. **Fluoridation. No Better Health Investment.** 1970. 4p. il. $0.10.
HE 20.3102:F 67/3.

477. **School Fluoridation, New Protection for a Child's Smile.** 1970. 4p. il.
$0.05. HE 20.3102:F 67.
This leaflet briefly discusses school fluoridation and how it can help children's teeth.

478. **Water Fluoridation, The Search and the Victory.** 1970. 302p. $3.25.
HE 20.3402:F 67.
Covers the major events and the research which provided the basis for water fluoridation. Brings together for the first time a chronological account of the many and varied facets of water fluoridation.

FLOWERS

See also—Gardening; Plant Pests and Diseases.

479. **Growing Azaleas and Rhododendrons.** 1969. 8p. il. $0.10.
A 1.77:71/3.

480. **Growing Camellias.** 1971. 12p. il. $0.15. A 1.77:86/5. S/N 0100-0866.
Describes species of camellias, and gives information on buying, planting, care, and disease and insect control.

481. **Growing Chrysanthemums in the Home Garden.** 1970. 8p. il. $0.10.
A 1.77:65/4.
Discusses planting and care of chrysanthemums and includes information on control of diseases and insect pests.

482. **Growing Dahlias.** 1970. 8p. il. $0.10. A 1.77:131/2.
Briefly describes classes of dahlias; discusses planting and care, propagation; and gives recommendations for control of diseases and insects.

483. **Growing Flowering Annuals.** 1970. 16p. il. $0.10. A 1.77:91/4.
Describes the characteristics and best ornamental use of common flowering annuals, and gives instructions for their proper planting and care. Also includes directions for starting plants indoors.

484. **Growing Flowering Perennials.** 1970. 32p. il. $0.25. A 1.77:114/3.
Contains information on how to select and plant flowering perennials for the home garden. Explains how to prepare soil; planting and setting plants; the care of the garden; and how to start plants indoors.

485. **Growing Hollies.** 1967. 8p. il. $0.05. A 1.77:130.

486. **Growing Iris in the Home Garden.** 1970. 8p. il. $0.10. A 1.77:66/6.
Describes the various types of irises, how they grow, the planting and care of the plants, propagation, diseases, and iris insects.

487. **Growing Magnolias.** 1968. 8p. il. $0.05. A 1.77:132.

488. **Growing Ornamentals in Urban Gardens.** 1971. 22p. il. $0.15. A 1.77:188.
Describes containers and other growing areas suitable for urban gardens, care of plants, natural and artificial lighting, signs of poor growing conditions, and air pollution problems.

489. **Growing Pansies.** 1970. 8p. il. $0.10. A 1.77:149/2.
Describes varieties of pansies and gives information on planting, care, disease and pest control.

490. **Growing Peonies.** 1971. 11p. il. $0.10. A 1.77:126/4.
This bulletin discusses the growing of peonies, how to buy and plant peonies, and how to care for the plants. Information on types of diseases, insects, and precautions to be taken when using pesticides is also given.

491. **Growing the Flowering Dogwood.** 1970. 8p. il. $0.10. A 1.77:88/5.
Briefly describes varieties of the flowering dogwood; discusses adaptation, planting and care, and gives recommendations for control of major diseases and insect pests.

492. **Roses for the Home.** 1970. 24p. il. $0.15. A 1.77:25/9.
Covers in detail the many types of roses grown in this country, and gives explicit instructions for their planting, pruning, care, and treatment. Numerous illustrations show how to prepare the soil for planting and how to take special care of the newly planted or transplanted bush. Included is a brief description of some of the types of diseases and insects that attack roses.

493. **Selecting and Growing House Plants.** 1968. 32p. il. $0.15. A 1.77:82/2.

Describes decorative plants suitable for home culture, gives directions for culture, and includes information on control of plant environment and on propagation.

FOODS

Included in this section are works dealing with foods and nutrition as related to diets and health. For more specific works, see the subheadings following this section. For related information, *see also—Child and Infant Care; Family Finances and Budgeting.*

Note that GPO publishes a separate Consumer Information Price List (No. 86, 5th ed., 1971. Free) which covers many aspects of consumer education including such areas as foods, nutrition, cookbooks, diet, etc.

494. **Calories and Weight, The USDA Pocket Guide.** 1968. 75p. il. $0.25. A 1.77:153.
Explains what to do to lose weight, and how to choose food for weight control and reduce calories. Includes a list of calories and a guide for estimating serving sizes of meat. A general index to the calorie tables is also included.

495. **Conserving the Nutritive Values in Foods.** 1971. 16p. il. $0.10. A 1.77:90/3. S/N 0100-0869.
Presents factors that affect losses in nutritive value that take place in foods; gives helpful information on how these nutritive losses can be minimized in the care and preparation of foods in the home; and briefly discusses conserving the nutritive value in canned and frozen foods.

496. **Dry Cereals.** 1970. iv + 284p. il. $1.25. Y 4.C 73/2:91—72.
Presents hearings held before the Consumer Subcommittee of the Senate Committee on Commerce on the nutritional content of dry breakfast cereals.

497. **Eat a Good Breakfast to Start a Good Day.** 1969. 8p. il. $0.05. A 1.35:268/5.

498. **Eat Well for You and Your Baby Who Is on the Way.** 1969. 4p. il. $0.10. FS 17.202:B 11/5.

499. **Facts About Nutrition.** 1969. 24p. il. $0.35. FS 2.22:N 95/968.
Discusses important food elements, good sources of vitamins and critical minerals, infant nutrition, nutrition in pregnancy, and nutrition in old age. Also gives a sample meal plan for an adequate diet, and sample menus for adults.

500. **Facts for Consumers, Food Additives.** 1964. 13p. il. $0.15. FS 13.111:10/2.

501. **Family Fare, A Guide to Good Nutrition.** 1970. 91p. il. $0.45.
A 1.77:1/6.
Includes a daily food guide, a simple, workable presentation of the kinds and
amounts of foods to have each day; tips on meal planning; facts about important nutrients, how they function in the body and where they are found in
foods; helpful information on buying, storing, measuring, and using foods;
a selection of recipes, main dishes, vegetables, salads, soups, sauces, breads,
sandwiches, desserts, plus variations of some of these recipes; menu suggestions; ways to use leftovers, and a list of cooking terms.

502. **Food for the Family with Young Childrei..** 1970. 16p. il. $0.10.
A 1.77:5/10.
Contains information on food for the family; planning meals; and sample
menus for a week. Also tells how to reduce food bills and provides a list
of food groups.

503. **Foods Your Children Need.** 1958. 16p. il. $0.10. HE 21.111:14.
Lists various kinds of foods that provide the daily requirements in children's
diets. Also discusses good eating habits for children.

504. **Include These Foods in the Lunch Each Day, Serve Each Child a
Real "Type A."** 1969. 10½ x 8 in. $0.15. A 98.9:4. **—Spanish Edition.**
1970. 10½ x 8 in. $0.15. A 98.9:4-S.
Colored chart depicting the type and amount of food a child should be
served for lunch each day.

505. **Nutritive Value of Foods.** 1970. 41p. il. $0.30. A 1.77:72/3.
Contains information on the food values of 615 foods commonly used in
this country, the yield of cooked meat per pound of raw meat, and recommended daily dietary allowances.

506. **Research Explores Nutrition and Dental Health.** 1970. 16p. il.
$0.30. HE 20.3402:N 95.
Discusses which foods promote or prevent tooth decay; periodontal (gum)
disease; malformations of the mouth; and other diseases of the mouth.

507. **Some Questions and Answers About Dietary Supplements. FDA
Fact Sheet.** 1969. 3p. Free. 7700-017.
Most frequently asked questions on multi-vitamin and multi-mineral prepara-
tions and on enriched and fortified foods. Available from Consumer Product
Information, Washington, D.C. 20407.

FOODS—BUYING GUIDES

A number of entries in this section are subtitled "A Guide for Consumers." These USDA guides provide tips on both the purchase of
these items and the actual cooking. The numerous recipes in each
booklet give instructions for the economical methods of serving
items in each food group.

508. Bargain Freezer Meats? There May Be a Catch to It! 1970. 15p. il. $0.10. FT 1.3/2:5.
The pamphlet warns the consumer about "bait-and-switch" operators and unscrupulous advertising.

509. Beef and Veal in Family Meals, A Guide for Consumers. 1970. 30p. il. $0.20. A 1.77:118/3.
Identifies the numerous cuts of beef and veal found in supermarkets and gives information on how to select and store these meats. Also tells how to suit the cooking method to the particular cut.

510. Cheese Varieties and Descriptions. 1969. 151p. $0.65. A 1.76: 54/969.

511. Eggs in Family Meals, A Guide for Consumers. 1967. 32p. il. $0.15. A 1.77:103/2.
Contains tips on buying and storing eggs. Tells how to poach, fry, bake, scramble, and cook eggs in the shell. Includes a wide assortment of recipes in which eggs are an essential ingredient, and information on the selection and use of dried and frozen egg products.

512. Fruits in Family Meals, A Guide for Consumers. 1970. 30p. il. $0.20. A 1.77:125/2.
Presents comprehensive information on buying, storing, and using fruits—fresh, frozen, canned, and dried. Includes up-to-date information on basic cookery of fruits, and recipes featuring fruits in appetizers, beverages, breads, desserts, salads, and sauces. Also gives number of calories per serving for each recipe.

513. How to Buy Meat for Your Freezer. 1969. 28p. il. $0.20. A 1.77: 166/2.

514. How to Buy Beef Steaks. 1968. 16p. il. $0.10. A 1.77:145.

515. How to Buy Beef Roasts. 1968. 16p. il. $0.10. A 1.77:146.

516. How to Buy Butter. 1968. 8p. il. $0.05. A 1.77:148.

517. How to Buy Canned and Frozen Vegetables. 1969. 24p. il. $0.30. A 1.77:167.

518. How to Buy Dry Beans, Peas, and Lentils. 1970. 12p. il. $0.25. A 1.77:177.

519. How to Buy Eggs. 1968. 8p. il. $0.10. A 1.77:144.

520. How to Buy Fresh Fruits. 1967. 24p. il. $0.15. A 1.77:141.

521. How to Buy Fresh Vegetables. 1967. 24p. il. $0.15. A 1.77:143.

522. How to Buy Poultry. 1968. 8p. il. $0.10. A 1.77:157.

523. **Milk in Family Meals, A Guide for Consumers.** 1967. 22p. il. $0.15. A 1.77:127.

524. **Pork in Family Meals, A Guide for Consumers.** 1969. Free. G 160. Available from U.S. Department of Agriculture, Office of Information, Washington, D.C. 20250.

525. **Poultry in Family Meals, A Guide for Consumers.** 1967. 30p. il. $0.15. A 1.77:110/2.

526. **Vegetables in Family Meals, A Guide for Consumers.** 1970. 32p. il. $0.20. A 1.77:105/4.

FOODS—PREPARATION

527. **How to Cook Clams.** 1960. 14p. il. $0.30. I 49.39:8.

528. **How to Cook Crabs.** 1956. 14p. il. $0.30. I 49.39:10.

529. **How to Cook Halibut.** 1956. 10p. il. $0.30. I 49.39:9.

530. **How to Cook Lobsters.** 1957. 14p. il. $0.30. I 49.39:11.

531. **How to Cook Ocean Perch.** 1952. 10p. il. $0.30. I 49.39:6.

532. **How to Cook Oysters.** 1961. 12p. il. $0.30. I 49.39:3/2.

533. **How to Cook Salmon.** 1951. 19p. il. $0.30. I 49.39:4.

534. **How to Cook Scallops.** 1959. 18p. il. $0.35. I 49.39:13.

535. **How to Cook Shrimp.** 1952. 14p. il. $0.20. I 49.39:7.

536. **How to Cook Tuna.** 1957. 14p. il. $0.20. I 49.39:12.

537. **Let's Cook Fish, A Complete Guide to Fish Cookery.** 1967. 55p. il. $0.60. I 49.49/2:8.

538. **Letters from the Captain's Wife. Portfolio of 12 Leaves.** 1966. 8p. il. $0.70. I 49.49/2:4.
On May 17, 1867, a mythical ship took a mythical trip with a mythical crew aboard. On this voyage, Lucy, the Captain's wife, an avid recipe collector, wrote a series of letters to her cousin who remained at home. The result is an unusual group of kitchen-tested seafood recipes which reflect the charm of a bygone era, yet whisper of today's convenience. These letters, reproduced in the original writing style, together with pen and ink sketches, are inserted in a portfolio.

539. **Money-Saving Main Dishes.** 1970. 48p. il. $0.30. A 1.77:43/5.
Contains recipes and suggestions for about 150 main dishes—easy to make, hearty, and economical. Most of the dishes give six liberal servings, while a few provide more. The recipes list the ingredients and cooking directions, provide ideas for variations, and suggest suitable foods to serve with each main dish.

540. **Potatoes in Popular Ways.** 1969. 22p. il. $0.20. A 1.77:55/4.

FOODS—PRESERVATION

541. **Freezing Meat and Fish in the Home.** 1970. 24p. il. $0.25. A 1.77:93/5.

542. **Home Canning of Fruits and Vegetables.** 1971. 31p. il. $0.20. A 1.77:8/7.

543. **Home Canning of Meat and Poultry.** 1970. 24p. il. $0.15. A 1.77: 106/3.

544. **Home Freezing of Fruits and Vegetables.** 1969. 48p. il. $0.20. A 1.77:10/6.

545. **Home Freezing of Poultry.** 1970. 24p. il. $0.15. A 1.77:70/4.

546. **How to Make Jellies, Jams, and Preserves at Home.** 1967. 30p. il. $0.15. A 1.77:56/3.

547. **Making and Preserving Apple Cider.** 1970. 14p. il. $0.10. A 1.9: 2125/4.

548. **Making Pickles and Relishes at Home.** 1970. 31p. il. $0.15. A 1.77: 92/4.

549. **Storing Perishable Foods in the Home.** 1971. 9p. il. $0.10. A 1.77: 78/4.
Gives specific directions on how to handle, prepare for storage, and under what conditions to store, a wide variety of foods. Up-to-date information on care of perishable foods in the home to delay spoilage and preserve nutritive value, quality, and flavor.

550. **Storing Vegetables and Fruits in Basements, Cellars, Outbuildings, and Pits.** 1970. 17p. il. $0.15. A 1.77:119/2.
Tells how to store vegetables and fruits without refrigeration in colder parts of the United States; discusses storage facilities, temperature and moisture control; and gives storage requirements of vegetables and fruits.

FOREIGN RELATIONS

See—International Relations.

FORESTRY AND FOREST PRODUCTS

See also—Trees.

In addition to the Forestry Price List (No. 43, available free from the Superintendent of Documents), the U.S. Forest Service, an agency of the Department of Agriculture, issues

a catalog of its publications. Often this catalog lists publications which are not included in any GPO bibliographies. For
a free copy of the Forest Service catalog, write to: Forest
Service, U.S. Department of Agriculture, Washington, D.C.
20250.

551.   **Demand and Price Situation for Forest Products.** 1970. 79p. il. $0.75.
A 1.38:1165.

552.   **Economic Importance of Timber in the United States.** 1963. 91p. il.
$0.50. A 1.38:941.

553.   **Forest Products Utilization and Marketing Assistance for Woodland
Owners, Loggers, Processors.** 1966. Folder PA-752.
Available from Forest Service, U.S. Department of Agriculture, Washington,
D.C. 20250.

554.   **Forest Regions of United States, Map with List of Principal Trees of
Forest Regions and General Description of the Forest Regions.** 1960. 1 sheet.
$0.10. A 13.28:F 76/2/960.

555.   **Forestry Activities. A Guide for Youth Group Leaders.** 1970. 31p. il.
$0.20. A 1.68:457/3.
Presents a variety of forestry projects to be used nationwide by youths in
helping to preserve our natural resources for future generations. A list of
materials to help teach forest conservation is also included.

556.   **Forestry Schools in the United States.** 1970. 24p. il. $0.15. A 13.2:
Sch 6/970.
A directory listing forestry schools by states.

557.   **Highlights in the History of Forest Conservation.** 1968. 40p. $0.20.
A 1.75:83/5.

558.   **In Your Service, The Work of Uncle Sam's Forest Rangers.** 1969.
24p. il. $0.25. A 1.75:136/4.

559.   **Lumber Production in the United States, 1799-1946.** H. B. Steer,
F.S. 1948. 233p. Misc. Pub. No. 669.
Available from Forest Service, Dept. of Agriculture, Washington, D.C. 20250.

560.   **Papermaking; Art and Craft.** 1968. 96p. $3.00. Z 663.15.P 3.
Available from Library of Congress, Information Office, Washington, D.C.
20540.

561.   **Products of American Forests.** 1969. 30p. il. $0.50. A 1.38:861/2.
Describes the many products coming from the American forests including
composite wood products such as house construction, veneer and plywood,
and furniture; wood chemical products and seasonal crops and extractive
materials.

562. **Tables for Estimating Board-Foot Volume of Timber.** 1956. 94p. $0.45. A 13.2:T 48/17.

563. **Wood . . . Colors and Kinds.** 1956. 36p. AH No. 101.
Descriptions, including range, properties, and principal uses, are provided for 18 hardwoods and 14 softwoods—the species most commonly found in retail lumber markets. Each description is accompanied by a full-color illustration showing grain pattern and other characteristics. End-grained, edge-grained (quarter-sawed), and flat-grained (plain-sawed) surfaces are all displayed in each illustration. A glossary is included which defines the terms used in the descriptions. Available from Forest Service, U.S. Department of Agriculture, Washington, D.C. 20250.

564. **Wood Handbook.** 1935. 325p.
Contains basic information on wood as a construction material with data for its use in design and specification. Covers many phases of the subject, including the structure of wood, physical properties of wood, strength values of clear woods and related factors, grades and sizes of lumber, gluing of wood, plywood, and other crossbanded products, control of moisture content and shrinkage of wood, fire resistance of wood construction, wood preservation, and thermal insulation. Available from Forest Service, U.S. Department of Agriculture, Washington, D.C. 20250.

FRUITS AND VEGETABLES

See also—Gardening.

565. **Blueberry Growing.** 1966. 33p. il. $0.15. A 1.9:1951/5.

566. **Dwarf Fruit Trees, Selection and Care.** 1971. 8p. il. $0.10. A 1.35:407/5.

567. **Growing American Bunch Grapes.** 1968. 22p. il. $0.15. A 1.9:2123/3.

568. **Growing Blackberries.** 1967. 10p. il. $0.10. A 1.9:2160/3.

569. **Growing Cauliflower and Broccoli.** 1969. 12p. il. $0.15. A 1.9:2239.

570. **Growing Eggplant.** 1968. 4p. il. $0.05. A 1.35:351/6.

571. **Growing Parsnips.** 1967. 4p. il. $0.05. A 1.35:545.

572. **Growing Pumpkins and Squashes.** 1969. 21p. il. $0.20. A 1.9:2086/6.

573. **Growing Raspberries.** 1970. 14p. il. $0.10. A 1.9:2165/4.
Describes the various types and varieties of raspberries; discusses adaptation, cultivation, harvesting, irrigation and propagation; and includes information on preventing winter injury and the control of diseases and insects.

574. **Minigardens for Vegetables.** 1970. 12p. $0.15. 0100-0821.
For the home gardener with limited planting space, instructions for growing vegetables in containers; includes information on selection, planting, and care. Available from Consumer Product Information, Washington, D.C. 20407.

575. **Muskmelons for the Garden.** 1968. 6p. il. $0.05. A 1.35:509/3.

576. **Strawberry Varieties in the United States.** 1967. 16p. il. $0.10.
A 1.9:1043/12.

577. **Suburban and Farm Vegetable Gardens.** 1970. 46p. il. $0.40.
A 1.77:9/5.
Gives simple instructions on garden preparation and soil improvement; planning and arranging the garden; obtaining the seed and quantity of seed required; starting of plants in hotbeds and other plant growing devices; care of the garden; time of planting; and culture of specific crops.

578. **Watermelons for the Garden.** 1966. 8p. il. $0.05. A 1.35:528/2.

GARDENING

See also—Botany; Flowers; Fruits and Vegetables; Insects;
Plant Pests and Diseases; Trees; Weeds.

579. **How Much Fertilizer Shall I Use?** 1963. 6p. $0.05. A 1.35:307/3.
A gardener's guide for converting tons or pounds per acre into pints, cups, tablespoons, or teaspoons per row or plant.

580. **How to Buy Lawn Seed.** 1969. 6p. il. $0.10. A 1.77:169.

581. **Selecting Fertilizers for Lawns and Gardens.** 1971. 8p. il. $0.10.
A 1.77:89/3.
Briefly describes types of fertilizers available to home gardeners and the advantages of each. Brief information given on obtaining recommendations for specific problems regarding soil fertility.

GARDENING—LANDSCAPING

582. **Better Lawns.** 1971. 30p. il. $0.25. A 1.77:51/8. S/N 0100-1102.
Tells how to establish, maintain, and renovate a lawn; gives suggestions for coping with lawn problems, such as weeds, diseases, and insects; and provides descriptions of various grasses and ground cover plants.

583. **Landscape Development.** 1967. 128p. il. $0.75. I 20.12/2:L 23.
Discusses and illustrates the basic principles needed for landscaping; introduces reasons for beautifying, cleaning up, and then maintaining; deals with possible construction and planting details; explores ways of grading and preventing soil erosion; and discusses ways to maintain what is developed.

584. **Planting and Maintenance of Trees, Shrubs, and Vines.** 1959. 12p. il. $0.20. D 103.6/3:1110-1-323.
Prescribes standard practices and techniques for the planting and maintenance of trees, shrubs, and vines.

GEOGRAPHY

585. **Boundaries of the United States and the Several States.** 1966. 291p. il. map. $1.75. I 19.3:1212.
Gives information on the source and marking of the boundaries of the United States, individual states, and U.S. territories. Miscellaneous geographic information concerning area, altitudes, geographic centers, and a map of the United States showing routes of the principal explorers from 1501 to 1844 are also included.

586. **Dictionary of Alaska Place Names.** 1967. 1084p. il. 12 maps. $8.50. I 19.16:567.

587. **Islands of America.** 1970. [3] + 95p. il. $2.00. I 66.2:Is 4.
This illustrated book presents the first comprehensive inventory of the recreational, scenic, natural and historical values of America's islands. It also discusses those islands which remain in a natural or near-natural state, those which have been developed and those already protected by public ownership. Special mention is given to islands with outstanding recreation potential. Also includes recommendations for the protection and enhancement of our island resources.

588. **Our Caribbean Gems, The U.S. Virgin Islands.** 1969. 32p. il. $0.45. I 35.13/2:C 19/969.
This full-color booklet brings the beauty of these islands to prospective tourists, students, teachers, and armchair tourists. A wealth of information about the history, climate, educational opportunities, government, and tourist regulations is presented and sources for additional information on the Virgin Islands are listed.

GEOGRAPHY—MAPS AND ATLASES

589. **Civil War Maps, An Annotated List.** 1961. 138p. $1.00. LC 5.2:C 49.

590. **Descriptive List of Treasure Maps and Charts in the Library of Congress.** 1964. 29p. $0.45. LC 5.2:T 71/964.

591. **The Look of Our Land, An Airphoto Atlas of the Rural United States: The East and South.** 1971. 99p. il. $1.25. A 1.76:406. S/N 0100-1279.
Presents airphoto index sheets and a stereo pair of contact prints to illustrate each of 42 land resource areas in the eastern and southern portions of the United States.

592. **The Look of Our Land, An Airphoto Atlas of the Rural United States: The Far West.** 1970. 48p. il. $0.60. A 1.76:372.
The aerial photographs in this bulletin show characteristics and use of land in three areas in California, Oregon, Washington, and Idaho. Accompanying the photographs of each area is a brief description of land use, climate, soils, and topography for the area which the photos illustrate.

593. **The Look of Our Land, An Airphoto Atlas of the Rural United States: The Mountains and Deserts.** 1971. 68p. il. $1.00. A 1.76:409.
Presents air-photo index sheets and a stereo pair of contact prints to illustrate each of 32 resource areas in 11 Western states. Accompanying the photos of each area is a brief description of land use, climate, soils, and topography.

594. **The Look of Our Land, An Airphoto Atlas of the Rural United States: North Central States.** 1970. 63p. il. $0.75. A 1.76:384. S/N 0100-1104.
The airphotos in this handbook were selected to show characteristics and land use in 28 resource areas in three regions comprising all or parts of 14 North Central states. Accompanying the photos of each area is a brief description of land use, climate, soils, and topography for that area.

595. **Maps Showing Explorers' Routes, Trails and Early Roads in the United States, An Annotated List.** 1962. 137p. map. $1.50. LC 5.2:Ex 7.

596. **Map Reading.** 1965. 134p. $1.25. D 101.20:21-26.
Fully illustrated guide to reading all types of maps, including aerial maps.

597. **Three-Dimensional Maps; An Annotated List of References Relating to the Construction and Use of Terrain Models.** 1964. 38p. $0.35.
LC 5.2:T 41/964.

598. **United States County Outline Map: 1970.** 1971. 1p. $0.20 (all black ed.); $0.25 (blue and black ed.). C 3.62/2.
These maps reflect changes to January 1, 1970, the last date on which boundary changes could be made effective for use in the 1970 census. The maps are printed at a scale of 1:5,000,000 (about 79 miles = 1 inch). The two editions are: all boundaries and county names printed in black ink; and state boundaries printed in black ink with county boundaries and names printed in light blue ink.

599. **Vietnam and Asian Continent Maps, Including Indexes and Economic and Topographic Maps.** 21 x 29 in., folded to 7¼ x 10½ in. 1967. $0.15.
90-1:H.doc. 147.
Provides useful, factual information (excluding any of the military aspects) on Vietnam and the Asian continent. The maps indicate the political boundaries and the topographic elevations of countries of Asia with enlargements of Southeast Asia, including an economic map illustrating the products of the various geographic areas. The large map of Vietnam and neighboring

countries—Laos, Thailand, Cambodia—presents brief facts about South
Vietnam; and contains indexes of the cities, towns, and physical features of
North and South Vietnam, Laos, and Cambodia.

GEOLOGY

600. **Atlantic Continental Shelf and Slope of the United States:**
  Color of Marine Sediments. 1969. 15p. il. $1.00. I 19.16:529-D.
  Geologic Background. 1966. 23p. il. $0.30. I 19.16:529-A
  Nineteenth Century Exploration. 1968. 12p. il. $0.30.
    I 19.16:529-F.

601. **Black Canyon of the Gunnison, Today and Yesterday.** 1965. 76p. il.
$0.50. I 19.3:1191.
This well-illustrated and simply written geological interpretation of the Black
Canyon of the Gunnison includes information on geological aspects of the
Canyon—its rocks, its age, and how it was formed.

602. **Descriptive Catalog of Selected Aerial Photographs of Geologic
Features in the United States.** 1968. 79p. 53 pl. (3 pl. in pocket). $2.25.
I 19.16:590.

603. **Earthquakes.** 1969. 16p. il. $0.30. C 52.2:Ea 7/2.
Describes how, why, and where earthquakes occur, how they are monitored
by modern seismology, and how they are rated as to size (intensity vs.
magnitude). Earthquake safety rules are included, along with a U.S. earthquake risk map.

604. **Gem Stones of United States.** 1968. 51p. $0.35. I 19.3:1042-G.

605. **Geologic Story of Mount Rainier.** 1969. 43p. il. $0.65. I 19.3:1292.
Traces the geologic past of one of America's most scenic volcanoes. Contains
many colorful pictures and discusses the changing landscape of this area
from 12 to 60 million years ago; what happened to the glaciers; the results
of recent eruptions; and landslides and mudflows—past, present, and future.

606. **Identification of Rock Types.** 1960. 17p. il. $0.20. C 37.6/2:R 59.

607. **Lexicon of Geologic Names of the United States for 1961-1967.**
1970. iv + 848p. $3.50. I19.3:1350. S/N 2401-0984.
Contains a compilation of the new geologic names introduced into the literature from 1961 to 1967, in the United States, its possessions, the trust
territory of the Pacific Islands, and the Panama Canal Zone.

608. **The River and the Rocks, The Geologic Story of Great Falls and the
Potomac River Gorge.** 1970. 46p. il. $0.40. I 19.2:R 52.
This booklet presents a brief account of the geology of Great Falls, summarizing what is known of the events that formed the rocks and shaped
the land.

GRAINS

See—Agriculture.

HEALTH

See—Medicine and Health.

HOBBIES

See also—Recreation

609. **Numismatics, An Ancient Science.** 1965. 102p. il. $1.00. SI 3.3:
229/paper 32.
A general survey of the history of numismatics, beginning with coin col-
lecting in ancient times and proceeding through the Middle Ages and
succeeding centuries to the trends and accomplishments of modern numis-
matic scholarship. Within each period, numismatists and their publications
are discussed. Illustrations appear throughout the text, and an index is
included.

610. **Sundials.** 1933. 6p. il. $0.05. C 13.4:402.
Tells how to construct a sundial for use in the yard or garden, explaining
exactly how to lay out the time lines, position the indicator, and place the
completed sundial outdoors. Several suggested mottoes for inscribing on the
dial are also given.

611. **United States Postage Stamps.** 1970. 287p. il. $2.00. P 4.10:970.
Includes an illustrated description of all United States postage and special
service stamps issued by the Post Office Department from July 1, 1874, to
June 30, 1970.

612. **Woodworking Tools, 1600-1900.** 1966. 48p. il. $1.25. SI 3.3:241/
paper 51.

HOME ECONOMICS

*See also—Child and Infant Care; Consumer Information; Family
Finances and Budgeting; Foods.*

613. **Clothing Repairs.** 1965. 30p. il. $0.25. A 1.77:107.
Contains information on equipment and aids for basic repairs on home
clothing, such as simple sewing, darning, and patches. Users should find
this booklet of value in holding down clothing replacements, saving money,
and preventing waste.

614. **How to Prevent and Remove Mildew, Home Methods.** 1970. 12p. il. $0.10. A 1.77:68/4.
Suggests ways to prevent mildew, and tells how to remove mildew from clothing and other household articles.

615. **Making Household Fabrics Flame Resistant.** 1967. 8p. il. $0.05. A 1.35:454/3.
Tells how household fabrics may be made flame resistant by treating them in the home with various flame-retardant solutions. It describes how to prepare and apply the solutions.

616. **Removing Stains from Fabrics, Home Methods.** 1968. 32p. il. $0.20. A 1.77:62/5.

617. **Soaps and Detergents for Home Laundering.** 1971. 8p. $0.10. A 1.77:139/2. S/N 0100-1318.
Presents essential facts in the choice and use of soaps and detergents for good results in home laundering.

HOME MAINTENANCE AND REPAIR

618. **Basic Handtools.** 1963. 227p. il. $1.50. D 208.11:H 19/963.

619. **An Economical and Efficient Heating System for Homes.** 1967. 26p. il. $0.20. A 1.84:99.

620. **Electrical Wiring.** 1957. 91p. il. $0.50. D 101.11:5-760.
Discusses in detail, design of interior wiring systems, construction methods, and tools and materials used by military electrical construction personnel. Includes information relating to methods of repair, remodeling, and extending existing wiring systems, and the necessary safety precautions to be taken in connection with electrical installations.

621. **Equipment for Cooling Your Home.** 1970. 8p. il. $0.10. A 1.77:100/3.
Details use of such equipment as fans, pumps, air systems, and water systems.

622. **Exterior Painting.** 1968. 12p. il. $0.10. A 1.77:155.
Selection of equipment and paint, surface preparation, and application.

623. **Fireplaces and Chimneys.** 1968. 24p. il. $0.20. A 1.9:1889/5.
Suggested designs and advice on building.

624. **Fixing Up Your Home: What to Do and How to Finance It.** 1970. 10p. Free. 7700-029.
Advice on selection of contractors and obtaining a loan. Available from Consumer Product Information, Washington, D.C. 20407.

625. **Floors, Care and Maintenance.** 1969. 35p. $0.30. P 1.31/3:3/2.

626. **How to Paint a Room, Step by Step.** 1962. 2p. il. $0.05. HH 3.6: P 16.

627. **Interior Painting.** 1971. 12p. $0.10. 0100-1171.
Selection of equipment and paint or finish, surface preparation, and application. Available from Consumer Product Information, Washington, D.C. 20407.

628. **Making Basements Dry.** 1970. 10p. il. $0.10. A 1.77:115/2.
Lists the causes of wet or damp basements and briefly explains how to build a dry basement or correct wet or damp conditions in an existing one.

629. **Preventing Cracks in New Wood Floors.** 1964. 8p. il. $0.05. A 1.35: 56.
Describes causes of cracking and how to prevent cracks.

630. **What to Do When Your Home Freezer Stops.** 1967. 8p. il. $0.05. A 1.35:321/3.

631. **When You Return to a Storm Damaged Home.** 1970. 12p. $0.10. HH 1.2:St 7.
Homes and furnishings damaged by flooding, windstorm, or tornado need prompt clean-up action. This pamphlet gives general instructions on precautions to take when entering damaged buildings; drying and cleaning; checking electrical and heating systems; water supply, plumbing and sanitation; household mechanical equipment; floors, woodwork, doors, roofs, and salvaging furniture.

632. **Wood Decay in Houses, How to Prevent and Control It.** 1969. 16p. il. $0.20. A 1.77:73/3.
Describes cause oт wood decay, general safeguards to prevent decay, how to safeguard woodwork close to the ground and parts of houses exposed to rain, and care of houses to stop ordinary decay and "dry rot."

633. **Wood Properties and Paint Durability.** 1962. 10p. il. $0.10. A 1.38: 629/2.

634. **Wood Siding, How to Install It, Paint It, Care for It.** 1956. 14p. il. $0.15. A 1.77:52.
Contains information on kinds of wood siding and how to install it, as well as how to paint and maintain it.

HOUSE CONSTRUCTION

635. **Bathrooms, House Planning Aid.** 1965. 4p. il. $0.05. A 1.38:988.
The space requirements and arrangements illustrated for bathrooms should be of help in planning adequate and convenient areas for new homes.

636. **Designs for Low-Cost Wood Homes.** 1969. 28p. il. $0.25. A 13.2: H 75/3.
All these designs can be constructed at considerably less than usual cost for homes of similar size and conveniences, basically because of design simplicity and the use of economical wood materials and new construction systems. Contains descriptive summary sheets for all 11 designs, and floor plans, interior and exterior sketches of houses, and special features and construction methods incorporated in each design.

637. **House Plan No. FS-FPL-1.** 1970. 9 sheets, each 18 x 24 in. $1.50/set. A 13.2:H 75/3/FPL-1.
A one-story, three-bedroom home (768 sq. ft.) for a family with three to five children. Features open living-dining-kitchen area which gives feeling of spaciousness to its relatively small size. A treated wood-post foundation permits construction on sloping sites without grading and masonry work.

638. **House Plan No. FS-FPL-2.** 1970. 9 sheets, each 18 x 24 in. $1.50/set. A 13.2:H 75/3/FPL-2.
A one and one-half story home (1,404 sq. ft.) for a large family of up to 12 children. First floor has three bedrooms, bath, and living-dining-kitchen area. Second floor consists of two large dormitory-type bedrooms, each divided by a wardrobe closet.

639. **House Plan No. FS-FPL-3.** 1970. 8 sheets, each 18 x 24 in. $1.50/set. A 13.2:H 75/3/FPL-3.
A home of 576 sq. ft. for a small family or for senior citizens who require only one main bedroom and small spare room. Kitchen and living room are open with a drop beam between. Plans include carport and porch.

640. **House Plan No. FS-FPL-4.** 1970. 9 sheets, each 18 x 24 in. $1.50/set. A 13.2:H 75/3/FPL-4.
An expandable home (768 or 1,228 sq. ft.). Steeply pitched roof allows room on second floor for two dormitory-type bedrooms to accommodate up to eight children, and a bath, if desired. The first floor provides a living room, compact kitchen and dining area, two bedrooms and bath.

641. **House Plan No. FS-FPL-5.** 1970. 10 sheets, each 18 x 24 in. $1.75/set. A 13.2:H 75/3/FPL-5.
Either a single-story two-bedroom home or a two-story home with two additional bedrooms on the second floor (672 or 1,042 sq. ft.). Second floor rooms can be finished with the rest of the house or left until later. In both versions, first floor plans include kitchen with dining area, living room, two bedrooms and bath.

642. **House Plan No. FS-SE-1.** 1970. 5 sheets, each 18 x 24 in. $1.25/set. A 13.2:H 75/3/SE-1.
Three-bedroom home (1,024 sq. ft.) for a flat site. Square shape provides a lot of usable interior space for house this size. Open kitchen, dining room,

living room area. Three bedrooms are multi-purpose rooms for playing, studying, and sleeping. Design also features novel floating-wood floor system.

643. **House Plan No. FS-SE-2.** 1970. 4 sheets, each 18 x 24 in. $1.00/set. A 13.2:H 75/3/SE-2.
A three-bedroom house (1,008 sq. ft.) with play area obtained through elimination of central hall. Large bedrooms also provide extra, multi-purpose space. When house is constructed on sloping sites, carport and storage area under house are bonus feature.

644. **House Plan No. FS-SE-3.** 1970. 5 sheets, each 18 x 24 in. $1.00/set. A 13.2:H 75/3/SE-3.
Three-bedroom house (1,008 sq. ft.) to accommodate large families without crowding. Sizeable open space of kitchen-dining-living area provides spacious feeling. Utility room next to bathroom. Pressure-treated wood poles support house. Carport and storage area available under house when it is constructed on sloping site.

645. **House Plan No. FS-SE-4.** 1970. 7 sheets, each 18 x 24 in. $1.25/set. A 13.2:H 75/3/SE-4.
A tubular home of 1,000 sq. ft., offering attractive living space within its curved walls. Primarily for sloping sites. Eight egg-shaped, glue-laminated wood ribs form the exterior of the two-story house. Plans provide kitchen, living and dining rooms on first floor, two bedrooms on second. Foamed-in-place polyurethane used for outside insulation and roof.

646. **House Plan No. FS-SE-5.** 1970. 6 sheets, each 18 x 24 in. $1.25/set. A 13.2:H 75/3/SE-5.
This unique round house provides a three-bedroom home (1,134 sq. ft.) for flat site. Interior walls spaced radially from central atrium hall. Open kitchen-living-dining area. Roof is foamed-in-place polyurethane. Clear plastic dome over atrium hall allows natural illumination.

647. **House Plan No. FS-SE-6.** 1970. 6 sheets, each 18 x 24 in. $1.25/set. A 13.2:H 75/3/SE-6.
Hillside duplex provides two-family home on sloping site, with 900 sq. ft. for each unit. Design is based on pole-frame structure combined with wood Gothic-type arches. Two units of two stories each provide complete privacy for each family. Kitchen, dining and living room areas on first floor; two bedrooms on second. Plans provide for wood deck, and balcony between the two units. One unit can be built separately for a single family.

648. **Fire Resistant Construction of the Home, of Farm Buildings.** 1967. 18p. il. $0.15. A 1.9:2227.

649. **House Construction, How to Reduce Costs.** 1970. 16p. il. $0.10. A 1.77:168/2.
Contains information on how to keep down home building costs. Discusses

location, style and design, interior arrangements, selecting material, construction, and utilities.

650. **Planning Your Home Lighting.** 1968. 22p. il. $0.20. A 1.77:138.

651. **Plumbing for the Home and Farmstead.** 1970. 20p. il. $0.15. A 1.9:2213/3.
Contains information on planning and installation of a plumbing system, and discusses piping, fixtures, and other components. Deals primarily with the installation of plumbing in new construction.

652. **Protecting Shade Trees During Home Construction.** 1965. 8p. il. $0.05. A 1.77:104.
How to prevent loss of valuable trees on home building sites.

653. **Technique of House Nailing.** 1947. 53p.
Available from Forest Service, U.S. Department of Agriculture, Washington, D.C. 20250.

IMMIGRATION AND NATURALIZATION

654. **Becoming a Citizen Series:**
> **Book 1. Our American Way of Life.** 105p. il. $0.65. J 21.9: C 49/4/bk. 1.
> **Book 2. Our United States.** 118p. il. $0.75. J 21.9:C 49/4/bk. 2.
> **Book 3. Our Government.** 137p. il. map. $1.25. J 21.9: C 49/4/bk. 3.
> **Teachers' Guide.** 23p. il. $0.25. J 21.9:C 49/4/guide.

655. **Federal Textbook on Citizenship, Home Study Course.**
Designed for persons who speak English but who have very limited skill in reading. Section 1 introduces a vocabulary relating to home and community living and provides practice in writing. Section 2 is devoted to a study of national government. Section 3 deals with state and local government, their relation to the national government, and the responsibility of the citizen in his community.
> **Sec. 1, English, Home and Community Life:**
> > **For the Student.** 108p. il. map. $1.25. J 21.9:En 3/sec. 1.
> > **For the Helper.** 56p. il. $0.40. J 21.9:En 3/2/sec. 1.
> **Sec. 2, English and Federal Government:**
> > **For the Student.** 172p. il. $1.75. J 21.9:En 3/sec. 2.
> > **For the Helper.** 99p. il. $1.00. J 21.9:En 3/2/sec. 2.
> **Sec. 3, English and State Government:**
> > **For the Student.** 121p. il. $1.25. J 21.9:En 3/sec. 3.
> > **For the Helper.** 76p. il. $0.75. J 21.9:En 3/2/sec. 3.

656. **Gateway to Citizenship.** 1962. 132p. $0.55. J 21.6/3:C 49/962.
Requirements and procedures for application to citizenship.

657. **Naturalization Laws, May 9, 1918—Dec. 23, 1963.** 1964. 403p.
$1.25. Y 1.2:N 21/3/964.

658. **Our Constitution and Government, Federal Textbook on Citizenship
[regular edition].** 400p. il. map. $2.25. J 21.9:C 76.
Lessons on the Constitution and government of the United States for use in
the public schools by candidates for citizenship.

659. **United States Immigration Laws, General Information.** 1971. 28p.
$0.20. J 21.5/2:Im 6/970. S/N 2702-0086.
Furnishes information to help solve the kind of problems met most frequently
under the provisions of the immigration laws relating to the entry of aliens.

INDIANS

See—North American Indians

INDOCHINA WAR

660. **American Prisoners of War in Southeast Asia, 1970.** 1970. 148p.
$0.60. Y 4.F 76/1:P 93/4.

661. **Background Information Relating to Southeast Asia and Vietnam.**
6th rev. ed. 1970. 455p. $1.75. Y 4.F 76/2:V 67/5/970.
Contains background information on the situation in Southeast Asia.

662. **Basic Data on North Viet-Nam.** 1970. 12p. il. $0.15. S 1.38:186.

663. **Cambodia Concluded, Now It's Time to Negotiate, A Report to the
Nation by Richard Nixon, President of the United States, June 30, 1970.**
1970. 28p. port. $0.25. S 1.38:193.

664. **The Cambodia Strike, Defensive Action for Peace, A Report to the
Nation by Richard Nixon, President of the United States, April 30, 1970.**
1970. 9p. $0.20. S 1.38:189.

665. **The Communist Insurgent Infrastructure in South Vietnam: A Study
of Organization and Strategy.** 1967. xxii + 469p. il. map. $6.00. D 101.22:
550-106. S/N 0820-0345.
Describes the infrastructure and concept of operation of the Communist-
dominated insurgency in South Vietnam during the period 1954-1965,
giving particular attention to matters of organization. Political, socio-
psychological, and paramilitary factors are analyzed.

666. **Impact of the War in Southeast Asia on the U.S. Economy, Part 1.**
1970. 121p. il. $0.50. Y 4.F 76/2:As 4/11/pt. 1.
First of a series of hearings to examine the impact of the Vietnam war on our

society and our economy and to inform the Congress and the public concerning the overall cost of the war to the American people in terms of both economic and human resources.

667. **Impact of the War in Southeast Asia on the U.S. Economy, Part 2.** 1970. iv + 123-458p. il. $1.25. Y 4.F 76/2:As 4/11/pt. 2.
Hearings on the impact of the war in Vietnam on the American people and the effect of the war on the cities.

668. **Investigation of the My Lai Incident.** 1970. 53p. map. $0.50. Y 4.Ar 5/2:M 99.
Presents report of the Armed Services Investigating Subcommittee on the investigation of the My Lai incident.

669. **Moral and Military Aspects of the War in Southeast Asia.** 1970. 108p. $0.45. Y 4.F 76/2:As 4/12.
Presents hearings on the impact of the war in Asia on our economy and our society, with emphasis on the impact of the war on America's basic moral values.

670. **Questions and Answers, The Situation in Cambodia.** 1970. 6p. $0.10. S 1.38:190.

671. **Seven Firefights in Vietnam.** 1970. 159p. il. $1.00. D 114.2:V 67.
A selection of accounts of fighting based on official Army records. Illustrates some of the events which have taken place in Vietnam since American troops were committed in force in 1965. Some of the subjects covered deal with human error, experimentation and innovation, and a new dimension in warfare afforded by the helicopter.

672. **Vietnam Information Notes.**
This series summarizes the significant available material on important aspects of the situation in Vietnam. Recently issued Notes are listed below:

> **Basic Data on South Vietnam.** 1970. 4p. il. $0.10. S 1.38:155/5.
> **Political Development in South Vietnam.** 1970. 8p. il. $0.10.
>   S 1.38:160/3.

INDUSTRY

See also—Labor; Small Business.

673. **Alcohol and Tobacco, Summary Statistics, Distilled Spirits, Wine, Beer, Tobacco, Enforcement, Taxes, Fiscal Year 1969.** 1970. 80p. $0.75. T 22.43:969.
Presents 89 tables of statistics relating to alcohol and tobacco industries for the fiscal year ended June 30, 1969. Tables are grouped under such topics as establishments and permits; distilled spirits (including alcohol); beer and cereal beverages; wines; tobacco; enforcement; label activity; claims; and collections.

674. **Construction Industry, Selected References 1960-69.** 1970. 13p.
Free.
A selective bibliography of works on the construction industry. Includes
works published from 1960 through 1969. Available from Library, U.S.
Department of Labor, Washington, D.C.

675. **The Housing Industry, A Challenge for the Nation, Report of the
Panel on Housing Technology.** 1970. 36p. il. $0.65. C 1.2:H 81/2.

676. **How to Improve Your Community by Attracting New Industry.**
1970. 44p. il. $0.35. C 46.8:In 2/2.

677. **Plant Tours for International Visitors to the United States.** 1969.
167p. $1.00. C 47.2:P 69/969-70.
A listing of plant tours, arranged by state and city, also classified by industry
for those who are interested in locating plants of a particular industry.

678. **Seasonal Unemployment in the Construction Industry. (Joint Study
by Departments of Labor and Commerce.)** 1970. 82p. Free.
Available from U.S. Department of Labor, Washington, D.C.

INSECTS

See also—Plant Pests and Diseases; Trees—Pests and Diseases.

679. **Beekeeping for Beginners.** 1968. 12p. il. $0.15. A 1.77:158.

680. **Beekeeping in the United States.** 1967. 147p. il. $1.00. A 1.76:335.

681. **The Caterpillar and the Butterfly.** By R. E. Snodgrass. 1961. 51p. il.
$0.75. Smithsonian Institution, Misc. Coll., Vol. 143, No. 6.
Generously illustrated account of how a caterpillar becomes a butterfly.
Order from the Smithsonian Institution, Washington, D.C.

682. **Collection and Preservation of Insects.** 1967. 42p. il. $0.25. A 1.38:
601/2.

683. **4-H Club Insect Manual.** 1954. 64p. il. $0.30. A 1.76:65.

684. **Insects that Carry Disease.** 1967. 16p. il. $0.10. FS 2.50:90/3.

685. **Insects: The Yearbook of Agriculture, 1952.** 1952. 952p. il. $6.50.
A 1.10:952.
Describes thousands of useful and harmful insects, and gives information on
insecticides (necessarily dated now). Includes livestock, cotton, crop, wildlife, vegetable, fruit, and ornamental plant pests.

INSECTS—HOUSEHOLD PESTS

686. **Ants in the Home and Garden, How to Control Them.** 1969. 8p. il.
$0.10. A 1.77:28/7.

687. **The Brown Recluse Spider.** 1970. 8p. il. $0.10. HE 20.1102:Sp 4.
Describes the spider, where it is likely to be found, how people are apt to be
bitten, and how it can be controlled.

688. **Chiggers: How to Fight Them.** 1966. 2p. $0.10. A 1.35:403.

689. **Cockroaches, How to Control Them.** 1970. 8p. il. $0.10. A 1.35:
430/7.
Describes cockroaches and their development. Discusses how to prevent
their entry and how to use sprays, dusts and other methods of control.

690. **Controlling Clover Mites around the House.** 1967. 4p. il. $0.05.
A 1.77:134.

691. **Controlling Household Pests.** 1964. 32p. il. $0.15. A 1.77:96.
Tells how to eliminate household pests which frequently survive normal
extermination methods.

692. **Controlling Mosquitoes in Your Home and on Your Premises.** 1970.
8p. il. $0.10. A 1.77:84/5. S/N 0100-1086.
Discusses the mosquito problem, describes breeding habits and the development of mosquitoes, gives detailed instructions for their control both indoors
and outdoors, and tells what precautions should be taken when using
insecticides.

693. **Controlling Wasps.** 1970. 8p. il. $0.10. A 1.77:122/3.
Presents information on wasps (hornets, yellow jackets, Polistes, mud
daubers, and the cicada killer) and their nests, how wasps develop, and how
to control them. Briefly describes precautions to be taken in using insecticides and the treatment of bee stings.

694. **Facts About Pest Control, War That Never Ends.** 1966. 11p. Free.
Available from Information Office, Department of Agriculture, Washington,
D.C. 20250.

695. **Fleas, How to Control Them.** 1964. 8p. il. $0.10. A 1.35:392.

696. **Grasshopper Control.** 1969. 12p. il. $0.10. A 1.9:2193/4.

697. **House Fly, How to Control It.** 1966. 8p. il. $0.05. A 1.35:390.

698. **How to Control Bed Bugs.** 1970. 7p. il. $0.10. A 1.35:453/4.
Describes what bed bugs look like, their feeding habits, how they develop,
their length of life, where they hide, and the kinds of insecticides to use to
control them in the home and in small animal and poultry houses.

699. **Old House Borer.** 1970. 8p. il. $0.10. A 1.35:501/3.
This leaflet describes the insect, its life cycle and habits, the damage it
causes, and methods of control.

700. **Protecting Woolens Against Clothes Moths and Carpet Beetles.** 1970.
8p. il. $0.20. A 1.77:113/3. S/N 0100-1087.

Describes pests that attack fabrics in the home; discusses their development, habits, spread; and gives detailed information on how to protect clothing and household furnishings against fabric insect damage.

701. **Silverfish and Firebrats, How to Control Them.** 1970. 6p. il. $0.10. A 1.35:412/7.
Provides a brief description of these insects and their habits, and places where they may be found. Also discusses the physical development of these pests and explains the uses of dusts and sprays for their control.

702. **Subterranean Termites: Their Prevention and Control in Buildings.** 1967. 30p. il. $0.15. A 1.77:64.

INSECTS—INSECTICIDES

703. **Farmer's Checklist for Pesticide Safety.** 1970. Free. PA 622.
Available from Office of Information, Department of Agriculture, Washington, D.C. 20250.

704. **Handbook of Toxicity of Pesticides to Wildlife.** 1970. 131p. $1.00. I 49.66:84.

705. **Hand Sprayers and Dusters.** 1967. 12p. il. $0.10. A 1.77:63/2.
Describes various kinds of hand sprayers and dusters and explains their operation and particular application.

706. **Pesticides—What are Pesticides?** 1967. 8p. $0.05. FS 2.50:112/2.
Discusses health protection, food protection, and the hazards of using pesticides for killing garden pests, ridding homes of insects or rodents, and defleaing or delousing pets.

707. **Power Sprayers and Dusters.** 1966. 18p. il. $0.15. A 1.9:2223.

708. **Safe Use of Agricultural and Household Pesticides.** 1967. 65p. il. $0.50. A 1.76:321.

709. **Suggested Guide for the Use of Insecticides to Control Insects Affecting Crops, Livestock, Households, Stored Products, Forests, and Forest Products, 1967.** 1968. $1.50. AH 331.

INSURANCE

Included in this section are works dealing with insurance in general and pension plans, as well as auto, home, mortgage, health, and life insurance. For items specifically concerned with health insurance covered under the Social Security Act (i.e., Medicare and Medicaid), *see—Medicare.*

710. **Digest of 100 Selected Health and Insurance Plans Under Collective Bargaining, Early 1966.** 1966. 152p. $1.00. L 2.3:1502.

711. **Digest of 100 Selected Pension Plans Under Collective Bargaining, Spring 1968.** 1969. 87p. $1.00. L 2.3:1597.

> —**Supplement to above. Benefits for Active and Retired Workers Age 65 and Over, Early 1968.** 1968. 33p. $0.40. L 2.3:1502-1.
> —**Supplement to above. Digest of 50 Health and Insurance Plans for Salaried Employees, Early 1969.** 1969. 126p. $1.25. L 2.3:1629.

712. **FHA Home Mortgage Insurance.** 1966. 8p. il. $0.10. HH 2.2: M 84/6/966.
Information on governmental aid for the potential home buyer, by the Federal Housing Administration.

713. **Insurance and Risk Management for Small Business.** 1963. 74p. $0.40. SBA 1.12:30.

714. **Public Attitudes Toward Auto Insurance, A Report of the Survey Research Center Institute for Social Research, The University of Michigan to the Department of Transportation, Staff Analysis of Consumer Complaint Letters Concerning Auto Insurance.** 1970. 266p. il. $1.25. TD 1.17:Au 8.
Reports on a survey of public attitudes towards automobile insurance. Also includes a compilation of selected consumer complaint letters regarding auto insurance reviewed by the Congress, the Department of Transportation, and other agencies.

715. **Understanding Life Insurance for the Family.** 1964. 12p. il. $0.10. A 43.2:In 7/2.
Brief summary of types of life insurance policies available for families.

716. **Welfare and Pension Plan Statistics: 100 Largest Retirement Plans 1960-68.** 1970. 31p. Free.
Available from Office of Labor-Management and Welfare-Pension Reports, U.S. Department of Labor, Washington, D.C.

INTERNATIONAL RELATIONS

717. **Africa: This New Dialogue.** 1970. 48p. il. $0.75. S 1.116:47.
Includes data on Africa, some of the problems faced by the new governments and their people, and a summary of U.S. relations with Africa.

718. **The Amerasia Papers: A Clue to the Catastrophe of China.**
Contains hundreds of official documents, many hitherto unpublished, which reflect the errors in the Far Eastern policy of the United States government in the closing months of World War II. The story of what happened to China prior to, during, and immediately following World War II continues as Part I of this introduction. Part II treats the controversial case of *Amerasia* magazine, or "Case of the Six" as it was called, when six American citizens

were suddenly arrested on charges of conspiring to commit espionage, and Part III presents an analysis of some of the documents, herein published in full text, which were written in 1943-1945 as official dispatches by one of the arrested six, John Stewart Service, then a young career diplomat on station in China.

Volume I. 1970. 1017p. il. $4.00. Y 4.J 89/2:Am 3/v. 1.
Volume II. 1970. 944p. $3.75. Y 4.J 89/2:Am 3/v. 2.

719. **American Foreign Policy, Current Documents, 1967.** 1969. 1380p. $6.75. S 1.71/2:967.
A collection of official papers which indicate the scope, goals, and implementation of the foreign policy of the United States. The volume also includes some documents on matters of major concern to this country, which were issued by other governments or by regional international organizations of which the United States is not a member.

720. **Aspects of Intellectual Ferment and Dissent in the Soviet Union.** 1968. 86p. $0.40. 90-2:S.doc. 106.

721. **Background Notes on the Countries of the World.** Subscription price: $3.50/year; $3.00 additional for foreign mailing; single copies vary in price. [BGN] S 1.123.
Subscription service includes approximately 75 updated or new Background Notes published during a 12-month period. These short factual pamphlets about various countries and territories include information on the country's land, people, history, government, political conditions, economy, and foreign relations.

A complete set of all currently available Background Notes may be purchased at $6.00 per set; $1.50 additional for foreign mailing; single copies vary in price. The set will include all Background Notes available at the time the order is processed. This can be supplemented by the subscription service listed above, which will insure receipt of revisions or additions to the series as they appear.

For a complete listing of individual notes on the various countries, write to the Superintendent of Documents, Government Printing Office, Washington, D.C. 20402. A two-piece binder with fasterners, for use with the subscription service or the complete set, may be purchased separately at $1.50 each; $0.40 additional for foreign mailing.

722. **Communist China.** 1969. 32p. il. $0.60. S 1.38:173-2.

—**Discussion Guide to Above.** 1969. 4p. $0.10. S 1.38:185.
Issues in United States foreign policy, No. 4.

723. **Communist China, A Bibliographic Survey.** 1971. x + 253p. il. pl. 14 maps (2 maps in pocket). $7.50. D 101.22:550-9. S/N 0820-0351.
Includes a wide range of source materials on a number of subjects that are

keys to a knowledge of the region and its peoples. Included are such subjects as: China's nuclear threat; global ambitions and objectives; foreign policy and international relations; the cultural revolution; and military posture. Two separate maps, printed in color, are included in a convenient pocket attached to the back cover.

724. **A Foreign Economic Policy for the 1970's, Part I—Survey of the Issues.** 1970. 160p. il. $0.60. Y 4.Ec 7:F 76/3/970/pt. 1.
Presents hearings concerning U.S. international economic policy.

725. **How Foreign Policy Is Made.** 1971. 28p. il. $0.50. S 1.71:195/4.
Discusses the role of the President, the Secretary of State, the Department of State, the Congress, and the American people in formulating foreign policy.

726. **Issues in United States Foreign Policy.**
A series of illustrated educational pamphlets designed to assist in identifying the elements of international problems, rather than to propose solutions— to define questions rather than answers. To this end, emphasis is given not primarily to policy decisions, but to the context within which decisions must be made.

> **No. 1, The Middle East.** 1968. 20p. il. $0.45. S 1.86:77.
> **No. 2, NATO and the Defense of Europe.** 1970. 32p. il. $0.60. S 1.70:87/2.
> **No. 3, Commitments of U.S. Power Abroad.** 1969. 20p. il. $0.40. S 1.71:235.
> **No. 4, Communist China.** 1969. 32p. il. $0.60. S 1.38:173-2.
> **No. 5, United Nations.** 1970. 48p. il. $1.00. S 1.70:93. S/N 4400-1314.
> **No. 6, Liberal Trade v. Protectionism.** 1971. 28p. il. $0.60. S 1.37:206. S/N 4400-1332.

727. **A Pocket Guide to Foreign Policy Information Materials and Services of the U.S. Department of State.** 1971. 18p. $0.20. S 1.40/2:F 76/971.

728. **The UN . . . Action Agency for Peace and Progress.** 1970. 12p. il. $0.10. S 1.70:55/7.
Lists the 126 members of the United Nations, shows its structure and discusses its role with respect to peace, arms control and disarmament, human rights, international services, food and population, trade and development, and education and work.

729. **U.S. and Africa in the 70's.** 1970. 9p. $0.25. S 1.116:48.
This reprint from the *Department of State Bulletin* presents the text of a statement submitted to President Nixon by Secretary of State William Rogers, together with an exchange of letters concerning the report.

730. **U.S. Foreign Policy for the 1970's, A New Strategy for Peace.** 1970. 160p. il. $0.75. Pr 37.2:F 76.
This February 18, 1970, report to the Congress by President Nixon presents a comprehensive statement on his Administration's stewardship of foreign affairs. It covers what has been accomplished so far, and new approaches to the challenges and opportunities of the world of the 1970's.

731. **U.S. Foreign Policy for the 1970's, Building for Peace. A Report to the Congress by Richard Nixon, President of the United States, February 25, 1971.** 1971. 235p. $1.00. Pr 37.2:F 76/971.
This report covers such topics as the Nixon doctrine, international economic policy, arms control, the U.N., the National Security Council, and the relationship between the national interests of the United States and those of European, Middle East, and Asiatic countries.

INTERNATIONAL TRADE

732. **Dictionary of International Agricultural Trade.** 1971. 170p. $1.50. A 1.76:411. S/N 0100-1364.
Gives definitions of terms identified with the international agricultural trade.

733. **Essential United States Foreign Trade Routes.** 1970. 81p. il. map. $1.00. C 39.202:F 76/969.
By providing description and maps of the essential trade routes, and the listings of U.S. steamship lines and commodities moving over them, this booklet provides information basic to an understanding and appreciation of the importance of the contribution made by the U.S. Merchant Marine to U.S. trade.

734. **Foreign Business Practices, Materials on Practical Aspects of Exporting, Investing, and Licensing Abroad.** 1971. 75p. il. $0.60. C 42.8/A: F 761/971.
Provides basic information on some of the laws and practices governing exporting, licensing, and investment abroad.

735. **Guide to Foreign Trade Statistics: 1971.** 1971. 190p. $1.50. C 3.6/ 2F 76/971.
This publication contains an explanation of the coverage of the statistics, and provides sample illustrations of the content and general arrangement of the data presented in individual foreign trade reports, tabulations, magnetic tapes, punch cards, and microfilm offered for public reference. It is intended to serve as a guide to the various sources of foreign trade statistics and to make it possible to utilize these sources to better advantage. The reports and tabulations described represent current plans for the release of foreign trade statistical data during 1971.

JUVENILE DELINQUENCY

736. **Delinquency Prevention Strategies.** 1970. iv + 20p. $0.20. HE
17.802:D 37/3. S/N 1766-0004.
Briefly describes a concept of delinquency prevention and includes some
suggestions as to how a prevention program may become operational.

737. **Delinquency Today, A Guide for Community Action.** 1971. 23p. il.
$0.20. HE 17.808:D 37.
Relates an overview of the problem of delinquency and offers a suggested
blueprint of community action programs to cope with the problem.

738. **The Effectiveness of Delinquency Prevention Programs.** 1966. 50p.
$0.25. FS 14.111:350.

739. **Juvenile Justice and Corrections, Third Report by the Select
Committee on Crime, House of Representatives.** 1971. v + 85p. $0.40.
91-2:H.rp. 1806. S/N 5271-0208.
This report examines youth living conditions, education, family responsibility,
service organizations, and their relationship to the fight against juvenile
crime, and the problems and duties of the police, juvenile court judges,
and probation personnel involved.

740. **A Look at Juvenile Delinquency.** 1963. 50p. il. $0.25. FS 14.111:
380.
This booklet deals with several aspects of juvenile delinquency, including
what it means, the extent of the problem, causes of delinquency, prevention
methods and their effectiveness, and programs for helping delinquent
children.

741. **The Prevention of Juvenile Delinquency: A Selected, Annotated
Bibliography.** Compiled by Lincoln Daniels. 1968. 15p. $0.30. FS 17.212:
J 98.
Lists books and journal articles about the prevention of juvenile delinquency
and is designed to serve as an introduction to recent developments in the
field.

742. **Toward a Political Definition of Juvenile Delinquency.** 1970. iii +
17p. $0.25. HE 17.802:D 37/2. S/N 1766-0003.
Examines the juvenile justice system, especially the relationship between that
system and those most affected by its decisions.

KOREAN WAR

743. **Combat Actions in Korea.** 1970. 252p. il. $2.75. D 114.2:K 84/4.
This book is a collection of accounts describing the Korean combat action of
small Army units—squads and platoons, companies and batteries. The stories
have been selected as representative of the important battles of the Korean

conflict. In chronological sequence, they follow the fighting beginning on the second day of the participation of the United States troops and continuing until the war settled into a static defense of fortified lines.

744. **History of United States Naval Operations, Korea.** 1962. 499p. il. $4.25. D 207.10/2:K 84.

745. **South to the Naktong, North to the Yalu.** By Roy E. Appleman. 1961. 813p. tables. maps. bibliog. index. $11.25. D 114.2:K 84/2/v. 1. Volume one of the series, *United States Army in the Korean War,* contains a detailed account of the first five months of the Korean War, vividly describing the disheartening days of setback and withdrawal to the Pusan perimeter, MacArthur's landing at Inch'on and his drive northward that crushed the North Koreans, and the ominous stiffening of enemy resistance as the United Nations forces neared the Yalu River and the Manchurian border.

746. **Truce Tent and Fighting Front.** 1966. 571p. il. maps. $6.00. D 114.2:K 84/2/v. 2. This is volume two of the series, *United States Army in the Korean War,* published by the Chief of Military History. It provides a detailed account of the truce negotiations over a two-year period. Information is given concerning the arguments, issues, and personnel involved. The events that influenced the United Nations' side of the negotiations are fully explained. Photographs, maps, and charts complement the text.

LABOR

See also—Occupations.

747. **Important Events in American Labor History, 1778-1968.** 1969. 32p. il. $0.25. L 1.2:H 62/2/778-968. A handy reference source for students and researchers, this chronology lists and describes important events in American labor history.

LABOR—AGRICULTURAL WORKERS

748. **Domestic Migratory Farmworkers, Personal and Economic Characteristics.** 1967. 32p. $0.25. A 93.28:121.

749. **Farmworker—Want a Job with Good Housing?** 1970. **—Spanish Edition.** 1970. Available free from Manpower Administration, U.S. Department of Labor, Washington, D.C.

750. **The Hired Farm Working Force of 1970: A Statistical Report.** 1971. 31p. Agricultural Economic Report No. 201. Available from Government Printing Office, Washington, D.C.

751. **The Hired Farm Working Force of 1969, A Statistical Report.** 1970. 30p. il. $0.25. A 93.28:180.

752. **Housing for Migrant Agricultural Workers.** 1970. 43p. il. $0.50. A 1.76:383.
Intended as an aid to employers in meeting federal, state, and local government requirements for adequate housing for migrant workers, this handbook contains housing plans, materials and construction methods, lighting, heating, toilet facilities, health units, child care centers and many additional ideas conducive to good housing.

LABOR—INTERNATIONAL

753. **Labor Law and Practice in:**

Afghanistan. 1969. 23p. il. $0.35. L 2.71:357.
Argentina. 1969. 65p. il. $0.65. L 2.71:344.
Belgium. 1970. 85p. $1.00. L 2.71:372.
Bolivia. 1962. 38p. il. $0.30. L 2.71:218.
Botswana. 1968. 29p. il. $0.40. L 2.71:337.
Chile. 1969. 70p. il. $0.70. L 2.71:339.
The Dominican Republic. 1968. 39p. il. $0.50. L 2.71:343.
Empire of Ethiopia. 1966. 55p. il. $0.40. L 2.71:298.
Guyana. 1968. 44p. il. $0.35. L 2.71:324.
The Hashemite Kingdom of Jordan. 1967. 70p. il. $0.45. L 2.71:322.
Iceland. 1970. 38p. $0.50. L 2.71:371.
India. 1967. 97p. $0.50. L 2.71:303.
Indonesia. 1968. 40p. il. map. $0.50. L 2.71:336.
Jamaica. 1967. 57p. il. $0.40. L 2.71:320.
Japan. 1970. 64p. $0.65. L 2.71:376.
Kingdom of Greece. 1968. 139p. il. $0.70. L 2.71:325.
Kingdom of Laos. 1965. 50p. il. $0.40. L 2.71:290.
Lebanon. 1966. 98p. il. $0.50. L 2.71:304.
Malaysia and Singapore. 1965. 105p. il. $0.55. L 2.71:274.
Morocco. 1965. 73p. il. $0.45. L 2.71:282.
New Zealand. 1967. 89p. il. $0.60. L 2.71:321.
Panama. 1970. 48p. il. $0.65. L 2.71:356.
Peru. 1968. 76p. il. $0.75. L 2.71:338.
Philippines. 1963. 85p. il. $0.50. L 2.71:253.
The Republic of Korea. 1969. 45p. il. $0.50. L 2.71:361.
Republic of Viet-Nam (South Viet-Nam). 1968. 85p. il. $0.50. L 2.71:327.
Spain. 1965. 58p. il. pl. $0.50. L 2.71:289.
Tunisia. 1965. 68p. il. $0.40. L 2.71:294.

754. **Special Job Creation for the Hard-to-Employ in Western Europe.**
1970. 44p. il. $0.50. L 1.39/3:14.
Since World War II, under the pressure of labor shortages, several countries
of northwestern Europe have pioneered in assisting the hard-to-employ to
find jobs in competitive labor markets. Some Western European countries
deliberately create jobs for the least successful candidates for jobs. This
booklet describes such jobs created through special public works, such as
public road maintenance, building factories, repairs of lighthouses, docks,
work on railway tracks, etc. Also included are descriptions of jobs
created for the severely handicapped, how such programs began, their growth,
organization, and finance.

LABOR—LABOR/MANAGEMENT RELATIONS

755. **Know Your Employment Rights.** 1970. 14p. il. $0.20. L 1.2:Em
7/4/970. S/N 2900-0091.
Discusses the rights of equal treatment in employment and what can be done
if these rights are violated.

756. **Labor-Management Policies for States and Local Government.** 1969.
263p. il. $2.00. Y 3.Ad 9/8:2L 11.

757. **Labor-Management Relations in the Federal Service, Report and
Recommendations, Executive Order 11491.** 1969. 56p. $0.60. L 1.2:
L 11/25.

LABOR—MANPOWER

758. **Counselor's Guide to Manpower Information, An Annotated
Bibliography of Government Publications.** 1968. 101p. $1.00. L 2.3:1598.
Publications are listed under broad subject categories. Information on how
to order publications is provided in the appendix.

759. **Developing Your Manpower.** 1970. 53p. il. $0.60. L 1.2:M 31/57.
This booklet is designed to help employers build and maintain an efficient
and dependable work force, to make better use of the available labor
resources, to meet employment problems, and to become manpower
developers. Suggestions are made on manpower utilization, both urban and
rural, that may be readily adaptable for use in businesses.

760. **Executive Management Bulletin, Analyzing Manpower Requirements
Using Statistical Estimates.** 1970. 19p. il. $0.20. PrEx 2.3/3:M 31.

761. **Facts for Manpower Trainees.** 1968. 8p. il. $0.10. FS 5.287:87029.
This brochure answers such questions as: How can I get a good job? How
and where will I be trained? How much will manpower training cost me?
I have trouble with reading, writing, and arithmetic; can I get manpower
training?

762. **Man, His Job, and the Environment: A Review and Annotated Bibliography of Selected Recent Research on Human Performance.** 1970. vi + 101p. $1.00. C 13.10:319.
Presents findings from a study on human reactions to work and environmental stress. Includes an extensive bibliography, and detailed abstracts of 190 research reports.

763. **Selected Readings in Employment and Manpower, Compiled for the Subcommittee on Employment and Manpower of the Committee on Labor and Public Welfare, Senate, 88th Cong., 2d sess.:**

Vol. 5, History of Employment and Manpower Policy in the United States: pt. 1-2, Depression Experience, Proposals, and Programs. 1965. p. 1585-2053. il. $1.25. Y 4.L 11/2: Em 7/7/v. 5.

Vol. 6, History of Employment and Manpower Policy in the United States: pt. 3-4, Looking Ahead to Postwar Economy and Concept of Full Employment in Congress. 1965. p. 2055-2504. il. $1.25. Y 4.L 11/2:Em 7/7/v. 6.

Vol. 7, History of Employment and Manpower Policy in the United States, 20 Years of Experience Under the Employment Act of 1946, Subcommittee on Employment and Manpower of the Committee on Labor and Public Welfare, Senate, 89th Cong., 2d sess.:
Pt. 1. 1966. p. 1-470. il. $1.25. Y 4.L 11/2:Em 7/7/v. 7/pt. 1.
Pt. 2. 1966. p. 471-944. il. $1.25. Y 4.L 11/2:Em 7/7/v. 7/pt.2.

LABOR—MINORITIES

764. **Finding Jobs for Negroes, A Kit of Ideas for Management.** 1970. 13p. $0.30. L 1.39/3:9.

765. **Negro Women in the Population and in the Labor Force.** 1968. 41p. il. $0.30. L 13.2:N 31/3/967.

766. **The Negro's Occupational Progress.** 1967. 8p. il. $0.10. L 2.70/4a: N 312.
Reprinted from *Occupational Outlook Quarterly,* vol. 10, no. 4, December 1966.

767. **Older Workers, Manpower Programs for Senior Citizens.** 1969. 8p. il. $0.15. L 1.2:Ol 1/3.

768. **Preliminary Report of Minority Group Employment in the Federal Government, 1969.** 1970. 78p. il. $0.75. CS 1.48:Sm 70-69A.
This report gives information on such subjects as the size and geographic distribution of the federal civilian work force, the extent of minority group representation, how this work force is paid, how the pay of minority group

employees compares with that of non-minority group employees. Included
in this census are Negroes, persons with Spanish surnames, American Indians,
Orientals, Aleuts, and Eskimos. All pay systems are represented as are all
states, foreign countries and territories, except Hawaii and Puerto Rico.

769. **Selective Placement, Hiring the Handicapped According to Their
Abilities.** 1963. 25p. il. $0.15. CS 1.58:9/2.

770. **Study of Minority Group Employment in the Federal Government,
November 30, 1969.** 1970. vii + 644p. il. $5.50. CS 1.48:SM 70-69B.
S/N 0600-0508.
The data contained in this study cover the size and geographic distribution
of the federal civilian work force, the extent of minority group representation,
a comparison of wages earned by minority and non-minority employees and
other related areas. Included in this census are Negroes, persons with Spanish
surnames, American Indians, Orientals, Aleuts, and Eskimos.

LABOR—STATISTICS

771. **Employment and Earnings Statistics for States and Areas, 1939-68.**
1969. 621p. il. $5.25. L 2.3:1370-6.
Prepared by the U.S. Department of Labor, Bureau of Labor Statistics, this
bulletin contains employment and earnings data for all states and detailed
industry data on 212 major labor areas—most are Standard Metropolitan
Statistical Areas. Employment data are related to the nonfarm sector of
the economy, and exclude proprietors, the self-employed, domestic workers
in private homes, and unpaid family workers. Hours and earnings for
manufacturing and mining relate to production workers, for contract
construction to construction workers, and for the remaining nonagricultural
components to non-supervisory workers. A special section containing
analytical and summary data is included.

772. **Handbook of Labor Statistics, 1970.** 1970. 400p. $3.50. L 2.3:1666.
Historical volume of major statistical series produced by the Bureau of Labor
Statistics. Related series from other governmental agencies and foreign
countries. Contains 175 tables, each starting at the earliest point in time
from which a continuous, reliable and consistent series can be carried.

LABOR—UNIONS

773. **A Brief History of the American Labor Movement.** 1970. 143p. il.
$1.00. L 2.3:1000/4.
Introduces the reader to the mainstream of trade unionism in the United
States. It presents simply and in general terms the role of labor organizations
in American history and economic life. An appendix covering important
events in American labor history from 1778 through 1969 is also included.

774. **Directory of Labor Organizations: Asia and Australasia.** 1963. 2v. $3.50. L 29.9:As 4/963/v. 1, 2.
Arranged alphabetically by countries and names of major organizations. Provides names of officers, addresses, membership statistics, and related information.

775. **Directory of Labor Organizations, Europe.** 1965. 2v. 1030p. $6.50/ set. L 29.9:Eu 7/965/v. 1, 2.
Similar in form and content to the directory above.

776. **Directory of National and International Labor Unions in the United States, 1969, Listing of National and International Unions, State Labor Organizations, Developments Since 1967, Structure and Membership.** 1970. 125p. $1.25. L 2.3:1665.

777. **Electing Union Officers.** 1970. 49p. il. $0.25. L 1.48:5/3.

778. **Individual Rights Under Collective Agreements.** By Madis Sulg, Office of the Chief of Staff, U.S. Department of the Army. In *Monthly Labor Review*, 1969, pp. 40-42. Free.
Both state and federal courts and the NLRB agree that union members have the right to be represented by their unions. However, controversy has existed between the courts and the NLRB and within the academic community in their methods of handling cases where an individual has charged violation of the duty of fair representation or breach of contract. Available from Bureau of Labor Statistics, U.S. Department of Labor, Washington, D.C. 20212.

779. **A Labor Historian Views Changes in the Trade Union Movement.** By Professor Philip Taft, Graduate School of Business, University of Chicago. In *Monthly Labor Review,* September 1969, pp. 8-11. Free.
The direction of the American labor movement, as expressed by Samuel Gompers, continues to be the keystone of today's labor philosophy. Since the 1930s, the movement differs on many points but shows similarity of outlook and practice in others. The labor organizations of the present place more emphasis on fringe benefits and their main direction is still towards increases in wages and other job-connected benefits.

Two important conditions which differentiate the environment of the current labor movement from the one existing prior to the 1930s are: (a) The right to organize and (b) the requirement that employers deal with the representatives of their employees.

Available from Bureau of Labor Standards, U.S. Department of Labor, Washington, D.C. 20212.

LABOR—WAGES

780. **Area Wage Survey, Selected Metropolitan Areas, 1968-69, Occupational Earnings, 88 Areas, Supplementary Provisions, 45 Areas.** 1970. 92p. $1.00. L 2.3:1625-90.

781. **Employment and Earnings.** (Monthly.) Subscription price: $10.00/yr.; $1.00/copy. L 2.41/2:vols.
Presents the most current information available on trends and levels of employment, hours of work, earnings, and labor turnover. It gives not only overall trends, but also shows developments in particular industries in the States, and in local metropolitan areas. Subscriptions are accepted for one, two, or three years.

782. **Employment and Earnings, United States 1909-70.** 1971. 602p. il. $4.25. L 2.3:1312-71. S/N 2901-0513.
Presents detailed industry statistics on the nation's nonagricultural work force, including monthly and annual averages on employment covering all employees, women, production workers in manufacturing and mining, construction workers in contract construction, and nonsupervisory workers in the remaining private nonmanufacturing industries; average weekly and hourly earnings; average weekly and overtime hours; and labor turnover rates.

783. **Glossary of Current Industrial Relations and Wage Terms.** 1965. 103p. $0.45. L 2.3:1438.
Lists and defines current non-technical terms.

784. **Pensions and Severance Pay for Displaced Defense Workers.** 1969. 173p. il. $1.50. AC 1.2:P 38.
This is the latest in a series of research studies devoted to exploring the implications of reductions in defense demand on the domestic economy. Reports on a study made to ascertain whether and under what circumstances there might be justification for special policies on pensions and other related fringe benefits for defense workers. Significant questions and definitive data are presented.

785. **State Minimum Wage Laws.** 1970. 10p. Free.
Available from Bureau of Labor Standards, Workplace Standards Administration, U.S. Department of Labor, Washington, D.C. 20210.

LABOR—YOUTH

786. **Getting Hired, Getting Trained, A Study of Industry Practices and Policies on Youth Employment.** 1965. 112p. $0.40. FS 14.2:H 61.

787. **Giving a Guy a Chance.** 1968. 6p. il. $0.05. A 1.68:884.
Briefly describes the Job Corps program for disadvantaged young men carried

out in Civilian Conservation Centers by the Forest Service of the Department of Agriculture and conservation agencies of the Department of Interior.

788. **Handbook for Young Workers, Labor Laws, Training Opportunities, Sources of Help.** 1965. 29p. il. $0.20. L 16.3:271.

789. **The Job Corps, Residential Training for Disadvantaged Youth.** 1970. 10p. il. $0.15. L 1.2:J 57/9.
Describes the purposes of the Job Corps and how it operates; the typical Job Corps enrollee; types of residential centers; education and work opportunities; and the effect of Job Corps education on the nation.

790. **The Neighborhood Youth Corps, A Review of Research.** 1970. 56p. $0.60. L 1.39/3:13.

791. **Summer Jobs for Students and How to Find Them.** 1969. Free. Available from Manpower Administration, U.S. Department of Labor, Washington, D.C.

792. **Work Training in Industry, Training Out-of-School Youth for Available Jobs.** 1969. 7p. il. $0.15. L 1.2:W 89/8.

793. **Working Children, A Report on Child Labor.** 1970. 19p. Available from Wage and Hour Division, Workplace Standards Administration, U.S. Department of Labor, Washington, D.C.

794. **Youth Opportunity Centers, Focus on Youth and Jobs.** 1969. 8p. $0.15. L 1.2:Y 8/5.

795. **Youth Unemployment and Minimum Wages.** 1970. 189p. $1.50. L 2.3:1657.

LIBRARIES

796. **Automated Approach to Technical Information Retrieval, Library Applications.** 1964. 44p. il. $0.30. D 211.2:Au 8.

797. **It's the Latest, It's the Greatest, It's the Li-ber-ee; From Buttermilk to Gum Log.** 1967. 11p. il. $0.15. FS 5.215:15064.
Reprinted from *American Education*, June 1967, this publication contains two articles describing how the Brooklyn Public Library and the Arkansas River Valley Regional Library are managing to distribute library books to the deprived sections of the areas they serve.

798. **Liaison Librarian.** 1968. 3p. il. $0.10. FS 5.215:15066.
Reprinted from *American Education,* December 1967—January 1968, this publication discusses the need for a better working relationship between public libraries and schools.

799. **Library Facilities for Elementary and Secondary Schools.** 1965. 44p. il. $0.40. FS 5.215:15050.

800. **Library Manpower, Occupational Characteristics of Public and School Librarians.** 1966. 36p. $0.30. FS 5.215:15061.

801. **Library Service for Rural People.** 1963. 20p. il. $0.15. A 1.9:2142/2.

802. **Library Statistics, 1966-67, A Preliminary Report on Academic Libraries.** 1967. 38p. $0.30. FS 5.215:15065.

803. **Library Statistics of Colleges and Universities, Data for Individual Institutions:**
    Fall 1967. 1969. 346p. il. $2.50. FS 5.215:15023-67.
    Fall 1968. 1969. 172p. $1.75. FS 5.215:15023-68.
In this series the Office of Education presents general management data on the libraries of individual institutions of higher education. The data provided are of maximum use to administrators, librarians, and others, particularly in budget-making operations. The series presents information for 1,841 college and university libraries and seven joint libraries.

804. **National Library of Medicine Classification, A Scheme for the Shelf Arrangement of Books in the Field of Medicine and its Related Sciences, 3d edition (With 1969 Supplementary Pages Added).** 1969. 323p. $2.75. HE 20.3602:C 56/969.

805. **Planning for a Nationwide System of Library Statistics.** 1971. 117p. $1.25. HE 5.215:15070.
Presents guidelines designed to serve as directions toward development of a nationwide system of library statistics, focused on the collection, evaluation, and dissemination of pertinent, meaningful, complete, and accurate library statistics.

806. **Procurement of Library Materials in the Federal Government.** 1968. 42p. $0.50. LC 1.32/2:L 61.

807. **Statistics of Public Libraries Serving Communities with at least 25,000 Inhabitants.** $1.50. HE 5.215:15068-68.

808. **Survey of Special Libraries Serving the Federal Government.** 1968. 108p. $0.75. FS 5.215:15067.
Presents detailed data on the special libraries which are serving the federal government in the United States.

LITERATURE

809. **Carl Sandburg, by Mark Van Doren, with a Bibliography of Sandburg Materials in the Collections of the Library of Congress.** 1969. 83p. $0.50. LC 29.9:V 28.

810. **Chaos and Control in Poetry, A Lecture Delivered at the Library of Congress by Stephen Spender, October 11, 1965.** 1966. 14p. $0.15. LC 29.9:Sp 3/2.

811. Dante Alighieri, Three Lectures; The Interest in Dante Shown by Nineteenth-Century American Men of Letters, by J. Chesley Mathews; On Reading Dante in 1965, the Divine Comedy as a "Bridge Across Time," by Francis Ferguson; The Relevance of the Inferno, by John Ciardi. 1965. 53p. il. $0.25. LC 29.9:M 42.

812. Fables from Incunabula to Modern Picture Books. 1966. 85p. il. $0.40. LC 2.2:F 11.
Consideration of the dissemination and variants of fables is the subject matter of this selective annotated bibliography.

813. Literary Recordings, A Checklist of the Archive of Recorded Poetry and Literature in the Library of Congress. 1966. 190p. $0.70. LC 2.2: P 75/5/966.

814. Louisa May Alcott, A Centennial for Little Women, An Annotated Selected Bibliography. 1969. 91p. il. $0.55. LC 2.2:Al 1/2.
This selective bibliography of works by Louisa May Alcott lists only first editions or later editions which are significant for the illustrations.

815. Metaphor as Pure Adventure. 1968. 20p. $0.25. LC 1.14:D 55/2.
A lecture delivered at the Library of Congress, Dec. 4, 1967, by James Dickey.

816. Randall Jarrell, Lecture Presented under Auspices of Gertrude Clarke Whittall Poetry and Literature Fund, with Bibliography of Jarrell Materials in the Collections of the Library of Congress. 1967. 47p. $0.25. LC 29.9:Sh 2.

817. Robert Frost, Backward Look, by Louis Untermeyer, Lecture Presented under Auspices of Gertrude Clarke Whittall Poetry and Literature Fund, with Selective Bibliography of Frost Manuscripts, Separately Published Works, Recordings, and Motion Pictures in Collections of Library of Congress. 1964. 40p. $0.30. LC 29.9:Un 8.

818. Thomas Mann's Addresses, Delivered at the Library of Congress, 1942-1949. 1963. 132p. $0.50. LC 1.14:M 31.

819. Walt Whitman: Man, Poet, Philosopher. 1969. 53p. $0.25. LC 29.2:W 59/2.

MEDICARE

820. A Brief Explanation of Medicare, Health Insurance for People 65 and Over. 1971. 12p. $0.10. HE 3.52:43/6.
This leaflet explains briefly the benefits Medicare provides.

821. Directory, Medicare Providers and Suppliers of Services, Hospitals, Extended Care Facilities, Home Health Agencies, Outpatient Physical Therapy, Independent Laboratories. 1970. 702p. $4.75. HE 3.51/5:970.

A compilation of the names and addresses of some health agencies, hospitals, extended care facilities, and independent laboratories which are participating as providers of services in the Health Insurance for the Aged Program. The directory was prepared to furnish identifying information regarding the availability of these services covered under Title XVIII of the Social Security Act. To facilitate reference, the directories are arranged in alphabetical sequence by state, by city within the state, and by the participating agency.

822. **How to Claim Benefits Under Medical Insurance.** SSI-37.
Gives brief explanation of how to fill out Form 1490, Request for Medicare Payment. Available from local Social Security Administration offices.

823. **Medicaid, Medicare, Which is Which?** 1970. 29p. $0.25. HE 17. 502:M 46/4.
Both Medicare and Medicaid help pay medical bills, are part of the Social Security Act, and work together. But Medicare and Medicaid are not the same. This book tells the difference.

824. **Medicare Information.**
The publications listed below provide a wealth of information covering all aspects of the Medicare program.

> **The Impact of Medicare, An Annotated Bibliography of Selected Sources.** 1970. 69p. $0.40. HE 3.38:M 46/2.
> Presents an annotated bibliography of selected references from periodicals, reports, and books published between August 1965 and December 1968.
> **Medicare and Medicaid, Problems, Issues, and Alternatives.** 1970. 323p. 4 pl. $2.00. Y 4.F 49:M 46/6.
> This report indicates major areas in which constructive changes, either in the statute itself or in the administration of the program, can prepare Medicare to meet the needs of the nation's elderly on a vastly more efficient and economical basis while improving the quality of care rendered under the program.

825. **Mental Health Benefits of Medicare and Medicaid.** 1970. 24p. il. $0.45. HE 20.2402:M 46.

826. **Your Medicare Handbook, Health Insurance Under Social Security, Hospital Insurance (Part A); Medical Insurance (Part B).** 1970. 32p. il. $0.40. HE 3.25:50/3.
For use by beneficiaries; gives comprehensive explanation of health insurance program and how to apply for benefits.

827. **Your Right to Question the Decision on Your Claim for Medical Insurance Benefits Under Medicare.** SSI-79.

Explains what a person may do if he feels that the decision made on his medical insurance claim is incorrect. Available from Social Security Administration offices.

MEDICINE AND HEALTH

See also—Cancer; Mental Health; Public Health.

828. **Arthritis, Source Book.** 1966. 73p. il. $0.50. FS 2.2:Ar 7/3.

829. **Bacteria, The Littlest Cells.** 1970. 18p. il. $0.30. HE 20.3252:B 13.
This booklet, by the National Institutes of Health, gives information on bacteria, such as their nature, bacteria at work, environmental needs, reproduction, control, useful bacteria, bacteria and disease, man's defenses and antibacterial treatment, diagnosis of bacterial disease, and research on bacteria.

830. **Bibliography of the History of Medicine, No. 4, 1968.** 1970. 299p. $2.75. HE 20.3615:4.
A bibliography of materials, within the collection of the National Library of Medicine's History of Medicine Division, related to the history of medicine and allied sciences, professions, and institutions.

831. **The Child with Epilepsy.** 1969. 17p. il. $0.20. FS 17.215:35.

832. **The Child with Rheumatic Fever.** 1955. 13p. $0.10. Children's Bureau Folder 42.
Emphasizes the importance of early diagnosis and treatment of strep infections in preventing rheumatic fever. Lists signs to help parents care for the child who has the disease.

833. **Diabetes and You.** 1968. 16p. il. $0.25. FS 2.2:D 54/7/968.
Prepared especially for the person who has diabetes and for his family, this publication discusses insulin and its use, urine testing, care of the feet, insulin reactions, oral drugs, and diabetic comas. It also contains suggestions on planning meals, shopping for food, and eating away from home, and provides food exchange lists.

834. **Diabetes Source Book.** 1969. 80p. il. $0.75. FS 2.2:D 54/13/968.
Contains information which is believed to be valuable to all those interested in diabetes. This booklet discusses the prevalence of diabetes by age, sex, geographic areas, and color; casefindings; factors associated with diabetes; other chronic conditions prevalent among diabetics; longevity; and mortality by trends, sex, and color.

835. **Diet and Arthritis.** 1969. 8p. il. $0.10. FS 2.2:D 56/4.

836. **Don't Gamble with Your Health, Glaucoma, 3 Minutes of Your Time Could Save Your Eyesight.** 1968. 8p. $0.05. FS 2.50/2:G 46.

837. **Don't Gamble with Your Health, Heart Disease.** 1968. 8p. $0.05. FS 2.50/2:H 35.

838. **Emphysema, The Battle to Breathe.** 1967. 28p. il. $0.35. FS 2.2: Em 7/6.

839. **Health Information Series.** Public Health Service. FS 2.50:nos. and HE 20.10:nos.
The titles listed below concern general health care and, in certain cases, specific ailments. Pamphlets are generally six to eight pages in length, and the information is designed for the layman. Stress is always placed on seeking the advice of doctors for medical problems. Each pamphlet describes disorders and diseases, the symptoms, causes, methods of treatment, and progress of research.

6. **Ringworm, Including Athlete's Foot.** $0.05.
7. **Swimming.** $0.05.
9. **Arthritis and Rheumatism.** $0.05.
11. **Scabies.** $0.05.
15. **Menopause.** $0.05.
17. **Hay Fever.** $0.05.
19. **Asthma.** $0.15.
21. **Home Care of the Sick.** $0.05.
22. **Mumps.** $0.05.
24. **Measles (Rubeola).** $0.05.
26. **Louse Infestation.** $0.05.
27. **Smallpox.** $0.05.
30. **Rabies.** $0.05.
33. **Tuberculosis Today.** $0.10.
33-A. **Development of Present Knowledge about Tuberculosis.** $0.10.
35. **Psoriasis.** $0.10.
37. **Diphtheria.** $0.05.
38. **Chickenpox.** $0.05.
41. **Malaria.** $0.05.
43. **Constipation.** $0.05.
46. **Meningococcal Meningitis.** $0.05.
47. **Trichinosis.** $0.05.
48. **Tapeworm.** $0.05.
50. **Varicose Veins, What Can Be Done About Them.** $0.15.
51. **Pinworms.** $0.05.
52. **Hookworm Disease.** $0.05.
53. **Hearing Loss, Hope Through Research.** $0.25.
55. **Anemia.** $0.05.
62. **Neuralgia and Neuritis.** $0.05.
65. **Poison Ivy.** $0.05.
67. **Rheumatic Fever and Its Prevention.** $0.05.

69. High Blood Pressure. $0.05.
70. Diabetes. $0.05.
71. Peptic Ulcer. $0.15.
72. Typhoid Fever. $0.05.
82. Hepatitis. $0.05.
83. Healthy Teeth, for a Happy Smile, for Good Health, for Good Looks. $0.15.
88. What Is Mental Illness. $0.10.
89. Food You Eat and Heart Disease. $0.10.
92. Multiple Sclerosis, Hope Through Research. $0.05.
94. Mongolism (Down's Syndrome), Hope Through Research. $0.05. —Spanish Edition. $0.05.
95. Cerebral Palsy, Hope Through Research. $0.10.
96. Septic Tank Care. $0.05.
98. Blood and the Rh Factor. $0.15.
99. Cataract and Glaucoma, Hope Through Research. $0.25.
100. Parkinson's Disease, Hope Through Research. $0.20.
102. Hodgkins Disease. $0.05.
103. Spina Bifida, A Birth Defect, Hope Through Research. $0.10.
104. Headache, Hope Through Research. $0.10.
105. Epilepsy, Hope Through Research. $0.20.
106. Muscular Dystrophy, Hope Through Research. $0.15.
108. Congestive Heart Failure, A Guide for the Patient. $0.10.
111. CF, Facts about Cystic Fibrosis. $0.05.
113. What about Radiation. $0.05.
114. Mental Retardation, Its Biological Factors, Hope Through Research. $0.15.
116. Cerebral Vascular Disease and Strokes. $0.20.
117. Inborn (Congenital) Heart Defects. $0.10.
121. Cold Facts about Home Food Protection. $0.05.
123. Kidney Disease. $0.15.
125. Shingles (Herpes Zoster). $0.05.
126. Canker Sores and Other Oral Ulcerations. $0.10.
128. How Doctors Diagnose Heart Disease. $0.10.
129. Hardening of the Arteries, Cause of Heart Attacks. $0.10.
130. Emphysema. $0.10.
131. Hemophilia. $0.10.
133. Research Explores Pyorrhea and Other Gum Diseases, Periodontal Disease. $0.20.
134. Research Explores Dental Decay. $0.20.
135. Research Explores Cleft Palate. $0.10.
139. Dizziness, Including Meniere's Disease, Hope Through Research. $0.20.
140. Learning Disabilities Due to Minimal Brain Dysfunction, Hope Through Research. $0.20.

143. **Spinal Cord Injury, Hope Through Research.** $0.20.
144. **Leukemia, Lymphonas and Multiple Myeloma.** $0.10.

840. **If You Have Emphysema or Chronic Bronchitis.** 1967. 20p. il. $0.15. FS 2.2:Em 7/5.

841. **Man, Medicine and Work.** $0.40. 1964-0-728-169.
To acquaint all interested parties with basic historical facts concerning man's attempts to control his occupational environment and developments in occupational medicine.

842. **Organ Transplantation, Current Medical and Medical-Legal Status, The Problems of an Opportunity.** 1970. 106p. il. $1.00. HE 20.3302:Or 3.
Contains proceedings of a Maryland Academy of Sciences symposium on organ transplantation, current medical and medical-legal status, the problems of an opportunity.

843. **Pain.** 1968. 16p. $0.15. FS 2.22:P 16.
Contains information on the perception of pain, its psychological aspects, man's effort to alleviate pain; and research and training being used to find ways of controlling pain.

844. **Progress Against Leukemia.** 1968. 13p. $0.15. FS 2.22/32-2:L 57.

845. **Rubella.** 1970. 8p. $0.20. HE 20.2752:R 82.
Gives a description of Rubella, commonly known as German measles, its symptoms, damage to the fetus, diagnosis, vaccine, who should be vaccinated, care of affected infants, and progress of research.

846. **Sickle Cell Anemia.** 1969. 8p. il. $0.10. FS 2.22:An 3/2.
This leaflet contains some facts about anemia—what it is and does, what causes it, and how it can be cured.

847. **The Size and Shape of the Medical Care Dollar, Chart Book, 1970.** 1971. 36p. il. $0.35. HE 3.2:M 46/8/970.
The charts in this publication present the background facts relating to the medical care dollar—who pays, what and how much is bought, for whom it is spent, how and why it has grown. The charts provide the foundation for understanding the current crisis in medical care—providing quality care at a price the nation can afford.

848. **Strike Back at Stroke.** 1969. 37p. il. $0.40. FS 2.6:St 8.
This booklet has been prepared to help the doctor show what can be done for the stroke patient at home to help prevent or keep to a minimum the disability that often develops after a stroke. Tells how those caring for the stroke patient can help him and how the patient can help himself.

849. **Viruses on the Border of Life.** 1970. 15p. il. $0.30. HE 20.3252: V 81.
Presents information on bacteria and viruses such as viral infection, natural body defenses, medical defenses, "quiet" viruses, viruses and cancer, and research.

850. **What You Should Know About Paraplegia.** 1970. 12p. il. $0.25. HE 17.102:P 21.

MENTAL HEALTH

851. **Bold New Approach, The Community Mental Health Center.** 1970. 8p. il. $0.10. HE 20.2402:C 73/2.
This pamphlet gives background information on community health centers; building a center, staffing a center, what are the functions of the center; what type of care it offers a community, and how to get a center.

852. **Coping and Adaptation, A Behavioral Sciences Bibliography.** 1970. 231p. $1.75. HE 20.2417:C 79.
This bibliography brings together in one volume relevant contributions that are scattered through the research literature in the bibliographical, psychological, and social sciences.

853. **The Family in the Hospital.** 1970. 305p. il. $1.50. HE 20.2402:F 21.
This report discusses the development of family approaches to the care and treatment of the mentally ill and analyzes what part families play in the patient care of the institutionalized.

854. **From Witchcraft and Sorcery to Head Shrinking, Society's Concern about Mental Health.** 1969. 12p. il. $0.30. FS 2.22:W 77.

855. **Mental and Emotional Illnesses in the Young Child.** 1969. 11p. il. $0.25. FS 2.22:C 43/3.

856. **Mental Health Directory 1971.** 1971. $3.75. HE 20.2418:971. S/N 1724-0136.
A listing, by state, of nationally established agencies which provide mental health prevention, treatment, and rehabilitation services (more than 3,000 agencies). Types of clients for each are listed, as well as types of financial agreements which can be made.

857. **Mental Health of Urban America.** $1.00. S/N 1740-0092.
Description of programs and activities in the field of urban mental health.

858. **Private Funds for Mental Health.** 1969. 31p. $0.25. FS 2.22:M 52/77.
An annotated list of foundations and other private granting agencies which support research, training or services in mental health and related disciplines.

859. **Voluntary Agency and Community Mental Health Services.** 1970. 27p. il. $0.20. HE 20.2402:V 88.
Primarily for the citizen concerned with the organization and delivery of community mental health services, this booklet contains a list of national voluntary agencies and a description of their services.

860. **What Is Mental Illness?** 1970. 10p. $0.10. HE 20.10:88. S/N 1702-0062.
Gives brief information on mental illness and its extent. Discusses what research is being done on mental illnesses, the chances for recovery, and what the average citizen can do about mental illness.

MENTAL RETARDATION

861. **Bibliography on Speech, Hearing and Language in Relation to Mental Retardation, 1900-1968.** 1970. 156p. $1.25. HE 20.2759:Sp 3/900-68.
Provides a compilation of references written in the English language during the period from 1900 to 1968 (some 1969 references are included). This bibliography was prepared to serve as a specialized but comprehensive reference guide for those concerned with the communicative processes of the mentally retarded.

862. **The Child Who Is Mentally Retarded.** 1956. 23p. $0.10. Children's Bureau Folder 43.
Makes suggestions for early training of mentally retarded children. Tells where parents can go for help.

863. **Mental Retardation Activities of the Department of Health, Education, and Welfare, January 1970.** 1970. 79p. $1.00. HE 1.23/5:970.
Describes the mental retardation program activities of the Department of Health, Education, and Welfare, and highlights the progress made in 1969.

864. **Mental Retardation, Its Biological Factors, Hope Through Research.** 1970. 24p. il. $0.15. HE 20.10:114.
The biological factors of mental retardation are the subject of this pamphlet. Discusses the various types of retardation, family plans for a retarded member, progress which has already been made through research, and what we hope to expect from future research.

865. **The Mentally Retarded Child at Home: A Manual for Parents.** By Laura L. Dittmann. 1959. 99p. $0.35. Children's Bureau Publication 374.
Designed to provide practical information about day-to-day care for the retarded child, from babyhood through the pre-school and later years. It discusses care and feeding, walking, toilet training, dressing, discipline, speech, play, and other parts of the child's growth and training.

866. **El Problema Del Retraso Mental.** 1970. 19p. $0.20. HE 1.2:M 52/12/970/Spanish.
Written in Spanish, this booklet serves as an introduction to the problem of mental retardation, giving a general description of mentally retarded persons. Mentioned also are services of the community for the mentally retarded, special education, rehabilitation, and preventive measures.

867. **Respite Care for the Retarded, An Interval of Relief for Families.**
1971. 24p. il. $0.25. HE 17.102:R 31. S/N 1761-0026.
This publication illustrates newly emerging services, across the United States,
which are directed primarily toward providing a measure of relief for the
families of the retarded.

868. **Selected Reading Suggestions, For Parents of Mentally Retarded
Children.** 1970. 58p. $0.60. HE 21.113:M 52/970.
Prepared primarily to help parents, families, and nonprofessionals who seek
information on mental retardation, these reading suggestions may also be
useful to professionals, especially those who are directly involved in helping
parents understand and accept their child's handicap.

MEXICAN-AMERICANS

869. **Mama Goes to Nursery School; School Bells for Migrants; Learn a
Lito Englich; Se Habla Espanol.** 1968. 11p. il. $0.15. FS 5.220:20190.
Reprinted from *American Education*, May 1967—March 1968. This publication presents four articles relating to the problems of Spanish-speaking
youngsters in the Southwestern United States.

870. **The Mexican American.** 1968. 69p.
A study done for the Civil Rights Commission by Helen Rowan, specialist
in Southwestern affairs, which delineates the type and range of problems
faced by the Mexican American community and indicates those which are
distinctive to it. Available from Office of the U.S. Commission on Civil
Rights, 1405 Eye Street, N.W., Washington, D.C. 20425.

871. **Mexican-Americans, A Handbook for Educators.** 1969. 34p. $0.45.
FS 5.6/2:M 57.
Provides an historical summary of the Mexican heritage in the United States,
and further discusses the Mexican-American way of life. A limited bibliography is included.

872. **Mexican Americans and the Administration of Justice in the Southwest, A Report of the United States Commission on Civil Rights, March 1970.**
1970. 135p. il. $1.25. CR 1.2:M 57/2.
Presents information on alleged discriminatory practices by law enforcement
agencies and judiciary bodies against Mexican Americans based on Commission hearings, state advisory committee meetings, and staff investigations.
Includes recommendations for specific federal legislation to eradicate
prevalent practices and institute procedures to further the civil rights of
Mexican Americans.

873. **Mexican Americans and the Administration of Justice in the Southwest, Summary of a Report of the United States Commission on Civil Rights,
1970.** 1970. 21p. $0.20. CR 1.10:26. S/N 0500-0044.
A summary of the report listed above.

874. **Speak Up, Chicano. The Mexican-American Fights for Educational Equality.** 1968. 4p. il. $0.10. FS 5.238:38007.
Reprinted from *American Education*, May 1968.

875. **Stranger in One's Land.** 1970. 49p. il. $0.35. CR 1.10:19.
This is an account, written by Ruben Salazar, a California journalist, of the hearings of the U.S. Commission on Civil Rights held in San Antonio, Texas, on issues of concern to Mexican Americans such as employment, education, the administration of justice, problems in housing and political representation.

876. **Viva la Raza, Mexican-American Education, A Search for Identity.** 1968. 18p. il. $0.35. FS 5.238:38011.
Reprinted from *American Education*, November 1968.

MILITARY SCIENCE

See also—United States—Armed Forces.

877. **Dictionary of United States Military Terms for Joint Usage (Short Title: JD).** 1968. 322p. $2.00. D 5.12:1/7.

878. **World Military Expenditures, 1969.** 1970. 26p. il. $0.60. AC 1.16:969.
Contains compiled information from all sources in order to assess the size and impact of the world's military expenditures. The survey covers 120 countries and also compares military expenditures with certain other public expenditures and with gross national product.

MINING AND MINERALOGY

See also—Geology.

879. **Dictionary of Mining, Mineral and Related Terms.** 1968. 1269p. $8.50. I 28.2:D 56.
An up-to-date and comprehensive dictionary of 150,000 authoritative definitions of mining, mineral, geologic, metallurgical, ceramic, and general scientific terms. Cites major sources of many items.

880. **Mineral Facts and Problems.** 1118p. $6.75. I 28.3:630.
Most complete one-volume encyclopedia ever prepared on all the important mineral commodities. Fact-filled book covers history, prices, uses, research. Will appeal to a wide audience, from students to professionals. Also available in separate chapters.

881. **Principal Gold-Producing Districts of the United States.** 1968. 283p. $4.75. I 19.16:610.

882. **Potential Sources of Aluminum.** 1967. 148p. il. $1.00. I 28.27:8335.

883. **Rare-Earth Minerals and Metals.** 1970. 8p. $0.10. I 28.37/a:R 182/969. S/N 2404-0086.
This preprint from the 1969 Bureau of Mines Minerals Yearbook discusses the domestic production of rare-earth minerals and metals, their consumption and uses, stocks, prices, foreign trade, and a review of world production and technology.

884. **Silver in the United States.** 1969. 34p. il. $0.45. I 28.27:8427.

885. **Socioeconomic Aspects of Mining in Selected Cities, Urbanization and Surface Mining, Atlanta, Ga.** 1970. 50p. il. $0.55. I 28.27:8477.

886. **Staking a Mining Claim on Federal Lands, Questions and Answers.** 1970. 17p. il. $0.15. I 53.2:M 66/4/970.

887. **Uranium.** 1968. 24p. il. $0.20. I 28.37/a:Ur 1/968.
Preprint from the 1968 Bureau of Mines Minerals Yearbook.

MINORITIES

See—Civil Rights; Mexican-Americans; Negroes; North American Indians.

MOTOR VEHICLES

888. **Automobiles Imported into the United States.** 1970. 12p. il. $0.10. T 17.2:Au 8/970.
This pamphlet explains the import requirements as they pertain to automobiles.

889. **Government Driver's Kit.** 1969. $1.75/set. T 1.10/2:D 83/2.
The government driver's guide contained in this kit explains how to avoid an accident and what to do if one occurs. Also included are suggestions on how to avoid common types of accidents, from the two-car collision to the run-off-the-road accident, how to adjust to adverse driving conditions, and how to handle emergencies. This kit consists of a government driver's guide and a complete set of accident forms.

890. **Maximum Safe Speed for Motor Vehicles.** 1969. 81p. il. $1.00. TD 2.202:Sp 3.

891. **Motorcycles in the United States, Popularity, Accidents, Injury Control.** 1968. 12p. il. $0.10. FS 2.300:UIH 7.

892. **National System of Interstate and Defense Highways.** 1970. 8p. il. $0.15. TD 2.2:In 8/2.
A map of the United States, showing highway status as of September 30, 1970. It outlines the national system of interstate and defense highways;

highways open to traffic, major toll roads under construction, engineering and right-of-way in progress, and preliminary status or not yet in progress.

893. **Read Before Driving.** 1969. 8p. $0.15. TD 2.202:D 83/2/970. This pamphlet lists the 1970 motor vehicle safety standards areas and provides some basic safe driving practices to follow.

894. **Your Motorcycling Fun and Personal Protection.** 1967. 6p. il. $0.05. FS 2.2:M 85/9.

NARCOTICS

See—Drugs.

NATIONAL PARKS

This section incorporates recreation areas, national monuments, and historical landmarks as well as national parks. The U.S. Forest Service, the National Park Service, and the Bureau of Outdoor Recreation are the major sources of information for material on this subject. For related information, *see—Recreation.*

895. **Cape Cod National Seashore.** $0.15. I 29.6/2:C 17.

896. **Developing the Self-Guiding Trail in the National Forests.** 1964. 18p. il. $0.20. A 1.38:968.

897. **Face of Half Dome, Yosemite National Park, California.** $0.40. I 29.20/2:Y 8.

898. **Glen Canyon Dam and National Recreation Area.** 1970. 24p. il. $0.20. I 27.2:G 48/5/970. This colorful folder on Glen Canyon Dam and National Recreation Area tells about the interesting sights to see, and the recreational opportunities and facilities in the area. A map and boating safety regulations are included.

899. **Great Smoky Mountains National Park, N.C. and Tenn.** $0.75. I 29.62:5. Explains the natural history of the scenic Great Smoky Mountains. Contains numerous photographs of the flowers, animals, and scenic views, as well as informative data on the area, wildlife, plants, climate, and other items of interest. A map of the area is also included in this handbook.

900. **Guides to Outdoor Recreation Areas and Facilities.** 1968. 116p. il. $0.55. I 66.15:G 94/968. Compiled as a reference guide, this booklet lists sources of various publications of interest to those seeking information on outdoor recreation areas and facilities. Consists of two sections—National Guides, and Regional and State Guides—cross-referenced for camping, canoeing, fishing, hiking, hunting.

901. **Historical Handbook Series.**

  1. **Custer Battlefield National Monument, Mont.** $1.25. I 29. 58:1/3.
     A new interpretation of Custer's expedition against the Indians in 1876, the battle of the Little Bighorn, including Indian participation accounts, a photographic essay, new maps, and drawing by the famed artist, Leonard Baskin.
  2. **Jamestown, Va., The Townsite and Its Story.** $0.40. I 29. 58:2.
     Relates the history of Jamestown, Virginia—site of the first permanent English settlement in America (1607).
  3. **Ford's Theatre and House Where Lincoln Died.** $0.50. I 29.58:3/4.
     This handbook, well illustrated with pictures and photographs, relates the story of the assassination and death of Abraham Lincoln, as well as the story of his life. New material on the restored theatre and new museum is included.
  4. **Saratoga National Historical Park, N.Y.** $0.30. I 29.58:4.
     Tells the story of the two battles of Saratoga, scene of the decisive American victory over Burgoyne, 1777, marking the turning point of the American Revolution. A decisive battle in world history.
  5. **Fort McHenry National Monument and Historic Shrine, Md.** $0.35. I 29.58:5.
     Relates the history of Fort McHenry, including the bombardment of the fort in September 1814, which inspired Francis Scott Key to write The Star Spangled Banner.
  6. **Custis-Lee Mansion, Robert E. Lee Memorial, Va.** $0.40. I 29.58:6.
     Tells the story of the Custis-Lee Mansion, a national memorial to one of America's greatest men, Robert E. Lee, and the lives of the families of George Washington Parke Custis and Robert E. Lee, who lived there.
  7. **Morristown National Historical Park, Military Capital of American Revolution.** $0.35. I 29.58:7.
     Presents the story of Morristown, site of Washington's military headquarters and the main encampment of his Continental Army during the winters of 1777 and 1779-80, during the American Revolution.
  8. **Hopewell Village National Historic Site, Pa.** $0.35. I 29.58:8.
     Relates the story of Hopewell Village—representative of early ironmaking communities from which developed the mighty iron and steel industry of modern masters of the 19th century, under whom the furnace enjoyed such growth and prosperity.

9. Gettysburg National Military Park, Pa. $0.40. I 29.58:9.
Relates the history of the campaign and battle of Gettysburg,
July 1-3, 1863, one of the great decisive battles of American
history. Also included is the story of the establishment and
dedication of the Cemetery, the famous Gettysburg Address,
delivered by Abraham Lincoln a few months after the battle,
and a short description of the historic points of interest in
the park.

10. Shiloh National Military Park, Tenn. $0.40. I 29.58:10.
Describes the preliminary campaign, the first and second day
of the battle, April 6 and 7, 1862, and the results of the Battle
of Shiloh. Also a brief description of the numbered markers
placed at points of interest in the park is given.

11. Statue of Liberty National Monument, Liberty Island, N.Y.
$0.35. I 29.58:11.
Gives the history of the construction, completion, and presentation of the Statue of Liberty, a complete description of the
great monument, and the story of the men who worked on it.

12. Fort Sumter National Monument, S.C. $0.25. I 29.58:12.
Describes in detail the construction of Fort Sumter, the
events leading to the firing of the "first shot" of the Civil
War, and the federal bombardment of the fort from 1863 to
1865. It is well illustrated with pictures, drawings, and
photographs relating to this historical monument.

14. Yorktown and Siege of 1781. $0.40. I 29.58:14.
Tells the story of the siege of Yorktown, 1781, and Lord
Cornwallis' surrender of the British Army, which virtually
ended the American Revolution.

15. Manassas (Bull Run) National Battlefield Park, Va. $0.35.
I 29.58:15.
Relates the history of two of the more famous battles of the
Civil War—the opening engagement of that great conflict,
the First Battle of Manassas, July 21, 1861, and the Second
Battle of Manassas, fought approximately a year later, which
paved the way for Lee's first invasion of the North. A short
description of the chief points of historic interest on the two
battlefields is included.

16. Fort Raleigh National Historic Site, N.C. $0.35. I 29.58:16.
Tells the story of Fort Raleigh—scene of the earliest English
colonizing attempts within the limits of the continental
United States. It was the birthplace of the first English
child born in the New World.

17. Independence National Historical Park, Philadelphia, Pa.
$0.40. I 29.58:17.

Relates the history of Independence Hall and the historical events which took place here—the adoption of the Declaration of Independence, the meeting place of the Continental Congress and the Constitutional Convention of 1787, and the seat of government of the United States from 1790 to 1800. A history of the Liberty Bell and descriptions of other points of interest are included.

18. **Fort Pulaski National Monument, Ga.** $0.40. I 29.58:18.
Tells the story of the construction of Fort Pulaski and the siege and surrender of this great fort in the Civil War in April 1862.

19. **Fort Necessity National Battlefield Site, Pa.** $0.35. I 29.58:19.
Relates the story of the opening engagement of the French and Indian War at Fort Necessity, July 3, 1754.

20. **Fort Laramie National Monument, Wyo.** $0.35. I 29.58:20.
Relates the history of Fort Laramie—site of fur trade post and principal military post guarding the covered wagon trails to Oregon, Utah, and California, 1834-1890. A short description of historic points of interest is included.

21. **Vicksburg National Military Park, Miss.** $0.40. I 29.58:21.
Gives the history of the campaign and siege of Vicksburg, the last stronghold on the Mississippi River in Confederate hands in June 1863. A short description of the chief points of historic interest is also included.

22. **Kings Mountain National Military Park, S.C.** $0.35. I 29.58:22.
Tells the story of the Battle of Kings Mountain, October 7, 1780. A short history of the lives of some of the leaders of this decisive victory for the patriots is also included.

23. **Bandelier National Monument, N. Mex.** $0.35. I 29.58:23.
Describes the principal ruins of the national monument, and gives information relating to the origins and life of the early people at Bandelier.

24. **Ocmulgee National Monument, Ga.** $0.25. I 29.58:24.
Relates the story of the life and culture of the early Indian as told from the excavation of the Indian mounds on the site now preserved as Ocmulgee National Monument.

25. **Chickamauga and Chattanooga Battlefields, Chickamauga and Chattanooga National Military Park, Ga.-Tenn.** $0.40. I 29.58:25.
Describes the Battle of Chickamauga, in September 1863, and the Siege of Chattanooga, in November 1863.

26. George Washington Birthplace National Monument, Va.
$0.25. I 29.58:26.
Relates the story of the Washington family, the Memorial
Mansion, and the Washington family burial ground.

27. Montezuma Castle National Monument, Ariz. $0.35.
I 29.58:27.
Relates the story of Montezuma Castle, a prehistoric Indian
cliff dwelling so perfectly preserved that ceiling timbers in
many of the rooms are still intact.

28. Scotts Bluff National Monument, Nebr. $0.40. I 29.58:28.
Presents the history of Scotts Bluff, a celebrated landmark on
the great North Platte Valley trunkline of the "Oregon Trail,"
the traditional route of overland migration to Oregon,
California, and Utah.

29. Chalmette National Historical Park, La. $0.40. I 29.58:29.
Describes the New Orleans Campaign and the Battle of New
Orleans, Jan. 8, 1815, the last major land battle of the War of
1812. A brief description of the numbered markers placed
at points of interest in the park is also given.

30. Guilford Courthouse National Military Park, N.C. $0.35.
I 29.58:30.
The Battle of Guilford Courthouse, fought March 15, 1781,
marked the beginning of the end of the Revolutionary
struggle. This historical handbook describes the campaign
leading to the battle, the Battle of Guilford Courthouse, and
the campaign after the battle. Short descriptions of the points
of interest in the park are included.

31. Antietam National Battlefield Site, Md. $0.40. I 29.58:31.
A historical handbook that not only describes the shrines
and memorials as they stand today but describes the historic battle between two great armies and the significant
events which made them famous. Also includes numerous
photographs and maps.

32. Vanderbilt Mansion National Historic Site, N.Y. $0.40.
I 29.58:32.
Presents the history of the Vanderbilt Mansion and the
Vanderbilt family, with a detailed, illustrated description of
the mansion and its grounds. A brief history of the estate,
prior to its purchase by the Vanderbilts, is also included.

33. Richmond National Battlefield Park, Va. $0.35. I 29.58:33.
A political, military, and manufacturing center of the South,
Richmond was long a military objective of the Union Army.
This well-illustrated handbook briefly describes some of the
events and battles that took place in the vicinity of the Con-
federate Capital.

34. Wright Brothers National Memorial, N.C. $0.40. I 29.58:34.
Tells the story of Wilbur and Orville Wright, the events leading
up to the world's first successful flight of a man-carrying,
power-driven, heavier-than-air machine on December 17,
1903, and of their experiences at Kitty Hawk and Kill
Devil Hills, North Carolina. A brief description of the points
of interest at the memorial is included. Numerous photographs and pictures illustrate the text.

35. Fort Union National Monument, N. Mex. $0.30. I 29.58:35.
As a base of operations for both military and civilian ventures
in New Mexico for 40 years, Fort Union played a key role
in shaping the destiny of the Southwest. This booklet, well
illustrated with pictures, photographs, drawings, and maps,
relates the story of the founding of Fort Union in 1851, the
part the Fort played as guardian of the Santa Fe Trail, and
its participation in the Apache War, the Ute War, the Civil
War, and other campaigns, until its abandonment in 1891.

36. Aztec Ruins National Monument, N. Mex. $0.30. I 29.58:36.
This historical handbook tells the story of the men in the
San Juan Valley—early hunters and gatherers, the Basket-
makers, the Pueblos, and the Aztec Pueblo. It describes the
explorations and excavations of these well-preserved ruins,
as well as the ruins as they are today.

37. Whitman Mission National Historic Site, Wash. $0.45.
I 29.58:37.
Tells the story of the Whitmans, founders of the Whitman
Mission, and of their devotion, nobility, and courage in
ministering to the Indians and assisting emigrants on the
Oregon Trail. The booklet contains brief informational and
descriptive material concerning the Whitman Mission National
Historic Site and includes photographs of the ruins being
excavated by archeologists.

38. Fort Davis National Historic Site, Tex. $0.30. I 29.58:38.
Tells the story of Fort Davis from the events leading to its
founding in 1854 to its establishment as a National Historic
Site in 1963. The booklet contains numerous photographs
and gives informational and descriptive material concerning
the fort.

**39. Where a Hundred Thousand Fell, The Battles of Fredericks-
burg, Chancellorsville, the Wilderness, and Spotsylvania Court
House.** $0.70. I 29.58:39.
Contains informative and descriptive material on some of the
scenes of four great Civil War battles, where, within the radius
of 17 miles, over 100,000 American casualties occurred in the

battles of Fredericksburg, Chancellorsville, the Wilderness,
and Spotsylvania Court House, all involving strategy and
tactics beyond the understanding of the average soldier.

40. Golden Spike. $0.60. I 29.58:40.

This centennial edition of the National Park Services' Historical Handbook, *Golden Spike*, including a number of interesting photographs, discusses the origin and building of the
Pacific Railroad, and describes the Great Railroad Race and
the driving of the last spike.

902. **Living History in the National Park System.** 1970. 20p. il. $0.30.
I 29.2:L 76.

This pamphlet lists the National Parks where the past is brought to life and
gives a brief resume of these demonstrations of the historic features of the
park.

903. **National Forest Vacations.** 1968. 60p. il. $0.45. A 13.2:V 13/4/968.
Presents information relating to campgrounds, picnic areas, resorts, summer
homes, wilderness areas, roads and trails, water sports, and winter sports.

904. **National Forest Wildernesses and Primitive Areas.** 1971. 12p. il.
$0.15. A 13.2:W 64/971.

905. **The National Park System.** 1970. 6p. il. $0.20. I 29.2:N 21/23.
Summarizes the natural, historical, and recreational areas of the National
Park System. The folder also includes a list of legislative enactments
creating the National Park Service and defining its mission.

906. **National Park System Descriptive Folders.**
Describing the various national parks, monuments, historic sites, and recreational areas located throughout the United States, these folders tell about the
interesting sights to see, the recreational opportunities, and the food and
lodging facilities available. They provide maps showing the roads, layouts,
and points of interest for each park.

> **Federal Hall National Memorial, New York.** 1970. 8p. il.
> $0.10. I 29.21:F 31/970.
> **Fort Caroline, Florida.** 1970. 8p. il. $0.10. I 29.21:F 77c/970.
> **Navajo National Monument, Arizona.** 1970. 6p. il. $0.10.
> I 29.21:N 22/970.
> **Theodore Roosevelt Birthplace, National Historic Site, New York.**
> 1970. 8p. il. $0.10. I 29.21:T 34/2/970.
> **Fort Pulaski National Monument, Georgia.** 1970. 12p. il. $0.10.
> I 29.21:F 77/p/4/970.
> **The United States Marine Corps War Memorial, The Netherlands
> Carillon, Arlington, Virginia.** 1969. 10p. il. $0.10. I 29.21:
> M 33/2/969.

Mound City Group National Monument, Ohio. 1970. 8p. il.
$0.10. I 29.21:M 86/3/970.

Oregon Caves National Monument. 1970. 6p. il. $0.10.
I 29.21:Or 3/970.

Wupatki and Sunset Crater National Monuments, Arizona. 1970.
8p. il. $0.10. I 29.21:W 96/3/970.

Curecanti National Recreation Area, Colorado. 1970. 12p. il.
$0.10. I 29.39:C 92/970.

The Cherry Blossoms, Washington, D.C. 1969. 8p. il. $0.10.
I 29.2:C 42/2/969.

Rock Creek Park, Washington, D.C. 1969. 12p. il. $0.10.
I 29.6:R 59/9/969.

Ozark National Scenic Riverways, Missouri. 1969. 16p. il.
$0.10. I 29.6/4:Oz 1.

Devils Tower National Monument, Wyoming. 1970. 10p. il.
$0.10. I 29.21:D 49/4/970.

Thomas Jefferson Memorial. 1969. 24p. il. $0.30. I 29.21:J
35/7/969. S/N 2405-0116.

John Muir National Historic Site, California. 1970. 6p. il.
$0.10. I 29.21:J 61/970. S/N 2405-0118.

Joshua Tree National Monument, California. 1970. 10p. il. $0.10.
I 29.21:J 78/2/970-2. S/N 2405-0248.

Nez Perce National Historical Park, Idaho. 1970. 10p. il. $0.10.
I 29.21:N 49/970. S/N 2405-0249.

Ocmulgee National Monument, Georgia. 1970. 10p. il. $0.10.
I 29.21:Oc 4/2/970. S/N 2405-0250.

907. **National Parks and Landmarks.** 1970. 141p. il. $0.60. I 29.66:970.
Gives the name, address, acreage, and outstanding characteristics and pertinent data for each of the National Parks, Monuments, Battlefields, Historic Sites, Recreation Areas, etc., administered by the National Park Service.

908. **National Parks of the United States.** (Packet of 8 maps in envelope.)
$1.50/packet. I 29.6:P 23.
More than 250 national parks, monuments, and recreational areas are scattered throughout the 50 states and the territories. New highways, improved accommodations, and expanded facilities and activities now make it possible to visit all of these parklands with greater ease, comfort, and enjoyment. The National Park Service has compiled this guide for travelers—a packet of eight maps, printed in color, locating the various parks, with descriptions, notes on camping, lodging, addresses, and suggested highway tours. Five of the eight maps divide the country into regions: Northeast, Southeast, Midwest, West, and Southwest. Two maps deal with major cities: the parks of New York City and vicinity, and Metropolitan Washington, D.C. A large color map covers the entire United States, showing all parks and the interstate highway system. The U.S. folder also features a 18½ x 24 in.

facilities-activities-accommodations chart, detailing up-to-date information important to the traveler and camper. The individual maps are sold separately as listed below:

> National Parks of:
> United States (includes a facilities, accommodations, and activities chart). $0.20. I 29.8:P 23/2.
> The Midwest (Colorado, Iowa, Kansas, Minnesota, Missouri, Montana, Nebraska, North Dakota, South Dakota, Utah, and Wyoming). $0.15. I 29.6:M 58.
> New York City (including Long Island). $0.10. I 29.6:N 42y.
> The Northeast (Indiana, Maine, Maryland, Massachusetts, Michigan, New Hampshire, New Jersey, New York, Ohio, Pennsylvania, and Rhode Island). $0.15. I 29.6:N 81e.
> The Southeast (Alabama, Arkansas, Florida, Georgia, Kentucky, Louisiana, Mississippi, North Carolina, Puerto Rico, South Carolina, Tennessee, Virginia, West Virginia, and Virgin Islands). $0.15. I 29.6:So 8e.
> The Southwest (Arizona, Colorado, Nevada, New Mexico, Oklahoma, Texas, and Utah). $0.15. I 29.6:So 8w.
> Washington, D.C. (includes Maryland and Virginia). $0.15. I 29.6:W 27.
> The West (Alaska, California, Hawaii, Idaho, Nevada, Oregon, and Washington). $0.15. I 29.6:W 52.

909. **National Scenic and Recreation Trails, Authorized by the National Trails System Act, Public Law 90-543, October 2, 1968.** 1970. 32p. il. $0.30. I 66.2:Sce 6.
This pamphlet describes national scenic trails designed primarily for hiking, and gives a description of the two already-established trails: Appalachian Trail and the Pacific Crest Trail. It also explains national recreation trails, connecting and side trails, and state and metropolitan area trails, how they are established, how they may be used, bikes, horses, etc.

910. **New England Heritage.** 92p. il. $1.00. I 66.2:C 75.
Recommendations regarding recreation potential of Connecticut River Valley in Connecticut, Massachusetts, Vermont, and New Hampshire.

911. **Olympic National Park, Washington.** $0.30. I 29.62:1.

912. **Reclamation's Recreational Opportunities.** 12p. il. $0.20. I 27.2: R 24/10/968.
For all vacationers, a complete listing of many dozens of Reclamation recreation spots in 17 Western states.

913. **Rocky Mountain National Park, Colorado.** $0.35. I 29.62:3.

914. **Room to Roam, Recreation Guide to Public Lands.** 1969. 32p. il. $0.75. I 53.7/2:R 53/969.
Here is a planning guide to adventure, a handsome book in full color for anyone traveling or hoping to travel through the West and in Alaska. It has more than 40 photos, six detailed regional maps, and 457 travel attractions, all briefly described.

915. **Trails for America, Report on the Nationwide Trail Study.** 1966. 155p. il. $3.00. I 66.2:T 68.
This book describes existing trail systems in the United States; assesses the adequacy of existing trail programs to serve present and future users; suggests the appropriate role for federal, state, and local governments and private groups in providing new trails; and recommends federal legislation to foster development of a balanced and adequate Nationwide System of Trails.

916. **United States of America, National Parks and Monuments, National Forests, Indian Reservations, Wildlife Refuges, Public Lands and Historical Boundaries [colored map].** Scale 1:3,168,000, 1 in. = 50 mi. 1964. 42 x 65 in. $2.00. I 53.11:Un 3/964.

917. **Virgin Islands National Park, St. John Islands, V. I.** $0.10. I 29.6: V 81.

918. **Yellowstone National Park, Wyoming, Montana, Idaho.** $0.15. I 29.6:Y 3/19.

NATURAL RESOURCES

919. **Atlas of River Basins of the United States, Drainage Areas of More Than 700 Square Miles, Land Resource Regions and Major Land Resource Areas.** 1970. 8p. 84 maps. $13.00. A 57.2:R 52.

920. **The Nation's River.** 1968. 128p. il. $1.75. I 1.2:P 84/5.
This report from the U.S. Department of the Interior, with recommendations for action by the Federal Interdepartmental Task Force on the Potomac, presents a program to preserve the Potomac as a model of scenic and recreation values for the entire country. Many photographs and illustrations of the Potomac, past and present, are included.

921. **Natural Resources of:**
These booklets provide general information as well as travel and recreation information. Generously illustrated and descriptively written, they take the reader on statewide tours of scenic beauty, industrial development, varied natural resources, and recreational opportunities. For the student, they cover a wealth of facts about the state's history, present development, and future progress. Included also is a summary of federal programs devoted to natural resources.

Alaska. 1966. 76p. il. $0.65. I 1.91:Al 1s.
Arizona. 1963. 52p. il. $0.45. I 1.91:Ar 4i.
California. 1967. 84p. il. $0.60. I 1.91:C 12/967.
Colorado. 1963. 72p. il. $0.50. I 1.91:C 71.
Idaho. 1965. 72p. il. $0.50. I 1.91:Id 1.
Indiana. 1967. 52p. il. $0.45. I 1.91:In 2.
Maryland. 1969. 54p. il. $0.75. I 1.91:M 36.
Minnesota. 1969. 46p. il. $0.60. I 1.91:M 66.
Montana. 1964. 70p. il. $0.50. I 1.91:M 76.
Nevada. 1964. 64p. il. $0.45. I 1.91:N 41.
New Mexico. 1964. 68p. il. $0.50. I 1.91:N 42m.
North Dakota. 1968. 46p. il. $0.60. I 1.91:N 81d.
Ohio. 1963. 56p. il. $0.45. I 1.91:Oh 3.
Oklahoma. 1969. 56p. il. $0.75. I 1.91:Ok 4.
Oregon. 1964. 68p. il. $0.50. I 1.91:Or 3.
Pennsylvania. 1968. 53p. il. $0.65. I 1.91:P 38.
South Dakota. 1967. 72p. il. $0.65. I 1.91:So 8d.
Texas. 1965. 64p. il. $0.45. I 1.91:T 31.
Utah. 1965. 57p. il. $0.45. I 1.91:Ut 1.
Washington. 1964. 71p. il. $1.00. I 1.91:W 27.
West Virginia. 1964. 64p. il. $0.45. I 1.91:W 52v.
Wyoming. 1966. 80p. il. $0.65. I 1.91:W 99.

NEGROES

922. **Afro-Americans in the Far West, A Handbook for Educators.** 1970. 106p. $0.60. HE 5.6/2:Af 8.

923. **The Black Panther Party, Its Origin and Development as Reflected in Its Official Weekly Newspaper, The Black Panther, Black Community News Service.** 1970. viii + 142 + xii p. il. $0.60. Y 4.In 8/15:B 56/2. S/N 5270-0939.
This staff study, prepared by the House Committee on Internal Security, 91st Cong., 2d sess., is a compilation of selected information which has appeared in the pages of *The Black Panther*, official publication of the Black Panther Party.

924. **Changing Characteristics of the Negro Population, A 1960 Census Monograph.** 1969. 259p. il. $2.75. C 3.30:N 31.

925. **How Anti-White Are Negro Youth?** 1968. 4p. $0.10. FS 5.238: 38006.
Reprinted from *American Education*, March 1968.

926. **Negroes in the United States, Their Economic and Social Situation.** 1966. 241p. il. $1.25. L 2.3:1511.

927. **The Negro in the United States, A Selected Bibliography.** 1970. 313p. $3.25. LC 1.12/2:N 31.
Designed to meet the current needs of students, teachers, librarians, researchers, and the general public for introductory guidance to the study of the Negro in the United States.

928. **Social and Economic Status of Negroes in the United States, 1969.** 1970. 96p. $1.00. C 3.186:P–23/29.

929. **Testimony of Stokely Carmichael.** 1970. 29p. $0.20. Y 4.J 89/2: C 21.
Presents hearings held before the Subcommittee to Investigate the Administration of the Internal Security Act and Other Internal Security Laws of the Senate Committee on the Judiciary, 91st Cong., 2d sess., March 25, 1970.

NORTH AMERICAN INDIANS

930. **American Indian Calendar.** 1970. 40p. il. $0.25. I 20.2:C 12/2/970.
Designed to acquaint the tourist with interesting events scheduled on Indian reservations, this calendar lists alphabetically by state the time of year the event is held, the name of the celebration or event, and the location.

931. **Answers to Your Questions about American Indians.** 1970. 42p. il. $0.35. I 20.2:In 2/21/970.
Fact-filled booklet about Indians.

932. **Bark Canoes and Skin Boats of North America.** 1968. 242p. il. $3.75. SI 3.3:230.
Contains descriptions of material and tools employed by the Indians and Eskimos to build their highly efficient watercraft, including detailed descriptions of actual procedures used. This publication has 224 illustrations, including nearly 100 line drawings and construction sketches of actual canoes which outdoorsmen can use to build their own craft. Many unique photos of Indians building canoes and of skin boats in use are shown as well as an illustrated appendix on how to "roll" an Eskimo kayak.

933. **Economic Development of American Indians and Eskimos, 1930-1967, A Bibliography.** 1969. 263p. $2.00. I 20.48:Ec 7/930-67.
Arranged by subject with publications listed by author but not annotated. Includes materials published in the United States from 1930 through 1967.

934. **Famous Indians, A Collection of Short Biographies.** 1966. 47p. il. $0.35. I 20.2:In 2/26.
Sketches the lives of 20 famous North American Indians. Includes a bibliography of sources for more extensive reading.

935. **Federal and State Indian Reservations, An EDA Handbook.** 1971. 428p. $3.75. C 46.8:In 2/3. S/N 0311-0049.
Presents detailed information on federal and state Indian reservations, giving

land status, history, culture, government, population profile, tribal economy, climate, transportation, utilities, and recreation.

936. **Folklore of the North American Indians.** 1968. 126p. il. $2.25. LC 2.2:In 25.
In the vast accumulation of recorded folklore, including much that is important to children for their reading and to storytellers for their repertoires, there are many tales of the North American Indians, which come down to us in government reports, folklore journals, and publications of learned societies. This bibliography aims to reveal a selection from these extensive resources. In the present bibliography items representing 11 Indian culture areas are included.

937. **Graphic Arts of the Alaskan Eskimo.** 1969. 87p. il. $1.00. I 1.84/4:2.

938. **Indian and Eskimo Children.** 1970. 48p. il. $0.50. I 20.2:C 43/5/969.
This is primarily a picture book for small children. Written in easy-to-understand language, the text and pictures show how American Indian and Eskimo children live, the work their fathers do, types of homes they live in, how families work and play together, and how they go to school.

939. **Indian Images, Photographs of North American Indians, 1847-1928.** 1970. 31p. il. $0.60. SI 3.2:In 2.
A catalog of selected North American Indian photographs in the Smithsonian's National Anthropological Archives. A short essay points out the misconceptions and superstitions which resulted in stereotypes of the Indian that persist even today.

940. **Indian Land Areas.** 1965. 26 x 36 in. $0.30. I 20.47:In 2/2.
This useful, three-color map shows Indian lands under federal responsibility. Approximately 4 x 8 in. folded, it fits into glove compartment or suitcase for traveling. Listed are field offices of the Bureau of Indian Affairs, and the tribes within their jurisdictions.

941. **Indian Series.**
The booklets listed below discuss the history and early life of Indians of the United States, including Eskimos and Aleuts.

> **Indians, Eskimos and Aleuts of Alaska.** 1968. 16p. il. $0.15. I 20.51:Al 1s/968.
> **Indians of Arizona.** 1968. 24p. $0.15. I 20.51:Ar 4i/968.
> **Indians of Montana and Wyoming.** 1968. 20p. il. $0.15. I 20.51:M 76/968.
> **Indians of New Mexico.** 1968. 20p. il. $0.20. I 20.51:N 42m/968.
> **Indians of the Central Plains** [Kansas, Nebraska and Iowa]. 1968. 20p. il. $0.15. I 20.51:C 33.

Indians of the Dakotas. 1968. 20p. il. $0.15. I 20.51:D 14/968.
Indians of the Eastern Seaboard [Maine, New Hampshire,
Massachusetts, Connecticut, Rhode Island, New York,
Delaware, New Jersey, Maryland, Pennsylvania, Virginia,
The Carolinas, Georgia, and Florida]. 1967. 28p. il. $0.15.
I 20.51:Ea 7.
Indians of the Great Lakes Area [Ohio, Michigan, Minnesota,
and Wisconsin]. 1968. 24p. il. $0.20. I 20.51:G 79/968.
Indians of the Gulf Coast States [Florida, Alabama, Mississippi,
Louisiana, and Texas]. 1968. 20p. il. $0.20. I 20.51:G
95/968.
Indians of the Lower Plateau [Colorado, Nevada, and Utah].
1968. 24p. il. $0.15. I 20.51:L 95/968.
Indians of the Northwest [Washington, Oregon and Idaho].
1968. 16p. il. $0.15. I 20.51:N 819/968.

942. **Suicide Among the American Indians.** 1969. 37p. $0.50. FS 2.22:
Su 3/2.
The long history of social and cultural turmoil that has confronted the
American Indian has created unique problems, and one of the outcomes is an
increase in suicide and other self-destructive behavior. This publication
presents papers from two workshops concerning suicide among American
Indians.

NUTRITION

See—Foods; Home Economics.

OCEANOGRAPHY AND MARINE SCIENCES

943. **Films on Oceanography.** 1969. 99p. il. $1.00. D 203.24:C—4/3.

944. **Glossary of Oceanographic Terms.** 1966. 204p. il. $3.50. D 203.22/
3:35.

945. **Inner Space, Sea of Opportunity.** 1966. 8p. il. $0.15. FS 5.256:
56020.
Reprinted from *American Education*, March 1965, this publication discusses
oceanography and opportunities available now and in the future in this field.

946. **Marine Science Activities of:**

Canada and the Nations of Europe. 1968. 160p. $0.55. PrEx
12.2:C 16.
The Nations of Africa. 1968. 76p. $0.35. PrEx 12.2:Af 8.
The Nations of East Asia. 1968. 80p. $0.35. PrEx 12.2:Ea 7a.
The Nations of Latin America. 1968. 76p. $0.35. PrEx
12.2:L 34.

The Nations of the Near East and South Asia. 1968. 55p. $0.30.
PrEx 12.2:N 27e.

947. Mobilizing to Use the Seas, The Report of the President's Task
Force on Oceanography. 1970. 12p. $0.15. Pr 37.8:Oc 2/R 29.
Discusses the total use of the marine environment for the security, economic
well-being, and welfare of the nation. It recommends the establishment of a
new agency for marine affairs.

948. Oceanographic Ships, Fore and Aft. 1971. 240p. il. $4.50. D 218.2:
Sh 6. S/N 0842-0050.
Contains historical data, specifications, and illustrations covering about 218
oceanographic ships from the 1800s through 1967. Appendixes listing
current inventory of major oceanographic ships and pertinent abbreviations
and symbols are included.

949. Questions About the Oceans. 1969. 121p. il. $2.00. D 203.24:G-13.
A book of 100 questions and answers that will hold the interest of students
of all ages. It presents factual material on the marine sciences for use by
young people at all grade levels and supplies teachers with a suitable introduction to selected marine subjects with specific references for additional
information on each topic. All answers were thoroughly researched and
guides to further reading on each question are supplied.

950. Selected Readings in the Marine Sciences. 1969. 32p. $0.45.
D 203.22/3:129.
Designed for the general reader with an interest in marine sciences. Although
this bibliography is not annotated, interest levels (juvenile, adult, technical)
are given.

OCCUPATIONS

See also—Labor; United States—Civil Service.

951. Careers for Women, Why Not Be:

An Apprentice? And Become a Skilled Craftsman. 1970. 10p. il.
$0.10. L 13.11:52.
An Engineer? 1971. 8p. il. $0.10. L 13.11:41.
A Mathematician? 1968. 8p. il. $0.10. L 13.11:45.
A Medical Technologist? 1971. 8p. il. $0.10. L 13.11:44.
An Optometrist? 1968. 7p. il. $0.10. L 13.11:42.
A Personnel Specialist? 1968. 8p. il. $0.10. L 13.11:48.
A Pharmacist? 1968. 7p. il. $0.10. L 13.11:43.
A Public Relations Worker? 1970. 7p. il. $0.10. L 13.11:46/2.
A Technical Writer? 1971. 8p. il. $0.05. L 13.11:47.
An Urban Planner? 1970. 8p. il. $0.10. L 13.11:49.

952. **Deseas Una Colocación?** 1970. 8p. il. $0.15. L 1.2:J 57/4/Spanish. Written in Spanish, this booklet explains the functions of the local employment service offices and what happens when you go there in search of a job.

953. **How to Prepare Yourself for Job Interviews.** 1965. 8p. il. $0.10. L 7.2:J 57/20.

954. **Job Guide for Young Workers, 1969-70 Edition.** 1969. 200p. il. $1.50. L 1.7/6:969-70.
Designed especially for the high school graduate, this job guide provides a host of job-related information. It lists the names of places to go and people to see for information and advice. In addition, this guide discusses some of the benefits of a good education and tells how to get financial aid to continue education. Information about the many job-training programs available for young job-seekers is included.

955. **Jobfinding Techniques for Mature Women.** 1970. 40p. $0.30. L 13.19:11.
Designed as a step-by-step guide to assist them to prepare for and to find employment. It is also aimed at the woman who has worked for many years in one firm, and then suddenly finds herself having to seek a new job, but lacks experience in the techniques of finding one.

956. **Jobs for which Apprenticeship Training Is Available.** 1968. 10p. il. $0.10. L 2.2:J 57/6.

957. **Jobs for which:**

> **College Education Is Usually Required.** 9p.
> **High School Education Is Generally Required.** 8p.

Available free from Bureau of Labor Statistics, U.S. Department of Labor, Washington, D.C.

958. **Merchandising Your Job Talents.** 1969. 26p. il. $0.25. L 1.7/2: J 57/3.
This booklet presents some of the basic principles and techniques for organizing a job-hunting campaign. It offers tips on scheduling, taking tests, and learning to profit from job interviews.

959. **New Careers for the Subprofessional.** 1970. 23p. il. $0.30. HE 5.211:11028. S/N 1780-0714.
Presents the results of a conference held in July 1969 to explore the expanding role of subprofessionals, the research and development needed to provide career ladder models and appropriate training programs, and ways to increase and improve the employment of subprofessionals in three human service fields—health, education, and welfare.

960. **Occupational Outlook Handbook.** 1970. 859p. il. $6.25. L 2.3:1650.
Prepared by the U.S. Department of Labor's Bureau of Labor Statistics, this handbook contains career information for use in guidance. It covers the

nature of work, education and training requirements, employment outlook, places of employment, and earnings and working conditions for over 700 occupations.

The following job profiles are reprints from the 1970-71 *Occupational Outlook Handbook.* They are arranged by subject.

AGRICULTURE

> **Employment Outlook, Agriculture.** $0.20. L 2.3:1650-106. Includes opportunities on farms, opportunities on specific types of farms, occupations relating to agriculture, cooperative extension service workers, soil conservationists, soil scientists, other professional workers, and farm service jobs.

ARCHITECTURE

> **Employment Outlook, Architects.** $0.10. L 2.3:1650-28.

> **Employment Outlook, Landscape Architects.** $0.10. L 2.3: 1650-34.

ATOMIC ENERGY

> **Employment Outlook, The Atomic Energy Field.** $0.15. L 2.3:1650-111.

AUTOMOTIVE

> **Employment Outlook: Automobile Salesmen.** $0.10. L 2.3: 1650-56.

> **Employment Outlook for Automobile Service and Sales Occupations: Automobile, Truck, and Bus Mechanics; Body Repairmen, Painters, Upholsterers; Gas Station Attendants; Salesmen; Parts Countermen; Service Advisors.** $0.15. L 2.3: 1550-6.

> **Employment Outlook, Driving Occupations, Over-the-Road and Local Truckdrivers, Routemen, Intercity and Local Busdrivers, Taxi Drivers.** $0.20. L 2.3:1650-94.

> **Employment Outlook for Motor Vehicle and Equipment Manufacturing.** $0.10. L 2.3:1550-111.

AVIATION

> **Employment Outlook, Aircraft, Missile, and Spacecraft Manufacturing.** $0.15. L 2.3:1650-108.

BANKING

> **Employment Outlook, Banking, Bank Clerks, Tellers, Bank Officers.** $0.10. L 2.3:1650-124.

CARPENTRY

Employment Outlook, Carpenters, Painters and Paperhangers, Glaziers. $0.20. L 2.3:1650-70.

CONSTRUCTION

Employment Outlook, Laborers (Construction). $0.15. L 2.3:1650-72.

Employment Outlook, Operating Engineers (Construction). $0.15. L 2.3:1650-76.

DRAFTING

Employment Outlook, Technicians, Engineering and Science Technicians, Draftsmen. $0.15. L 2.3:1650-27.

ELECTRICITY

Employment Outlook, Electric Power Industry. $0.15. L 2.3:1650-118.
Includes electric utility occupations, powerplant occupations, transmission and distribution occupations, and customer service occupations.

Employment Outlook, Electric Sign Servicemen. $0.10. L 2.3:1650-85.

Employment Outlook, Electricians (Construction). $0.15. L 2.3:1650-73.

Employment Outlook, Maintenance Electricians, Industrial Machinery Repairmen, Millwrights. $0.15. L 2.3:1650-86.

ELECTRONICS

Employment Outlook, Electronics Manufacturing. $0.15. L 2.3:1650-112.

Employment Outlook, Programmers, Systems Analysts, Electronic Computer Operating Personnel. $0.15. L 2.3:1650-41.

FACTORIES

Employment Outlook, Factory Operatives, Assemblers, Electroplaters, Inspectors, Power Truck Operators, Production Painters. $0.15. L 2.3:1650-95.

FIREFIGHTING

Employment Outlook, Firefighters. $0.10. L 2.3:1650-65.

FLOOR COVERINGS

Employment Outlook, Floor Covering Installers. $0.15. L 2.3:1650-75.

FURNITURE UPHOLSTERING

> **Employment Outlook, Furniture Upholsterer.** $0.10. L 2.3: 1650-97.

GUIDANCE AND COUNSELING

> **Employment Outlook, Counseling and Placement Occupations, School Counselors, Rehabilitation Counselors, Employment Counselors, College Placement Officers.** $0.15. L 2.3: 1650-32.

HEALTH AND MEDICAL SERVICES

> **Employment Outlook for:**

> **Chiropractors.** $0.10. L 2.3:1650-13.

> **Dental Hygienists, Dental Assistants, Dental Laboratory Technicians.** $0.15. L 2.3:1650-8.

> **Dentists.** $0.10. L 2.3:1650-7.

> **Dietitians.** $0.10. L 2.3:1650-19.

> **Dispensing Opticians, Optical Mechanics.** $0.10. L 2.3: 1650-93.

> **Hospital Administrators.** $0.10. L 2.3:1650-20.

> **Medical Laboratory Workers.** $0.10. L 2.3:1650-16.

> **Medical Record Librarians.** $0.10. L 2.3:1650-18.

> **Occupational Therapists, Physical Therapists.** $0.10. L 2.3:1650-14.

> **Optometrists.** $0.10. L 2.3:1650-10.

> **Pharmacists.** $0.10. L 2.3:1650-11.

> **Physicians, Osteopathic Physicians.** $0.10. L 2.3:1650-6.

> **Podiatrists.** $0.10. L 2.3:1650-12.

> **Psychologists.** $0.10. L 2.3:1650-42.

> **Radiologic Technologists.** $0.10. L 2.3:1650-17.

> **Registered Nurses, Licensed Practical Nurses, Hospital Attendants.** $0.15. L 2.3:1650-9.

> **Sanitarians.** $0.10. L 2.3:1650-21.

> **Speech Pathologists and Audiologists.** $0.10. L 2.3:1650-15.

HOME ECONOMICS

> **Employment Outlook, Home Economists.** $0.10. L 2.3: 1650-33.

HOTEL AND RESTAURANT SERVICES

Employment Outlook, Cooks and Chefs, Waiters and Waitresses. $0.10. L 2.3:1650-63.

Employment Outlook, Hotels. $0.15. L 2.3:1650-126. Includes bellmen and bell captains, front office clerks, housekeepers and assistants, managers and assistants.

Employment Outlook, Restaurants. $0.10. L 2.3:1650-123.

INDUSTRIAL DESIGN

Employment Outlook, Commercial Artists, Industrial Designers and Interior Designers and Decorators. $0.15. L 2.3: 1650-30.

INSULATION WORK

Employment Outlook, Asbestos and Insulating Workers. $0.15. L 2.3:1650-68.

INSURANCE

Employment Outlook, Insurance Agents and Brokers. $0.10. L 2.3:1650-57.

INTERIOR DECORATION

Employment Outlook, Commercial Artists, Industrial Designers, Interior Designers and Decorators. $0.15. L 2.3:1650-30.

IRON AND STEEL

Employment Outlook, The Iron and Steel Industry. $0.15. L 2.3:1650-114.

LAW

Employment Outlook, Lawyers. $0.10. L 2.3:1650-35.

LIBRARIES

Employment Outlook, Librarians, Library Technicians. $0.15. L 2.3:1650-36.

MACHINERY

Employment Outlook for Business Machine Servicemen. $0.15. L 2.3:1650-83.

MASONRY

Employment Outlook, Bricklayers, Stonemasons, Marble Setters, Tile Setters, Terrazzo Workers. $0.20. L 2.3: 1650-69.

Employment Outlook, Cement Masons, Lathers, Plasterers. $0.20. L 2.3:1650-71.

MATHEMATICS

Employment Outlook, Mathematicians and Related Occupations, Mathematicians, Statisticians, Actuaries. $0.15. L 2.3:1650-37.

MENTAL HEALTH SERVICES

Career Opportunities in the Field of Mental Retardation. 1969. 30p. il. $0.25. HE 1.2:M 52/14.

Employment Outlook, Psychologists. $0.10. L 2.3:1650-42.

Nursing Careers in Mental Health. 1969. 15p. il. $0.30. FS 2.22:N 93/4/968.

Occupations in Care and Rehabilitation of the Mentally Retarded. 1966. 76p. il. $0.35. L 7.2:M 52.

METALWORKING

Employment Outlook, Blacksmiths. $0.10. L 2.3:1650-91.

Employment Outlook, Boilermaking Occupations. $0.10. L 2.3:1650-92.

Employment Outlook, Elevator Constructors, Structural and Other Iron Workers. $0.15. L 2.3:1650-74.

Employment Outlook, Machining Occupations, All-Round Machinists, Machine Tool Operators, Tool and Die Makers, Instrument Makers (Mechanical), Setup Men (Machine Tools), Layout Men. $0.15. L 2.3:1650-98.

Employment Outlook, Roofers, Sheet-Metal Workers. $0.15. L 2.3:1650-78.

Welders, Oxygen and Arc Cutters. $0.10. L 2.3:1650-105.

PERFORMING ARTS

Employment Outlook, Performing Arts Occupations. $0.15. L 2.3:1650-39.
Includes actors and actresses; dancers; musicians and music teachers; singers and singing teachers.

PETROLEUM INDUSTRY

Employment Outlook, Petroleum and Natural Gas Production and Processing, Petroleum Refining. $0.15. L 2.3:1650-107.

PHOTOGRAPHY

Employment Outlook, Photographers, Photographic Laboratory Occupations. $0.15. L 2.3:1650-40.

PLUMBING AND PIPEFITTING

Employment Outlook, Plumbers and Pipefitters. $0.15. L 2.3:
1650-77.

POLICE

Employment Outlook, Police Officers, State Police Officers.
$0.15. L 2.3:1650-66.

PUBLIC RELATIONS

Employment Outlook, Advertising Workers, Marketing Research
Workers, Public Relations Workers. $0.15. L 2.3:1650-3.

RADIO AND TV

Employment Outlook, Radio and Television Broadcasting.
$0.15. L 2.3:1650-120.
Includes radio and television announcers and broadcasting
technicians.

Employment Outlook, Television and Radio Service Technicians.
$0.10. L 2.3:1650-89.

RAILROADS

Employment Outlook, Railroads. $0.20. L 2.3:1650-121.
Includes locomotive engineers, locomotive firemen (helpers),
conductors, brakemen, telegraphers, telephoners, and tower-
men, station agents, clerks, shop trades, signal department
workers, track workers, bridge and building workers.

REAL ESTATE

Employment Outlook, Real Estate Salesmen and Brokers.
$0.10. L 2.3:1650-59.

RECREATION

Employment Outlook, Recreation Workers. $0.10. L 2.3:
1650-43.

SCIENCES

Employment Outlook, Environmental Scientists, Geologists,
Geophysicists, Meteorologists, Oceanographers. $0.15.
L 2.3:1650-24.

Employment Outlook, Life Science Occupations, Life Scientists,
Biochemists. $0.15. L 2.3:1650-25.

Employment Outlook, Physical Scientists, Chemists, Physicists,
Astronomers. $0.15. L 2.3:1650-26.

SOCIAL SCIENCES

Employment Outlook, Social Scientists, Anthropologists, Economists, Geographers, Historians, Political Scientists, Sociologists. $0.15. L 2.3:1650-44.

Employment Outlook, Social Workers. $0.10. L 2.3:1650-45.

TEACHING

Employment Outlook, Teachers. $0.15. L 2.3:1650-47. Includes kindergarten and elementary school teachers, secondary school teachers, college and university teachers.

Opportunities Abroad for Teachers, 1971-72, Teaching, Short-Term Seminars. 1970. 28p. $0.20. HE 5.214:14047-72.

TELEPHONE INDUSTRY

Employment Outlook, Telephone Industry, Central Office Craftsmen, Central Office Equipment Installers, Linemen and Cable Splicers, Telephone and PBX Installers and Repairmen. $0.15. L 2.3:1650-122.

Employment Outlook, Telephone Operators. $0.10. L 2.3: 1650-55.

URBAN PLANNING

Employment Outlook, Urban Planner. $0.10. L 2.3:1650-48.

WATER TREATMENT

Employment Outlook, Waste Water Treatment Plant Operators. $0.10. L 2.3:1650-104.

WRITING

Employment Outlook, Writing Occupations, Newspaper Reporters, Technical Writers. $0.15. L 2.3:1650-49.

PETS

961. **Hamster Raising.** 1960. 6p. il. $0.05. A 1.35:250/2.
This pamphlet describes the hamster, its uses, management, breeding and growth, and briefly discusses causes of death in hamsters.

962. **How to Import Pets But Not Disease.** 1968. 6p. $0.05. FS 2.60/2: P 44.

963. **Raising Guinea Pigs.** 1970. 6p. il. $0.10. A 1.35:466/3.
This leaflet describes guinea pigs and discusses buying and selling, housing, feeding, growth, breeding, health, disease prevention, and control of lice.

964. **Raising Rabbits.** 1964. 24p. il. $0.15. A 1.9:2131/3.

965. **Selection and Care of Common Household Pets.** 1968. 24p. il. $0.15.
A 1.75:332.
This pamphlet is designed to help in the selection of a household pet. It
describes the physical characteristics and traits of some of the more popular
household pets including hamsters, rabbits, parakeets, and various breeds of
cats and dogs. Information is provided on feeding, training, health, and
other aspects of pet care.

PLANETS

See—Space Sciences

PLANT PESTS AND DISEASES

See also—Insects; Trees—Pests and Diseases.

966. **Blight of Pears, Apples, and Quinces.** 1970. 6p. il. $0.10. A 1.35:
187/7.
Describes characteristics of blight of pears, apples, and quinces; tells how it
spreads; and gives effective control methods.

967. **Boll Weevil, How to Control It.** 1969. 12p. il. $0.10. A 1.9:2147/3.

968. **Cabbage Insects, How to Control Them in the Home Garden, on
Cabbage, Broccoli, Cauliflower, Kale, Brussels Sprouts, Collards, Kohlrabi.**
1969. 8p. il. $0.10. A 1.77:44/7.

969. **Controlling Diseases of Raspberries and Blackberries.** 13p. $0.15.
F 2208.
Major diseases which may afflict raspberries and blackberries are described in
this revised bulletin, and control information is brought up to date. It
includes information on cultural and chemical control of these diseases and
also provides new information on nematode damage and control. Available
from Office of Information, U.S. Department of Agriculture, Washington,
D.C. 20250.

970. **Controlling Insects on Flowers.** 1967. $0.45. AB 237.

971. **Controlling Pink Bollworm on Cotton.** 1968. 12p. il. $0.20. A 1.9:
2207/2.

972. **Controlling Potato Insects.** 1970. 15p. il. $0.10. A 1.9:2168/5.
This pamphlet lists recommended kinds and amounts of insecticides to use
for the control of potato insects, with suggestions on selecting, mixing and
applying these insecticides. Cultural and natural controls of potato insects
are also briefly discussed as well as precautions to be taken.

973. **Controlling the Japanese Beetle.** 1970. 16p. il. $0.25. A 1.77:159/2.
Contains a description of the beetle and describes its habits and the damage

which it can do. Natural controls, control of grubs and beetles, and precautions to be taken when applying insecticides are also discussed.

974. **Corn Diseases in the United States and Their Control.** 1966. 44p. il.
$0.35. A 1.76:199/966.

975. **Cotton Insects.** 1965. 19p. $0.15. Pr 35.8:Sci 2/C 82.

976. **Gypsy Moth Menaces Our Living Resources: Shade Trees and Forests,
Recreational Areas, Wild-Life Habitats.** 1963. PA 530.

977. **Insects Affecting Sweetpotatoes.** 1967. 28p. il. $0.25. A 1.76:329.

978. **Insects and Diseases of Vegetables in the Home Garden.** 1971. 50p. il.
$0.40. A 1.77:46/9. S/N 0100-1160.
This bulletin, prepared for home gardeners, tells how to recognize the more
common insects and diseases that attack vegetables in the continental
United States, and how to prevent the damage they cause.

979. **Insects and Related Pests of House Plants, How to Control Them.**
1970. 16p. il. $0.10. A 1.77:67/6.
Tells how to recognize and control the most common insects and related
pests that attack plants in homes and home greenhouses throughout the
United States. The insecticides recommended are those that are considered
most widely useful on indoor plants, least hazardous to handle, and most
generally available.

980. **Insects in Farm Stored Wheat: How to Control Them.** 1966. 8p. il.
$0.05. A 1.35:345.

981. **The Japanese Beetle in the United States.** 1970. 30p. il. $0.25.
A 1.76:236/970.
This handbook was prepared to acquaint people with the appearance, life
history, habits, and economic importance of the insect, and with its native
and imported natural enemies. It does not tell in specific detail how to
combat the beetle. Recommendations on the use of insecticides to protect
plants from attack by the adult beetle and to destroy grubs in the soil are
modified periodically as more effective materials are developed.

982. **Lawn Diseases, How to Control Them.** 1967. 16p. il. $0.20. A 1.77:
61/4.

983. **Lawn Insects: How to Control Them.** 1969. $0.15. G 53.

984. **Pea Aphid on Alfalfa, How to Control It.** 1967. 6p. il. $0.05.
A 1.35:529/2.

985. **Potato Insects, Their Biology and Biological and Cultural Control.**
1964. 61p. il. $0.30. A 1.76:264.

986. **Stored Grain Pests.** 1962. 46p. il. $0.25. A 1.9:1260.
Primarily describes the four main pests found in stored grain: granary weevil,
rice or black weevil, lesser grain borer or Australian wheat weevil, and
Angoumas grain moth.

POISONOUS PLANTS / 135

987. **Strawberry Diseases.** 1970. 26p. il. $0.20. A 1.9:2140/4.
Covers the diseases that attack the entire plant; root diseases; foliage, bud
and flower diseases; and berry diseases. The symptoms and type of damage
are discussed, along with what to do if the disease occurs and the type of
prevention to be used. Soil fumigation and fungicides are also covered.

988. **Strawberry Insects, How to Control Them.** 1971. 17p. il. $0.20.
A 1.9:2184/5. S/N 0100-1032.
Provides illustrated descriptions of the most important pests of strawberries
in the United States, and tells how to control them by the use of insecticides
and other control measures.

989. **Sugarbeet Insects, How to Control Them.** 1968. 25p. il. $0.15.
A 1.9:2219/2.

990. **Tomato Fruitworm, How to Control It.** 1968. 6p. il. $0.05. A 1.35:
367/6.

991. **Wood Ticks: How to Control Them in Infested Places; Diseases They
Spread; Insecticides, Repellants; Ticks in Homes.** 1963. 8p. il. $0.05.
A 1.35:387.

POISONOUS PLANTS

992. **Common Poisonous Plants of New England.** 1964. 23p. $0.35. FS
2.2:P 75/5.
Provides a useful way of identifying poisonous plants commonly found in
the New England states and in many other states. First aid information is
given for the layman and medical data are provided for the physician called
upon to treat patients who have eaten or contacted the plants described. A
color photograph of each poisonous plant discussed is also included.

993. **Poison-Ivy, Poison-Oak and Poison Sumac, Identification, Precautions, Eradication.** 1968. 16p. $0.15. A 1.9:1972/7.
Contains information relating to poisoning by these plants, precautions
against poisoning, and treatment for poisoning.

994. **Poisonous Plants.** W. A. Dayton. USDA. 1948. Yrbk. Sep. No. 2100.
Available from Forest Service, U.S. Department of Agriculture, 12th and
Independence Avenue, S.W., Washington, D.C. 20250.

995. **3 Leaves Mean Poison Ivy.** 1970. 12p. il. $0.10. A 1.68:839.
Illustrations show how to identify poison ivy and poison oak leaves.
Describes how and where they grow and methods of eradication.

996. **22 Plants Poisonous to Livestock in the Western States.** 1968. 64p.
$0.45. A 1.75:327.
Covers such plants as arrowgrass, bracken fern, chokecherry, copperweed,
death camas, greasewood, halogeton, horsebrush, Indian hemp, larkspur,
locoweed, lupine, milkweed, oak, poison hemlock, rubberweed, etc.

POISONS

997. Carbon Monoxide, CO, Odorless, Tasteless, Colorless, Deadly. 1970. 6p. il. $0.10. HE 20.1802:C 18.
Each year carbon monoxide kills 1,500 people in the United States. This pamphlet describes some of the dangers of carbon monoxide and discusses safety precautions to be taken to avoid these dangers.

998. Directory, Poison Control Centers. 1971. 50p. $0.35. HE 20.4005: P 75/971.
Gives the name, address, and director of the facilities, alphabetically by state, which provide for the medical profession, on a 24-hour basis, information concerning the treatment and prevention of accidents involving ingestion of poisonous and potentially poisonous substances.

999. Lead Poisoning in Children. 1970. 25p. $0.25. HE 20.2752:L 46.
Discusses the many facts of lead poisoning in children including its consequences, its diagnosis, screening methods, factors contributing to lead poisoning, and a plan of approach to control and prevention.

1000. Volatile Substances—Some Questions and Answers. 1971. 6p. Free. 7700-043.
Hazards associated with inhaling household cleaners and aerosols to produce intoxication are discussed. Among these substances are airplane glue, nail polish remover, insecticides, hair spray, etc. Available from Consumer Product Information, Washington, D.C. 20407.

POLITICAL AND SOCIAL DISSENT

See also—Civil Disorders.

1001. Anatomy of a Revolutionary Movement: "Students for a Democratic Society." 1970. vii + 175 + xiii p. $0.70. 91-2:H.rp. 1565.
This report by the House Committee on Internal Security discusses the origin, history, organization, character, objectives, and activities of the Students for a Democratic Society.

1002. Extent of Subversion in the "New Left."
Presents hearings on the so-called New Left, subversive and militant organizations, their objectives and activities.

> **Part 1, Extent of Subversion in the "New Left," Testimony of Robert J. Thoms, January 20, 1970.** 1970. 59p. il. $0.45. Y 4.J 89/2:L 52/3/pt. 1.
> **Part 2, Testimony of Inspector Cecil M. Pharris, San Francisco Police Department, January 21, 1970.** 1970. p. 61-185. il. $0.55. Y 4.J 89/2:L 52/3/pt. 2.

Part 3, Testimony of Marjorie King and Mike Soto, March 31,
1970. 1970. p. 187-236. $0.30. Y 4.J 89/2:L 52/3/pt. 3.

Part 4, Testimony of Charles Siragusa and Ronald L. Brooks,
June 10, 1970. 1970. ii + 237-759 + iv p. il. $2.00. Y 4.J
89/2:L 52/3/pt. 4.

Part 5, Fall River, Massachusetts, June 11 and July 9, 1970.
1970. iii + 761-881 + v p. il. $0.55. Y 4.J 89/2:L 52/3/pt. 5.

Part 6, Testimony of James W. Rutherford, Louis Szabo and
Charles H. Gilmore, July 1, 1970. 1970. p. 883-1051. il.
$0.70. Y 4.J 89/2:L 52/3/pt. 6.

Part 7, Testimony of Hugh Patrick Feely and Harry F. Port, Jr.,
August 3, 1970. 1970. p. 1051-1110. il. $0.30. Y 4.J 89/2:
L 52/3/pt. 7.

Part 8, Testimony of Clifford A. Murray and Richard M. Schave,
September 25, 1970. 1971. 131p. il. $0.55. Y 4.J 89/2:L
52/3/pt. 8.

Part 9, Testimony of Allen Crouter and Paul Chambers,
August 6, 1970. 1971. 110p. il. $0.45. Y 4.J 89/2:L 52/3/
pt. 9.

1003. Investigation of Students for a Democratic Society.
Contains hearings held before the House Committee on Internal Security pertaining to investigation of Students for a Democratic Society, as listed
below:

Part 1-A, Georgetown University, June 3-4, 1969. 1969. 266p.
il. $1.00. Y 4.In 8/15:St 9/pt. 1-A.

Part 1-B, Georgetown University, June 5-17, 1969. 1969.
p. 267-474. il. $1.00. Y 4.In 8/15:St 9/pt. 1-B.

Part 2, Kent State University, June 24-25, 1969. 1969.
p. 475-642. il. $0.70. Y 4.In 8/15:St 9/pt. 2.

Part 3-A, George Washington University, July 22, 1969. 1969.
p. 643-869. il. $1.00. Y 4.In 8/15:St 9/pt. 3-A.

Part 3-B, George Washington University. 1969. p. 871-1047.
il. $0.70. Y 4.In 8/15:St 9/pt. 3-B.

Part 4, The American University, July 24, 1969. 1969. p. 1049-
1145. il. $0.45. Y 4.In 8/15:St 9/pt. 4.

Part 5, University of Chicago; Communist Party Efforts With
Regard to SDS, August 6-7, 1969. 1969. p. 1653-1742.
il. $0.45. Y 4.In 8/15:St 9/pt. 5.

Part 6-A, Columbus, Ohio, High Schools, October 20-22, 1969.
1970. p. 1743-1923. il. $0.70. Y 4.In 8/15:St 9/pt. 6-A.

Part 6-B, Akron, Ohio; Detroit, Mich.; and Pittsburgh, Pa.,
October 28-30, 1969. 1970. p. 1925-2183. il. $1.00.
Y 4.In 8/15:St 9/pt. 6-B.

> **Part 7-A, Return of Prisoners of War, and Data Concerning Camera News, Inc., "Newsreel," December 9-11 and 16, 1969.** 1970. p. 2185-2430. il. $1.00. Y 4.In 8/15:St 9/pt. 7-A.
>
> **Part 7-B, SDS Activities at Fort Dix, N.J.; Washington, D.C.; and Chicago, Ill., December 17 and 18, 1969.** 1970. p. 2431-2612. il. $0.70. Y 4.In 8/15:St 9/pt. 7-B.

1004. **SDS Plans for America's High Schools.** 1969. 13p. $0.15. Y 4.In 8/15:St 9/2.
Prepared by the House Committee on Internal Security, this document presents a report on the SDS plans for America's high schools.

1005. **Subversive Involvement in the Origin, Leadership, and Activities of the New Mobilization Committee to End the War in Vietnam and Its Predecessor Organizations.** 1970. 70p. il. $0.45. Y 4.In 8/15:N 42m.
This study reveals how the New Mobe has operated from its inception with significant domestic and international Communist support, and it details for the interested reader "the basic pattern of Communist participation that has remained a characteristic of all Mobe activity."

POLLUTION—AIR

1006. **Air Pollutants Affecting the Performance of Domestic Animals, A Literature Review.** 1970. iv + 109p. $1.00. A 1.76:380.
Describes the effects of air pollution, smoke and automobile exhausts on domestic animals; also, specific air pollutants found in the air; smoke and automobile exhausts are described. The term "domestic animals" as referred to in the report includes cattle, sheep, goats, swine, horses, chickens, turkeys, ducks, geese, pigeons, Japanese quail, dogs, cats, rabbits, and honey bees.

1007. **Air Pollution Publications, A Selected Bibliography with Abstracts, 1966-1968.** 1969. 552p. $4.50. FS 2.24:Ai 7/966-68.
Contains 1,000 entries for the period 1966-1968, arranged in 12 broad subject categories such as emission sources, measurement, and legal aspects.

1008. **Automotive Fuels and Air Pollution.** 1971. iv + 32p. $0.40. C 1.2:Au 8/2.
This report deals with the influence of fuel composition, including additions, on the amount and nature of emissions from automotive vehicles.

1009. **Compilation of Selected Air Pollution Emission Control Regulations and Ordinances.** 1968. 146p. il. $0.75. FS 2.300:AP-43.

1010. **Danger in the Air: Sulfur Oxides and Particulates.** 1970. 16p. il. $0.40. HE 20.1302:Su 5.
This booklet describes the many dangers caused by these pollutants such as

damage to human health, causing both temporary and permanent injury, destruction to property and vegetation, reduced visibility and effect on the weather.

1011. **Free Films on Air Pollution on Loan for Group Showing.** 1967. 16p. il. $0.10. FS 2.2:Ai 7/30/967.

1012. **Reduction of Air Pollutants from Gas Burner Flames Including Related Reaction Kinetics.** 1969. 67p. il. $0.70. I 28.3:653.

POLLUTION—WATER

1013. **Laws of the United States Relating to Water Pollution Control and Environmental Quality.** 1970. 265p. $1.00. Y 4.P 96/11:91-33.
Presents an updated compilation of legislation developed by the Committee on Public Works in the field of water pollution control and environmental quality.

1014. **Fish Kills Caused by Pollution.** 1970. 20p. il. $0.20. I 67.9:969. S/N 2417-0089.
Water pollution killed an estimated 41 million fish in 45 states in 1969. This report provides statistical information on fish kills in the United States and discusses some of the causes.

1015. **International Joint Commission, Canada and United States, Pollution of Lake Erie, Lake Ontario and the International Section of the St. Lawrence River.** 1971. iv + 174p. il. $1.50. S 3.23:P 76/8. S/N 4400-1335.
Discusses pollution problems, potential oil pollution, sources of pollution, effects of pollutants, jurisdictional and legal problems, remedial measures, and conclusions.

1016. **Ocean Dumping, A National Policy.** 1970. x + 43p. $0.55. PrEx 14.2:Oc 2.
This report to the President by the Council on Environmental Quality recognizes a critical need for a national policy on ocean dumping. It discusses sites, amounts, and composition of wastes dumped in the ocean; effects of these waste materials on marine environment and man; alternatives to ocean dumping in terms of costs, availability and effectiveness; state and federal agencies and authorities that deal with specific aspects of dumping; and the international implications of ocean dumping.

1017. **Phosphates in Detergents and the Eutrophication of America's Waters.** 1970. 88p. il. $0.40. 91-2:H.rp. 1004.

1018. **What You Can Do about Water Pollution.** 1968. 8p. il. $0.15. I 67.2:P 76/968.

1019. **Wild and Scenic Rivers.** 1970. 28p. il. $0.25. I 66.2:R 52/2. S/N 2416-0037.
Discusses the National Wild and Scenic Rivers System and its efforts to preserve the quality of the waters.

POPULATION AND THE ENVIRONMENT

1020. **Effects of Population Growth on Natural Resources and the Environment, Hearings Before a Subcommittee on the Committee on Government Operations, House, 91st Cong., 1st sess., Sept. 15-16, 1969.** 1969. 256p. $1.00. Y 4.G 74/7:P 81.

1021. **Family Planning Service Programs, An Operational Analysis.** 1970. 109p. il. $1.00. HE 1.29:970/1.

1022. **The Population Challenge, What It Means to America, U.S. Department of the Interior Conservation Yearbook.** 1970. 80p. il. $2.00. I 1.95:2. Presents in vivid color the dramatic story of the demands our expanding population is placing on our natural resources, contrasts America the beautiful with America the wasteland, illustrates the necessity to preserve and stretch our resources if the future is to see our way of life continue.

1023. **Population Growth and America's Future (Interim Report of the Commission on Population Growth and America's Future).** 1971. 56p. $0.40. Y 3.P 81:1/971. S/N 5258-0001. This report outlines the population situation in the United States and the issues it poses; raises questions about the probable impact of future population growth and distribution, and describes how the Commission is developing answers to these questions.

1024. **Protecting the World Environment in the Light of Population Increase, A Report to the President.** 1970. viii + 36p. $0.50. PrEx 8.2:En 8/2. S/N 4106-0026. This report concerns actions which the United States might take to improve the world environment, taking into account current domestic programs. It describes the nature and extent of the problems of the world environment, discusses areas needing attention, and recommends actions to meet these needs.

1025. **Report on the Oral Contraceptives. 1st edition.** 1966. 104p. $0.55. FS 13.102:C 76/2. **—2nd edition.** 1969. 88p. $1.00. FS 13.102:C 76/2/ 969.

1026. **Report on Intrauterine Contraceptive Devices.** 1968. 101p. il. $0.55. FS 13.102:C 76/3.

POVERTY

1027. **Education, An Answer to Poverty, School Programs Which May Be Eligible for Federal Aid.** 1966. 76p. il. $0.40. FS 5.237:37000.

1028. **Growing Up Poor, An Over-View and Analysis of Childrearing and Family Life Patterns Associated with Poverty, Implications for the Mental Health, Educational Achievement, Social Behavior, Family Stability of**

Very Poor Parents and Their Children, Suggestions for Action Programs, Guide-Lines to Further Research. 1966. 117p. $0.45. FS 14.2:P 79.

1029. **The Poor, A Selected Bibliography.** 1969. 56p. $0.60. A 1.38:1145.
A selected compilation of literature dealing with many aspects of poverty such as psychology, sociology, demography, economics, physical and mental health.

1030. **Slums and Social Insecurity, An Appraisal of the Effectiveness of Housing Policies in Helping to Eliminate Poverty in the United States.** 1966. 168p. $0.70. FS 3.49:1.

1031. **Toward Better Housing for Low Income Families, The Report of the President's Task Force on Low Income Housing, May 1970.** 1970. 20p. $0.25. Pr 37.8:H 81/R 29.
Concentrates on certain key recommendations which it is believed will help improve the housing conditions of low-income families and help produce a better all-round performance for the nation in the housing area. Discusses such areas as financing, land, modern technology and the provision of low-cost housing, federal housing programs, discrimination, and income maintenance.

POVERTY—PROGRAMS

1032. **Characteristics of General Assistance in the United States.** 1970. 122p. $1.25. HE 17.19:39. S/N 1760-0091.
Lists alphabetically by state 20 items of characteristics of general assistance, grouped into five sections: general description; conditions of eligibility; standards of assistance and payment; administration; and other aid from public funds.

1033. **Child Welfare Services.** 1966. 44p. il. $0.25. FS 14.111:406.

1034. **Food Stamp and Food Donation Program:**

> **Food Stamp Program, More Food, Better Diets for Low-Income Families.** 1969. 6p. il. $0.10. A 1.68:930.
> **How to Plan a Self-Service Food Donation Center.** 1969. 7p. il. $0.10. A 1.68:936.
> **You Can Help Fight Hunger in America, Donated Foods Handbook for Volunteers.** 1969. 11p. $0.15. A 88.40/2:76.
> **You're in Good Company, Millions of Americans Use USDA Food Stamps.** 1969. 12p. il. $0.20. A 1.68:922.
> **Your Family Food Donation Program.** 1969. 6p. il. $0.10. A 98.2:F 21.

1035. **Food Stamps to End Hunger.** 1970. 8p. il. $0.15. A 1.68:911/2.
This leaflet discusses the Food Stamp Program as it helps to get more food to low-income families in the United States. Information provided in this

publication tells what the Food Stamp Program is, where it is needed, who is eligible, and what goes on in a neighborhood when the Food Stamp Program is initiated.

1036. **Highlights of Welfare Reform, Reform, Renewal for the 70's.** 1971. 26p. il. $0.40. PrEx 15.2:W 45. S/N 4101-0056.

1037. **Perspectives in Public Welfare, A History.** 1969. 107p. il. $0.70. FS 17.2:P 96/3.
Knowledge of the history of the Anglo-American law is essential to an understanding of America's attempt to wage war on poverty. This succinct and informative review of poor relief policies and practices from the medieval period through the 1920s will be welcomed by all students of social welfare history. This account helps to put the current scrutiny and reappraisal of public welfare into historical perspective.

1038. **Poverty Amid Plenty, The American Paradox, The Report of the President's Commission on Income Maintenance Programs.** 1969. 155p. il. $1.75. Pr 36.8:In 2/P 86.
This Report of the President's Commission on Income Maintenance Programs discusses and reviews the operations of welfare and related programs. Further, this Report is noted for its recommendation of the adoption of a new program of income supplementation for all Americans in need.

PUBLIC HEALTH

See also—Drug Abuse; Medicine and Health.

The U.S. Public Health Service makes available a large number of pamphlets, books, and charts. These cover a wide variety of health-related subjects and range in appeal from the elementary school level through the very technical medical works. Many of their publications will be sent free on direct request or are available for purchase from the Superintendent of Documents.

1039. **About Syphilis and Gonorrhea.** 1970. 6p. $0.10. HE 20.10:84.
This pamphlet describes these diseases, tells how they look, how they affect a person, what their effects can be, and advice on treatment.

1040. **Biological Factors in Domestic Rodent Control.** 1969. 32p. il. $0.40. FS 2.60/7:R 61.
Deals with individual rats and mice, their identification, distribution, and life history, as well as the characteristics of rodent populations and the principles of rodent control.

1041. **Control of Domestic Rats and Mice.** 1969. 41p. il. $0.50. FS 2.6/2: R 18.
One of a series of training guides on procedures for control of rats and mice.

1042. **Emergency Health Services Digest.** 1970. vii + 55-135p. $0.50. HE 20.2013/2:2. S/N 1701-0380.
Emergency health services are an integral part of day-to-day comprehensive health care as well as the cornerstone of disaster preparedness for a catastrophe of any magnitude, whether local accident or national emergency.

1043. **Facts about Microwave Oven Radiation.** 1970. 9p. Free. 7700-003.
Safety aspects in use and maintenance. Available from Consumer Product Information, Washington, D.C. 20407.

1044. **Facts of Life and Death.** 1970. iv + 39p. il. $0.50. HE 20.2202: L 62. S/N 1701-0299.
The statistics in this report have been assembled to answer questions frequently asked about vital and health statistics for the United States. Information is included on births, deaths, marriage, divorces, life expectancy, estimates for selected health conditions, chronic conditions, persons injured, days of disability, health personnel data, and reported cases of communicable diseases.

1045. **From Hand to Mouth [Story of Food, Flies, Fingers, and Such, Brief Account of the Things You Can and Must Do to Prevent Spread of Disease].** 1961. 48p. il. $0.20. FS 2.2:H 19/961.

1046. **Man's Health and the Environment—Some Research Needs, Report of the Task Force on Research Planning in Environmental Health Science.** 1970. 258p. $1.25. HE 20.3552:M 31.
This report contains studies and recommendations of a special Task Force of the National Institute of Environmental Health Sciences on specific environmental problem areas, such as air pollution, food and water; on specific disease conditions; and on social and behavioral sciences, technological trends, training and organizational needs.

1047. **National Medical Audiovisual Center, Catalog, 1970.** 1970. 114p. $1.25. HE 20.3608/4:970. S/N 1752-0126.
The audiovisuals described in this catalog include motion picture films, filmstrips, videotapes, audiotapes, and slide sets. All deal with some aspect of a medical or health-related problem area, and are made available on a short-term loan basis from the National Medical Audiovisual Center to the biomedical professions.

1048. **Rats, Let's Get Rid of Them.** 1968. 8p. il. $0.05. I 49.4:22/2.
Information on selection and use of traps and poisons.

1049. **Rurality, Poverty, and Health, Medical Problems in Rural Areas.** 1970. 10p. il. $0.15. A 93.28:172.

1050. **Smallfry Smiles, A Guide for Teaching Dental Health in Community Care Programs.** 1970. 58p. il. $0.55. HE 20.3108:Sm 4/970.

1051. **Strictly for Teenagers.** 1964. 8p. il. $0.05. FS 2.2:T 22/2/964.
This leaflet, which presents some important facts about venereal diseases, has been prepared to answer many of the questions modern teenagers ask about this important topic.

1052. **What About Radiation?** 1964. 2p. $0.05. FS 2.50:113.
Contains brief answers to some of the questions that are frequently asked about certain radiation sources—removal of strontium 90 from milk, X-rays for medical and dental purposes, mass chest X-ray programs, shoe-fitting fluoroscopes, television sets, radium dial watches and clocks, radioactive tableware.

1053. **What's Being Done about X-Rays from Home TV Sets?** 1971. 12p. $0.10. HE 20.1500:T 23.
Discusses the causes of X-ray emission, reflects on the potential public health hazard, summarizes federal activities to control TV X-radiation emission, discusses the radiation safety of sets today, and offers advice to consumers.

REAL ESTATE

1054. **How to Buy Public Lands.** 1968. 4p. $0.10. I 53.9:4/2.
Answers the questions most frequently asked by persons interested in buying property from the Bureau of Land Management.

1055. **Inventory Report on Real Property Owned by the United States Throughout the World, As of June 30, 1969.** 1970. 90p. il. $0.55. GS 1.15:969.
Summarizes detailed data on all land, buildings, and other structures and facilities owned by the United States (including wholly owned government corporations) throughout the world, as of June 30, 1969.

1056. **What about Land in Alaska?** 1969. 4p. il. $0.10. I 53.9:2/5.

1057. **What Are "The Public Lands"?** 1968. 4p. il. $0.10. I 53.9:1/5.
Here are the answers to most-asked questions about America's 460 million acres of public domain lands administred by Interior's Bureau of Land Management. A map showing general location of public lands in 11 Western states is included in this folder.

RECREATION

Included in this section are works on fishing, hunting, camping, winter sports, and recreation in general. For specific national recreation areas, *see—National Parks. See also—Boating.*

1058. **Anglers' Guide to Sharks of the Northeastern United States, Maine to Chesapeake Bay.** 1964. 32p. il. $0.25. I 49.4:179.

1059. **The Appalachian Trail.** 1964. 8p. il. $0.05. A 1.38:951.

1060. **Backpacking in the National Forest Wilderness, A Family Adventure.**
1971. 28p. il. $0.25. A 1.68:585/3.
Written for those families of the cities who dream of exploring the vast
National Forest Wilderness of our country, this manual for backpacking
campers is designed for those who want to do it but don't quite know how.
It tells what equipment is needed and the procedures to follow for family
backpacking, gives sample menus for meals, and lists organizations that
might give further information.

1061. **Camping on the Public Lands.** 1968. 7p. $0.05. I 53.9:3/5.

1062. **Camping the National Forests, America's Playgrounds.** 1969. 16p. il.
$0.20. A 1.68:502/3.
Highlights the fun of camping for families and others on the National
Forests. Contains background information on facilities, answers to frequently asked questions about camping, and a description of some of the
playgrounds and natural wonders within the National Forests.

1063. **Camping in the National Park System.** 1970. 12p. il. $0.25. I 29.71:
970.
Lists camping accommodations in each area, name and address of area, and
name of camping site in the National Parks. Also gives pertinent information
for campers such as camping season, campground type, number of sites or
spaces, fees, water and toilet facilities, stores, swimming, boating, fishing
information, and includes a reference map.

1064. **Fishing in the National Park System.** 1969. 16p. il. $0.30. I 29.2:
F 53/3/969.

1065. **Handbook for Recreation.** 1960. 148p. il. $0.75. FS 17.210:231.
Provides plans for parties and picnics, instructions for hundreds of games for
indoors and outdoors, and detailed suggestions for such activities as dances,
dramas, storytelling, singing, and others.

1066. **Handling Your Big-Game Kill.** 1967. 12p.
A guide to prevent waste of meat or trophy, for novice hunters of deer, elk,
moose and other large game animals. Field dressing, cooling, butchering,
and storage are discussed. Available from Forest Service, U.S. Department of
Agriculture, 12th and Independence Avenue, N.W., Washington, D.C. 20250.

1067. **Outdoor Recreation in the National Forests, Resources, Opportunities, Activities, Management, Policy, Programs, Outlook.** 1965. 106p. il.
$0.60. A 1.75:301.
Recreation policies, programs, and objectives of the Forest Service are
described. There is also descriptive information on wilderness and primitive
areas in the National Forests.

1068. **Private Assistance in Outdoor Recreation, A Directory of Organiza-tions Providing Aid to Individuals and Public Groups.** 1970. 82p. $0.45. I 66.2:D 62/2/970.

1069. **Skiing the National Forests, America's Playgrounds.** 1970. 24p. il. $0.50. A 1.68:525/8.
Illustrated in color, this 24-page booklet contains a clip-out sheet showing the 12 standard national ski area signs developed for skier safety and con-venience. The "Skier's Courtesy Code" and a directory of the approximately 200 ski areas in the National Forests are also included.

1070. **Snowmobiles.** 1969. 10p. il. $0.10. C 41.2:Sn 6.
This pamphlet describes this new recreational vehicle, and discusses its growth, utilization, production and sales, industry structure, foreign trade, and markets.

1071. **Sport Fishing, U.S.A.** $10.00. I 49.2:F 52/7.

1072. **Vigor.** 1964. 24p. il. $0.25. Pr 35.8:P 56/V 68.
A complete physical fitness plan for boys age 12 to 18. Includes a basic workout, plus sections on isometric exercise and weight training. Tests help boys check their fitness against that of other boys their own age.

1073. **Vim.** 1964. 24p. il. $0.25. Pr 35.8:P 56/V 72.
A complete physical fitness plan for girls age 12 to 18. Includes a basic workout and tips on figure development, plus information on diet, weight control, and posture. Explains how being physically fit helps develop beauty and poise.

1074. **Winter Activities in the National Park System.** 1970. 24p. il. $0.35. I 29.2:W 73.
Besides skiing, both cross country and downhill, there are parks providing ice skating and sliding on innertubes and platters, popular with children. For those desiring more strenuous exercise there are areas for mountaineering and snowshoeing. For the less agile, ice fishing and snowmobiling are avail-able. This pamphlet provides detailed information on the National Parks which offer winter activities.

RURAL LIFE

See also—Agriculture; Farms and Farming.

1075. **Age of Transition, Rural Youth in a Changing Society.** 1967. 92p. $0.75. A 1.76:347. —**Supplement.** 1967. 41p. $0.25. A 1.76:347/supp.

1076. **A New Life for the Country, The Report of the President's Task Force on Rural Development.** 1970. 51p. $0.35. Pr 37.8:R 88/L 62.

1077. **People of Rural America.** 1968. 289p. il. $3.50. C 3.30:R 88.
This monograph attempts to describe the rural population as reported in the 1960 Census of Population and to evaluate the residence categories used. Information on the age and sex composition of the rural population; differential fertility; educational status; employment of rural people; and rural income and earnings is also provided.

SAFETY MEASURES

1078. **Directory and Index of Safety and Health Laws and Codes.** 1969. 109p. il. $1.25. L 16.2:Sa 1/31.
This is a compilation of all known occupational safety and health regulations and laws which are administered by the states.

1079. **Electric Shock, Its Causes and Its Prevention.** 1954. 37p. il. $0.20. D 211.2:El 2.

1080. **Fire Extinguishing Equipment.** 1970. 3 + 26p. $0.25. P 1.31/3:10/2.
This handbook contains information on what you should know about fires and fire extinguishers—how to order, install, and keep fire extinguishers ready for use; characteristics, procurement, use maintenance, and inspection of fire hoses; sprinkler systems; and a checklist of very important points.

1081. **Safety and Survival in an Earthquake.** 1969. 12p. il. $0.10. I 19.2:Ea 7/3.
This publication tells what actions can be taken to reduce the dangers before, during, and after an earthquake occurs.

1082. **Skywarn, Tips for Tornado Safety.** 1970. 4p. il. $0.10. C 52.2: T 63/4.

1083. **Survival in a Hurricane.** 1970. 4p. il. $0.10. C 52.2:H 94/4.

1084. **Tornado Safety Rules [Poster].** 9 x 12 in. 1970. $0.10. C 55.106: T 63.

1085. **Winter Storm Safety Rules.** 9 x 12 in. 1970. $0.10. C 55.106:St 7. S/N 0318-0004.

SANITATION

1086. **Developing a State Solid Waste Management Plan.** 1970. 50p. il. $0.60. HE 20.1408:M 31.
This document describes basic features of the planning process and their utilization in the development of a state plan for its solid waste management. Purpose of this publication is to aid states in preparing comprehensive solid waste management plans.

1087. **Home Sanitation.** 1962. 6p. il. $0.05. FS 2.50:39/3.
This folder briefly presents information and suggestions on home sanitation—

water supply, sewage disposal, refuse disposal, flies, other insects, and rats, light and ventilation, heating, plumbing, refrigeration, and accident prevention.

1088. **Safe and Sanitary Home Refuse Storage.** 1968. 6p. il. $0.10. FS 2.2:R 25/968.
Explains how to handle garbage and rubbish, in order to have a safe and comfortable home, and an attractive and healthful community.

1089. **Septic Tank Care.** 1967. 6p. il. $0.05. FS 2.50:96/3.
Guide for the care and maintenance of septic tank soil absorption systems.

1090. **Solid Waste Processing, A State-of-the-Art Report on Unit Operations and Processes.** 1970. 72p. il. $0.75. HE 20.1102:So 4.

1091. **Swimming Pools and Natural Bathing Places.** $0.35. PHS 1586.
Annotated bibliography listing articles relating to the sanitation and safety problems of swimming pools and natural bathing places.

SENIOR CITIZENS

See—Aging.

SMALL BUSINESS

1092. **Advice for Persons Who Are Considering an Investment in a Franchise Business.** 1970. 11p. $0.10. FT 1.3/2:4.
Tells the consumer what pitfalls to watch for and what steps to take to protect himself as a prospective franchisee, while considering an investment in a franchise business.

1093. **Buying and Selling a Small Business.** 1969. 122p. $0.75. SBA 1.2: B 98.

1094. **Financial Recordkeeping for Small Stores.** 1966. 131p. $0.60. SBA 1.12:32.

1095. **Guide to Record Retention Requirements.** 1971. 92p. $1.00. GS 4.107/a:R 245/971.
This guide tells the user what records must be kept, who must keep them, and how long they must be kept. Each digest includes a reference to the full text of the basic law or regulation providing for such retention. The index, numbering over 2,200 items, lists for ready reference the categories of persons, companies, and products affected by federal record retention requirements.

1096. **Handbook for Small Business, A Survey of Small Business Programs of the Federal Government.** 1969. 200p. il. $1.75. 91-1:S.doc. 45.
Designed to present in one comprehensive volume information on programs of the federal government which are beneficial to small business. The

handbook describes the activities of various agencies pertaining to small
business and provides an overall view of the major areas of governmental
help to small businessmen.

1097. **Impact of Crime on Small Business, 1969-70, Hearings Before the
Select Committee on Small Business, Senate, 91st Cong., 1st and 2d sess.,
July 23, 1969—June 24, 1970, pt. 2.** 1970. p. 377-582. il. $1.00. Y 4.Sm
1/2:C 86/3/969-70/pt. 2.

1098. **Improving the Prospects of Small Business, The Report of the President's Task Force on Improving the Prospects of Small Business.** 1970. 30p.
$0.25. Pr 37.8:Sm 1/R 29.
This report presents an overview of the problems faced by small business
today, considering the problems that are likely to emerge in the years ahead
and recommending what might be done to improve the prospects of small
business in this country.

1099. **Selecting Advertising Media, A Guide for Small Business.** 1969. 114p.
il. $0.70. SBA 1.12:34.

1100. **Starting and Managing Series.**
This series, published by the Small Business Administration, contains a
number of guides for prospective business owners and operators, pointing
out problems which may be encountered and areas of information necessary.
The businesses covered are listed below:

>**Starting and Managing a:**
>**Carwash.** 1967. 76p. il. $0.45. SBA 1.15:14.
>**Pet Shop.** 1970. 40p. $0.30. SBA 1.15:19.
>**Retail Drugstore.** 1966. 103p. il. $0.40. SBA 1.15:11.
>**Retail Flower Shop.** 1970. 121p. il. $0.55. SBA 1.15:18.
>**Service Station.** 1961. 80p. il. $0.45. SBA 1.15:3/2d ed.
>**Small Automatic Vending Business.** 1967. 70p. il. $0.40.
>   SBA 1.15:13.
>**Small Bookkeeping Service.** 1962. 64p. il. $0.35. SBA 1.15:4.
>**Small Building Business.** 1962. 102p. il. $0.50. SBA 1.15:5.
>**Small Business of Your Own.** 1962. 49p. il. $0.35. SBA 1.15:1/2.
>**Small Credit Bureau and Collection Service.** 1959. 187p. il.
> $0.60. SBA 1.15:2.
>**Small Dry Cleaning Business.** 1966. 80p. il. $0.35. SBA 1.15:12.
>**Small Duplicating and Mailing Service.** 1963. 55p. il. $0.35.
>   SBA 1.15:8.
>**Small Motel.** 1963. 70p. il. $0.40. SBA 1.15:7.
>**Small Restaurant.** 1964. 116p. il. $0.65. SBA 1.15:9.
>**Small Retail Camera Shop.** 1969. 69p. $0.40. SBA 1.15:17.
>**Small Retail Jewelry Store.** 1971. 78p. il. $0.40. SBA 1.15:21.
>   S/N 4500-0099.

Small Retail Music Store. 1970. 81p. il. $0.55. SBA 1.15:20.
Small Shoe Service Shop. 1968. 86p. $0.45. SBA 1.15:16.
Swap Shop or Consignment Sale Shop. 1968. 78p. il. $0.35.
SBA 1.15:15.

1101. A Survey of Federal Government Publications of Interest to Small Business. 1969. 85p. $0.45. SBA 1.18/2:G 74/969.
From the vast output of booklets, pamphlets, and leaflets published by the various federal government agencies, those most likely to be of assistance to the small business sector are listed in this volume. Small business operators, prospective businessmen, or students will find helpful references on many subjects relating to small business management and operation.

SMOKING AND HEALTH

See also—Cancer.

1102. Bibliography on Smoking and Health, 1969 Cumulation, Part II. 1970. 362p. $3.25. HE 20.11:45/pt. 2.
Includes all of the items added to the Technical Information Center of the National Clearinghouse for Smoking and Health from January through December 1969.

1103. Chart Book on Smoking, Tobacco, and Health. 1969. 46p. il. $0.45. HE 20.2002:Sm 7.
Through the use of charts and narratives, this booklet describes and discusses cigarettes in our society, the relationship between cigarette smoking and health, cigarettes and the economy, cigarette manufacturing and marketing, and cigarettes as a tax source.

1104. Datos Sobre el Habito de Fumar y la Salud. 1970. 12p. il. $0.15. HE 20.2602:Sm 7/4/Spanish.
Written in Spanish, this leaflet presents a summary of the current knowledge about smoking and health. Discusses research and scientific studies which have been made and includes a chart showing the death rate of cigarette smokers versus non-smokers by selected diseases and further discusses each disease in relation to smoking and how to avoid increased health risks associated with cigarette smoking.

1105. The Facts about Smoking and Health. 1970. 12p. $0.15. HE 20. 2602:Sm 7/4.

1106. If You Must Smoke, 5 Ways to Reduce the Risks of Smoking. 1970. 6p. il. $0.10. HE 20.2602:Sm 7.
Lists and describes five ways to reduce the risks of smoking. Lung cancer, emphysema, chronic bronchitis, and coronary heart disease are discussed as they relate to smoking.

1107. Smoking and Lung Cancer. 1970. 6p. $0.10. HE 20.2602:Sm 7/2.
Contains information on symptoms, diagnosis, causes, treatment of lung
cancer. Also discusses the relationship between lung cancer and cigarettes
and ways of prevention.

1108. Smoking and Pregnancy. 1971. 25p. $0.20. HE 20.2002:Sm 7.
Discusses the effects of maternal smoking on infant birthweight and on
risk of abortion, stillbirth, and neonatal death.

1109. Smoking, Health, and You—Facts for Teenagers. 1964. 22p. il. $0.15.
FS 17.210:424.
The purpose of this pamphlet is to help the young person make a decision
regarding smoking that is satisfactory to himself. Divided into two sections—
questions and answers and medical evidence—it tells about the health
hazards of smoking in language the teenager can understand.

1110. Tar and Nicotine Content of Cigarettes. 1970. 1p. $0.05. HE
20.2602:T 17/970.
Chart lists name of cigarette, type of cigarette, and tar and nicotine content.

1111. What's New on Smoking in Print and on Film. 1971. 8p. $0.10.
HE 20.2602:Sm 7/6. S/N 1727-0018.
This folder presents films and filmstrips and educational materials on smoking
and health which have been issued by member organizations of the National
Interagency Council on Smoking and Health. It covers a wide range of
interests and is directed to many audiences, including young people and
adults, smokers, and nonsmokers.

SOCIAL SECURITY

See also—Insurance; Medicare.

1112. The Future Is Now. 24p. il. $0.25. FS 3.52:76.
Colorfully illustrated, this booklet provides, in an entertaining way, informa-
tion about some of the varied services rendered by the Social Security
Administration.

1113. If You Become Disabled. 1970. 32p. $0.15. HE 3.52:29/2.
This booklet tells you what you need to know about the social security
disability provisions, how they affect you and your family both now and
in the future.

**1114. If You're Self-Employed . . . Reporting Your Income for Social
Security.** 1970. 5p. $0.10. HE 3.52:22/2.
Gives specific information of interest to self-employed business or professional
people, how to figure net earnings, how to report earnings, family business
arrangements, a contribution rate schedule for the self-employed, and special
instructions for U.S. citizens working in this country for a foreign government.

1115. Information about Making Social Security Reports. SSI-99.
A basic pamphlet aimed at helping the employer report his employees'
earnings. Available from local Social Security Administration offices.

**1116. Social Security Benefits—How You Earn Them—How Much Credit
You Need—How to Estimate the Amount.** 1970. 14p. il. $0.15. HE 3.52.
47/3.
Explains how to earn social security credits; how many are required for payments at the retirement age; and how you estimate the amount of benefits
payable at retirement age to a worker and his family.

1117. Social Security Benefits for Students, 18-22. 1969. 8p. il. $0.10.
HE 3.52:48/2.
Tells how a student from 18 to 22 may now receive monthly cash social
security benefits. This pamphlet also explains the requirements necessary to
receive such benefits, the information needed when applying, and how and
where to apply.

1118. Social Security Information for Young Families. 1970. 19p. il. $0.15.
HE 3.52:35b/3.
This booklet is about the protection social security has for younger people,
how a worker earns this protection, the benefits that can be paid. It also
contains other information about social security of interest to younger
workers.

1119. Social Security Programs Throughout the World, 1969. 1970. xxx +
249p. $2.75. HE 3.49:31.
Presents an analysis of the principal provisions of social security programs in
all countries of the world. Countries are listed alphabetically and a separate
summary is given for each country. The larger part of the programs covered
are social insurance measures, but several related types of social security
programs are also included.

1120. Social Security Record Book. SSI-74. **—Seguro Social—Libro de
Record [Spanish Edition].** SSI-74SP.
For farm workers' use in recording work dates, hours worked, and wages.
Includes postcard form, OAR-7004 (Request for Statement of Earnings).
Available from local Social Security Administration offices.

**1121. Special Information for Self-Employed Farmers about Reporting
Their Income for Social Security.** 8p. $0.05. FS 3.52:25.

1122. Your Right to Question the Decision Made on Your Claim. SSI-58.
Explains what a person may do if he feels that the decision made on his
Social Security claim is not correct. A copy is sent with all letters of dis-
allowance. Available from local Social Security Administration offices.

1123. Your Social Security Earnings Record. 1970. 32p. $0.20. HE
3.52:44/4.
Explains how social security records are kept, how to get a statement of

one's social security record, what the statement shows, and other important points which relate to social security earnings records.

SPACE EXPLORATION

The National Aeronautics and Space Administration, in addition to its highly technical publications, issues pamphlets and charts designed for the general reader and some for children. The publications listed in this section without an NAS number are from NASA. All others are available from the Superintendent of Documents.

1124. **America in Space: The First Decade, Aeronautics.** 1970. 22p. il. $0.45. NAS 1.19:61.
This booklet discusses the field of aeronautics and includes such topics as aeronautical research, aeronautics in NASA, the X-15 research airplane, variable-sweep wings, the supersonic transport, hypersonic flight, helicopters and V/STOL aircraft.

1125. **Apollo 8, Man Around the Moon.** 1968. 24p. il. $0.50. NAS 1.19: 66.
The Apollo 8 flight around the moon by astronauts Borman, Lovell, and Anders is reported in this full-color booklet.

1126. **Apollo 13, "Houston, We've Got a Problem."** 25p. $0.75. NAS 1.19:76.
Failure of one of Apollo 13's oxygen tanks made it necessary to continue flight in an emergency mode to and around the Moon, and back to splashdown in the Pacific Ocean. The story of this dramatic flight is told mainly in excerpts from the conversations between the astronauts and Mission Control.

1127. **Apollo 14, Science at Fra Mauro.** $1.25. NAS 1.19:91. S/N 3300-0347.
Exploration of the upland Fra Mauro area of the moon incorporated the most extensive scientific observations in manned lunar exploration up to that time. The story of this mission is presented in text, a traverse map and color photographs.

1128. **Apollo 15 at Hadley Base.** $0.75. NAS 1.19:94. S/N 3300-0402.
This pamphlet gives an account of the Apollo 15 lunar explorations of Hadley Base. Photographs, many taken on the Moon, illustrate the different phases of the expedition from lift-off to splashdown.

1129. **Exploring Space with a Camera.** 1968. 214p. il. $4.25. NAS 1.21:168.
This is a collection of photographs taken from space during the first decade of space exploration. The significance of each photograph is fully explained. Many are in full color.

1130. **The First Lunar Landing as Told by the Astronauts.** $0.75. NAS 1.19:73.

1131. **Journey to the Moon.** 1968. 1 sheet, 21 x 48 in. [folded]. $0.30. NAS 1.20:NF-40.
Describes, in simplified terms, the lunar journey from launch to recovery.

1132. **Man in Space.** 30p. $0.55. EP-57.
A chronicle of the Mercury, Gemini, and Apollo Manned Space Flight programs.

1133. **Man in Space.** 28p. $1.00. EP-81.
This first booklet in a new series entitled "Space in the Seventies" discusses Apollo flights still to come, Skylab, the Shuttle and space stations, and takes a "long look ahead" at possibilities for lunar colonies and manned flight to Mars and other planets.

1134. **NASA Pictures:**

> **Apollo, in the Beginning.** 1969. 7 color lithographs, each 12 x 16 in. or 16 x 12 in. $1.25/set. NAS 1.43/2:1.
> Apollo—"In the beginning . . ." is a succinct story of manned Apollo missions, told in a collection of seven full-color lithographs.
> **Eyewitness to Space.** 1969. 12 color reproductions, each 16 x 20 in. $2.75/set. NAS 1.43/2:3.
> Twelve reproductions in full color of paintings of space program scenes by well-known artists.
> **Apollo, First Manned Lunar Landing.** 1969. 12 full-color pictures, each 11 x 14 in. or 14 x 11 in. $1.75/set. NAS 1.43/2:4.
> A 12-scene story of the epic journey of Apollo 11 and man's first visit to another celestial body. The preparation, the launch, and man and his Lunar Module on the very surface of the moon—all of these are included in this set.
> **Apollo, Man on the Moon.** 1969. 1 full-color picture, 16 x 20 in. $1.00. NAS 1.43/2:5.
> Selected by NASA as the single picture which best portrays the first moon landing.
> **Apollo 12, Pinpoint Landing on the Moon.** 1970. 8 full-color and 2 black and white pictures, each 11 x 14 in. $1.50/set. NAS 1.43/2:6.
> This set shows highlights of Apollo 12.

1135. **NASA Spacecraft.** 26p. $0.50. EP-54.
The present family of NASA spacecraft. All types are discussed—small, large, spin-oriented, accurately attitude-controlled, manned, automated, in low orbits, in trajectories to the Moon and the planets, free in space until they expire, or commanded to return to Earth or to land on the Moon.

1136. **The Pioneer Mission to Jupiter.** 1971. 46p. il. $0.30. NAS 1.21:268. S/N 3300-0387.
Presents a brief account of the objectives, demands, and potential rewards of the Pioneer program, and gives a highly condensed description of the complex scientific experiments to be undertaken, the spacecraft to be used, and the management of the mission.

1137. **Space Station: Key to the Future.** 1970. 40p. il. $0.45. NAS 1.19:75.

1138. **This Is NASA.** 20p. $0.45. EP-22.
An overview of NASA's programs in aeronautical research and space exploration. Illustrations are from the NASA Art Program.

1139. **This New Ocean: A History of the Project Mercury.** By Loyd S. Swenson, Jr., James M. Grimwood, and Charles C. Alexander. 1966. 680p. $5.50. NASA SP-4201.
A well-documented story of Project Mercury, the first U.S. manned space flight program, which spanned 55 months from authorization through Cooper's 22-orbit flight in May 1963 and which involved more than two million people.

1140. **Vanguard—A History.** 1970. xvi + 308p. il. $2.75. NAS 1.21:4202.
This book deals with the origin, course of development, and results of the first American earth satellite project.

SPACE SCIENCES

1141. **Aerospace Bibliography: 5th Edition.** 102p. $1.00. EP-48.
An annotated listing of books, pamphlets, audiovisual aids, and other resources, with a key indicating grade levels for which the various materials are suited.

1142. **Aids to Identification of Flying Objects.** 1968. 36p. il. $0.20. D 301.2:F 67.
Unidentified Flying Objects (UFOs) have been the subject of considerable interest on the part of the public, as well as the U.S. Air Force, for two decades. This booklet is intended to meet the needs of individuals seeking information on scientific observations and analyses. The section "Aids to Identification of Flying Objects" is more technical and should be of interest to persons desiring in-depth information on flying objects. The "Questions and Answers" section will help answer many of the questions commonly asked about UFOs.

1143. **Alvan Clark & Sons, Artists in Optics.** 1968. 120p. il. $1.75. SI 3.3: 274. S/N 4701-0066.
In 1800 there were no astronomical observatories in the United States, but by 1900 there were several hundred. This expansion of astronomical facilities was greatly aided by Alvan Clark and his sons, who produced many telescopes

of all sizes, culminating with the 40-inch Yerkes refractor, then and now the largest in the world. This book contains biographies of these three talented instrument makers, a discussion of their techniques, and a catalog of all the astronomical instruments made by them.

1144. **Astronomical Phenomena (Calendar) Year**.
These works, as listed below, provide the data required for the practice of astronomical navigation at sea.

> 1967. 33p. il. $0.35. D 213.8/3:967
> 1968. 33p. il. $0.35. D 213.8/3:968
> 1969. 33p. il. $0.35. D 213.8/3:969
> 1970. 39p. il. $0.40. D 213.8/3:970
> 1971. 39p. il. $0.45. D 213.8/3:971
> 1972. 71p. il. $0.55. D 213.8/3:972
> 1973. 79p. il. $0.60. D 213.8/3:973
> 1974. 71p. il. $0.55. D 213.8/3:974

1145. **Atlas of Cometary Forms, Structures Near the Nucleus.** 1969. 128p. il. $2.25. NAS 1.21:198.
This volume contains four sections of pictorial material. In the first section are drawings from visual telescopic observations of the central regions of comets made during the 19th and early 20th centuries; the second section is devoted to the two comets from which both visual and photographic observations are available—Comet Daniel 1907 IV and Comet Halley 1910 II; the third and fourth sections contain photographs of three of the bright comets of this century, Comet Morehouse 1908 III, Comet Halley 1910 II, and Comet Humason VIII, and photographs of six additional comets for which less extensive photographs of structure in the coma are visible.

1146. **The Book of Mars.** 1969. 315p. il. $5.25. NAS 1.21:179.
This book on Mars, published by NASA in support of the growing interest in the study of our solar system, is a one-volume compaction of information about Mars, gained over many years by many scientists throughout the world. A highly readable book designed to acquaint the scientific community and the intelligent layman with what is known about Mars. to support investigation by providing a forum of information, and to describe the problems and their solutions. Contains numerous photographs and illustrations. The book discusses historical observations, orbital characteristics, prebiological systems, clouds, polar caps, atmosphere and climatology, and other related subjects.

1147. **Handbook of the Physical Properties of the Planet Jupiter.** By C. M. Michaux et al. 1967. 142p. $0.60. NASA SP-3031.
The largest planet in the solar system is especially intriguing because of such features as its wandering Great Red Spot and erratic decameter radio noise storms. This volume presents the astronomer's findings and recent conclusions.

1148. **Handbook of the Physical Properties of the Planet Mars.** By C. M. Michaux. 1967. 167p. $0.70. NASA SP-3030.
Although observed from Earth at every opportunity for many years, Mars remains an enigma. This volume summarizes both observational and theoretical conclusions regarding its surface, structure, and the possible presence of life there.

1149. **Handbook of the Physical Properties of the Planet Venus.** By L. R. Koenig, F. W. Murray, C. M. Michaux, and H. A. Hyatt. 1967. 132p. $0.60. NASA SP-3029.
Radio and radar astronomy, and the flight of Mariner II, have added observational data to theoretical studies of Venus, the nearest planet to Earth. This volume reviews what is known of its surface, atmosphere, and other still-bewildering properties.

1150. **Short Glossary of Space Terms.** 1966. 52p. $0.25. NASA SP-1.
Brief definitions of frequently used space terms, selected from the *Dictionary of Technical Terms for Aerospace Use* (NASA SP-7).

1151. **Space, Environmental Vantage Point.** 1971. 36p. il. $0.70. C 55.2: Sp 1. S/N 0317-0009.
This book gives a history and description of satellites, beginning with Tiros I, and discusses the contribution each one has made to environmental science. Photographs and sketches accompany the text. Also included is a satellite performance chart.

1152. **Space Science, A Guide Outlining Understandings, Fundamental Concepts, and Activities.** 1969. 144p. il. $2.00. NAS 1.19:64.

1153. **UFOs and Related Subjects, An Annotated Bibliography.** 1970. 401p. il. $3.50. D 301.45/19-2:68-1656.
This very comprehensive bibliography cites over 1,600 works about UFOs.

SPORTS

See—Recreation.

SURVIVAL

See also—Civil Defense; Safety.

1154. **Disaster Control (Ashore and Afloat).** 1968. 291p. il. $2.00. D 208. 11/2:D 63/968.
Prepared by the Bureau of Naval Personnel, U.S. Navy, this book is intended to help answer questions and should prove useful to all who are concerned with disaster control. Discusses man-made disasters—nuclear, biological or chemical warfare attack—their characteristics, results, and how to combat them.

1155. If Disaster Strikes and There Is No Doctor, A 16-Hour Free Course for the General Public. 1967. 6p. il. $0.05. FS 2.2:M 46/15/967.
Tells how to obtain free teaching materials and necessary equipment for presentation of the Medical Self-Help Training Course, developed by the Public Health Service in cooperation with the Office of Civil Defense to help prepare people for survival if disaster strikes and there is no doctor.

1156. Survival, Search and Rescue. 1969. 159p. il. $1.50. D 301.7:64-5/3.
This Air Force manual is designed to aid and insure survival and rescue regardless of geographic location or climatic conditions. It describes the proper use of survival equipment and will serve as an aid in the identification and use of natural resources at hand.

1157. Survival, Training Edition. 1969. 408p. il. $4.25. D 301.7:64-3/3.
This manual is for student use in Air Force formal survival training courses. It describes climatic and topographical conditions and vegetation and animal life in all geographical areas—land and sea. It also explains what man must do to survive in these areas, and how and why he must do it. The will and ability to survive are also discussed.

1158. Survival Preparedness for Rural Areas. 1968. 228p. il. $2.25. A 13.2: Su 7/3.
This Forest Service programmed instruction publication is designed as a self-teaching progressive referral course. It teaches the basic steps toward preparing for and surviving a natural or nuclear disaster. The fundamentals learned should contribute to saving the life of the student and those around him in times of flood, hurricane, tornado or in the danger period following a nuclear attack.

TAXES

1159. Excise Tax Information on Imported Foreign-Made Automobiles. 1970. 6p. il. $0.10. T 22.2:Au 8.
Explains the federal excise tax laws which impose a tax on the import and use of a new or used foreign-made automobile by a U.S. resident for his personal use.

1160. Impact of the Property Tax, Its Economic Implication for Urban Problems. 1968. 48p. il. $0.20. Y 4.Ec 7:P 94/14.

1161. Road-User and Property Taxes on Selected Motor Vehicles, 1970. 1970. 66p. il. $0.65. TD 2.102:T 19/970.
Supplies basic information for 1970 from each state on the application of road-user taxes and property taxes to a selected group of vehicles. This report is intended to supply the means to measure and compare the annual payments that would be made for each of 14 carefully selected vehicles in each state. Highway-use taxes paid on each vehicle and total taxes paid are

compared from state to state in dollar amounts in the tables. Rank columns in each table aid in the comparison. Bar charts and maps are also presented to show amounts of taxes that would be paid to each state for each vehicle.

1162. State Forest Tax Law Digest—1967. By E. T. Williams, F.S. 1968. 56p. Misc. Pub. No. 1077.
Summarizes in non-technical language the essential features of 56 special forest tax laws effective in 33 states and Puerto Rico as of December 31, 1967. The last previous edition of the digest was issued in 1957. Forest Tax provisions are grouped under four headings: exemptions, modified property taxes, yield taxes, and severance taxes. Principal changes in forest tax provisions since publication of the 1957 edition are summarized. A table is included showing the forest area in private ownership classified under optional laws. Available from Forest Service, U.S. Department of Agriculture, 12th and Independence Avenue, S.W., Washington, D.C. 20250.

1163. State Tax Collections in 1970. 1970. 38p. $0.50. C 3.191/2:970/1.

1164. Tax Guide for Small Business, Individuals, Corporations, Partnerships, Income, Excise, and Employment Taxes. 1972. $0.75. S/N 4804-0387.

TAXES—INCOME TAXES

1165. All States Income Tax Guide Information for Service Personnel. 1970. 113p. $1.25. D 302.8:In 2/971.

1166. The Commuter and the Municipal Income Tax, A Background Paper. 1970. 32p. $0.25. Y 3.Ad 9/8:2C 73.

1167. Description of Principal Federal Tax Returns, Related Forms, and Publications. $0.50. T 22.2:T 19/11/971.

1168. Internal Revenue Service Tax Information Publications (by number):

Your Exemptions and Exemptions for Dependents. $0.10. T 22.44/2:501.
Deduction for Medical and Dental Expenses. $0.10. T 22.44/2:502.
Child Care and Disabled Dependent Care. $0.10. T 22.44/2:503.
Income Tax Deduction for Alimony Payment. $0.10. T 22.44/2:504.
Tax Withholding and Declaration of Estimated Tax. $0.10. T 22.44/2:505.
Computing Your Tax Under the Income Averaging Method. $0.15. T 22.44/2:506.
Tax Information on Scholarships and Fellowships. $0.10. T 22.44/2:507.

Tax Information on Educational Expenses. $0.10. T 22.44/2:
508.
Tax Calendar and Checklist. $0.15. T 22.44/2:509.
Information on Excise Taxes for 1971. $0.15. T 22.44/2:510.
Sales and Other Dispositions of Depreciable Property. $0.15.
T 22.44/2:511.
Credit Sales by Dealers in Personal Property. $0.10. T 22.44/2:
512.
Tax Information for Visitors to the United States. $0.10.
T 22.44/2:513.
Foreign Tax Credit for U.S. Citizens and Resident Aliens. $0.15.
T 22.44/2:514.
Withholding of Tax on Nonresident Aliens and Foreign Corpora-
tions. $0.15. T 22.44/2:515.
Tax Information for U.S. Government Civilian Employees
Stationed Abroad. $0.10. T 22.44/2:516.
Social Security for Clergymen and Religious Workers. $0.10.
T 22.44/2:517.
Foreign Scholars and Educational and Cultural Exchange
Visitors. $0.30. T 22.44/2:518.
United States Tax Guide for Aliens. $0.30. T 22.44/2:519.
Tax Information for American Scholars Abroad. $0.10. T 22.44/
2:520.
Tax Information on Moving Expenses. $0.10. T 22.44/2:521.
Adjustments to Income for Sick Pay. $0.15. T 22.44/2:522.
Tax Information on Selling Your Home. $0.15. T 22.44/2:523.
Retirement Income and Retirement Income Credit. $0.15.
T 22.44/2:524.
Taxable Income and Non-Taxable Income. $0.15. T 22.44/2:
525.
Income Tax Deductions for Contributions. $0.10. T 22.44/2:
526.
Rental Income and Royalty Income. $0.10. T 22.44/2:527.
Information on Filing Your Tax Return. $0.15. T 22.44/2:528.
Other Miscellaneous Deductions. $0.10. T 22.44/2:529.
Tax Information on Deductions for Homeowners. $0.10.
T 22.44/2:530.
Reporting Your Tips for Federal Tax Purposes. $0.10. T 22.44/
2:531.
Tax Information for Students and Parents. $0.10. T 22.44/2:
532.
Information on Self-Employment Tax. $0.10. T 22.44/2:533.
Depreciation, Amortization, and Depletion. $0.15. T 22.44/
2:534.

Tax Information on Business Expenses. $0.20. T 22.44/2:535.
Losses from Operating a Business. $0.10. T 22.44/2:536.
Installment and Deferred-Payment Sales. $0.15. T 22.44/2:537.
Tax Information on Accounting Periods and Methods. $0.15.
    T 22.44/2:538.
Withholding Taxes from Your Employee's Wages. $0.15. T 22.
    44/2:539.
Tax Information on Repairs, Replacements, and Improvements.
    $0.10. T 22.44/2:540.
Tax Information on Partnership Income and Losses. $0.15.
    T 22.44/2:541.
Corporations and the Federal Income Tax. $0.20. T 22.44/2:
    542.
Tax Information on the Sale of a Business. $0.10. T 22.44/2:
    543.
Sales and Exchanges of Assets. $0.25. T 22.44/2:544.
Income Tax Deduction for Interest Expense. $0.10. T 22.44/2:
    545.
Income Tax Deduction for Taxes. $0.10. T 22.44/2:546.
Tax Information on Disasters, Casualty Losses, and Thefts.
    $0.20. T 22.44/2:547.
Tax Information on Deduction for Bad Debts. $0.10. T 22.44/
    2:548.
Condemnations of Private Property for Public Use. $0.20.
    T 22.44/2:549.
Tax Information on Investment Income and Expenses. $0.25.
    T 22.44/2:550.
Tax Information on Cost or Other Basis of Assets. $0.10.
    T 22.44/2:551.
Recordkeeping Requirements and A Guide to Tax Publications.
    $0.10. T 22.44/2:552.
Highlights of Changes in the Tax Law. $0.10. T 22.44/2:553.
Tax Benefits for Older Americans. $0.20. T 22.44/2:554.
Community Property and the Federal Income Tax. $0.10.
    T 22.44/2:555.
Audit of Returns, Appeal Rights and Claims for Refund. $0.10.
    T 22.44/2:556.
How to Apply for Exemption for an Organization. $0.20.
    T 22.44/2:557.
Tax Information for Sponsors of Contests and Sporting Events.
    $0.10. T 22.44/2:558.
Federal Tax Guide for Survivors, Executors, and Administrators.
    $0.20. T 22.44/2:559.
Retirement Plans for Self-Employed Individuals. $0.15. T 22.44/
    2:560.

Valuation of Donated Property. $0.15. T 22.44/2:561.

Tax Return Filing Requirements for U.S. Citizens Abroad. $0.10. T 22.44/2:563.

Tax Information on Mutual Fund Distributions. $0.15. T 22. 44/2:564.

Tax Information on the Interest Equalization Tax. $0.20. T 22.44/2:565.

Questions and Answers on Retirement Plans for the Self-Employed. $0.10. T 22.44/2:566.

Tax Advice on Civil Service Disability Retirement Payments. $0.10. T 22.44/2:567.

Federal Tax Information for Civil Service Retirees. $0.10. T 22.44/2:568.

Questions Asked by U.S. Taxpayers Abroad. $0.15. T 22.44/2: 569.

Tax Guide for U.S. Citizens Employed in U.S. Possessions. $0.15. T 22.44/2:570.

Tax Sheltered Annuity Plans for Employees of Public Schools and Certain Tax-Exempt Organizations. $0.20. T 22.44/2:571.

Tax Information on Investment Credit. $0.10. T 22.44/2:572.

Interest Equalization Tax Highlights. $0.10. T 22.44/2:573.

Filing of U.S. Annual Return of Income Tax to Be Paid at Source. $0.10. T 22.44/2:574.

1169. **The Timber Owner and His Federal Income Tax.** By E. T. Williams, F. S. 1964. 49p.
Available from Forest Service, U.S. Department of Agriculture, 12th and Independence Avenue, S.W., Washington, D.C. 20250.

1170. **Your Federal Income Tax, 1972. Edition for Individuals.** 1971. $0.75. T 22.44:972. S/N 4804-0386.

TELEVISION AND RADIO

1171. **Broadcasting Stations of the World Corrected to 1970:**

Pt. 1, Amplitude Modulation Broadcasting Stations According to Country and City. $2.00. PrEx 7.9:970/pt. 1.

Pt. 2, Amplitude Modulation Broadcasting Stations According to Frequency. $2.00. PrEx 7.9:970/pt. 2.

Pt. 3, Frequency Modulation Broadcasting Stations. $1.75. PrEx 7.9:970/pt. 3.

Pt. 4, Television Stations. $2.75. PrEx 7.9:970/pt. 4.

Lists all known radio and television stations except those which broadcast in the United States on domestic channels.

1172. **Can Television Really Teach?** 1969. 8p. il. $0.20. FS 5.234:34044.
Reprinted from *American Education*, August-September 1969.

1173. **Educational Television, The Next 10 Years.** 1965. 375p. il. $1.25.
FS 5.234:34036.

1174. **Instructional Television Facilities, A Planning Guide.** 1969. 73p. il.
$1.00. HE 5.234:34043.
Contains information upon which to base decisions concerning instructional
television for school systems. This guide presents guidelines for planning
and selecting the best facilities.

TRAVEL

1175. **Air-Line Distance Between Cities in the United States.** 1967. 257p.
$1.50. C 4.19:238.

1176. **Customs Guide for Private Flyers.** 1970. 36p. $0.25. T 17.5/2:
F 67/970.

1177. **Fees Charged by Foreign Countries for the Visa of United States
Passports.** 1970. 8p. $0.10. S 1.2:V 82/2/970.
Aimed mainly at U.S. citizens traveling as tourists. Does not reflect adjust-
ments in rates of exchange.

1178. **Health Information for International Travel.** 1970. 16p. $0.10.
HE 20.2302:T 69.
This booklet is designed to assist the traveler in obtaining the required and
recommended vaccinations and prophylactic measures for entering foreign
countries and for returning to the United States. Contains a chart which
shows immunization requirements for entering most countries, as well as
recommended immunizations and other health precautions for international
travel.

1179. **Immunization Information for International Travel, 1967-68.** 1967.
120p. il. $0.40. FS 2.60:Im 6/967-68.
Includes information on vaccination requirements of foreign countries and
the United States, additional immunizations recommended for the traveler's
protection, and the international vaccination centers.

1180. **Information for Passport Applicants.** 1970. 4p. $0.10. S 1.2:P
26/26/970.
Contains information on applying for a passport; executing a passport application; proof of citizenship; identification; passport fees; mutilation and loss of
passports; vaccination and inoculation, and other related subjects.

1181. **Know Before You Go, Customs Hints for Returning U.S. Residents.**
1971. 24p. il. $0.35. T 17.2:C 96/3/971. S/N 4802-0024.
This brochure answers the most commonly asked questions which U.S.
residents have when planning a trip abroad.

1182. United States Customs Hints for Visitors (Non-Residents). 1970. 12p. il. $0.10. T 17.2:C 96/5/970.
Includes general hints about United States customs requirements. Use of these suggestions and information should enable U.S. customs inspectors to complete baggage examinations without delay.

> **—French Edition of above.** $0.10. T 17.2:C 96/5/967/French.
> **—German Edition of above.** $0.10. T 17.2:C 96/5/967/German.
> **—Italian Edition of above.** $0.10. T 17.2:C 96/5/967/Italian.
> **—Spanish Edition of above.** $0.10. T 17.2:C 96/5/967/Spanish.

1183. You and Your Passport. 1970. 14p. $0.10. S 1.69:127/6.
Gives information on application requirements, vaccinations, care of your passport, visas, and getting along abroad.

TRAVEL—HANDBOOKS AND GUIDES

1184. Area Handbooks.
These handbooks are designed for use by persons in need of sociological, political, economic, and military background information on the various countries. Extensive bibliographies note other sources for more detailed information in areas of special interest.

> **Area Handbook for Algeria.** 1970. 519p. il. $3.50. D 101.22: 550-44.
> **Area Handbook for Angola.** 1968. 439p. il. $2.25. D 101.22: 550-59.
> **Area Handbook for the Peripheral States of the Arabian Peninsula.** 1971. 201p. il. 5 maps. $2.50. D 101.22:550-92.
> **Area Handbook for Argentina.** 1969. 446p. il. $3.50. D 101.22: 550-73.
> **Area Handbook for Brazil.** 1971. 645p. il. $4.00. D 101.22: 550-20/2.
> **Area Handbook for Burma.** 1968. 375p. il. $2.50. D 101.22: 550-61.
> **Area Handbook for Burundi.** 1969. 203p. il. $2.75. D 101.22: 550-83.
> **Area Handbook for Cambodia.** 1968. 364p. il. pl. $3.00. D 101.22:550-50/2.
> **Area Handbook for Colombia.** 1970. xiv + 595p. il. $3.75. D 101.22:550-26/2.
> **Area Handbook for Communist China.** 1968. 672p. il. pl. 6 maps. $5.50. D 101.22:550-60.
> **Area Handbook for Congo (Kinshasa).** $3.75. D 101.22: 550-67.

Area Handbook for People's Republic of the Congo (Congo Brazzaville). 1971. 255p. il. $2.50. D 101.22:550-91.

Area Handbook for Costa Rica. 1970. xiv + 323p. $3.00. D 101.22:550-90.

Area Handbook for the Dominican Republic. 1967. 446p. il. $2.25. D 101.22:550-54.

U.S. Army Area Handbook for Germany. 1964. 955p. il. 8 pl. 6 maps. $6.25. D 101.22:550-29.

Area Handbook for Guatemala. 1970. xiv + 361p. il. $3.25. D 101.22:550-78.

Area Handbook for Guyana. 1969. 378p. il. $3.25. D 101.22: 550-82.

Area Handbook for India. 1970. xx + 791p. il. $4.50. D 101. 22:550-21/2.

Area Handbook for Indonesia. 1970. xviii + 569p. il. $4.00. D 101.22:550-39/2.

Area Handbook for Iran. $4.00. D 101.22:550-68.

Area Handbook for Iraq. 1969. 411p. il. $3.50. D 101.22: 550-31.

Area Handbook for Israel. 1970. xvi + 457p. il. $3.50. D 101. 22:550-25.

Area Handbook for Japan. 1969. 628p. il. $4.25. D 101.22: 550-30/2.

Area Handbook for the Hashemite Kingdom of Jordan. 1970. 370p. il. $3.25. D 101.22:550-34.

Area Handbook for Kenya. 1967. 707p. il. $2.25. D 101.22: 550-56.

Area Handbook for the Republic of Korea. 1969. 492p. il. $3.75. D 101.22:550-41/2.

Area Handbook for North Korea. 1969. 481p. il. $3.75. D 101. 22:550-81.

Area Handbook for Laos. 1968. 349p. il. $2.00. D 101.22: 550-58.

Area Handbook for Lebanon. 1969. 352p. il. $3.25. D 101.22: 550-24.

Area Handbook for Liberia. 1966. 418p. il. $3.50. D 101.22: 550-38.

Area Handbook for Libya. 1969. xiv + 307p. il. $3.00. D 101.22:550-85.

Area Handbook for Malaysia. 1970. xvi + 639p. il. $4.00. D 101.22:550-45/2.

Area Handbook for Mongolia. 1970. xvi + 500p. il. $3.75. D 101.22:550-76.

Area Handbook for Morocco. 1969. 459p. il. $3.25. D 101.22: 550-49.

Area Handbook for Mozambique. 1969. 351p. il. $3.25. D 101.22:550-64.

Area Handbook for Nicaragua. 1970. xvi + 393p. il. $3.25. D 101.22:550-88.

Area Handbook for Oceania. 1971. 55p. il. $4.00. D 101.22: 550-94.

Area Handbook for Pakistan. 1965. 607p. il. $3.25. D 101. 22:550-48.

Area Handbook for the Philippines. 1969. 413p. il. $3.50. D 101.22:550-72.

Area Handbook for Rwanda. 1969. 212p. il. $2.75. D 101.22: 550-84.

Area Handbook for Saudi Arabia. 1970. 371p. il. $3.25. D 101.22:550-51.

Area Handbook for Somalia. 1970. 455p. il. $3.25. D 101.22: 550-86.

Area Handbook for the Republic of South Africa. 1971. 845p. il. $4.75. D 101.22:550-93.

U.S. Army Area Handbook for Syria. 1965. 394p. il. $3.50. D 101.22:550-47.

Area Handbook for Tanzania. 1968. 552p. $3.75. D 101.22: 550-62.

Area Handbook for Thailand. 1968. 558p. $4.00. D 101.22: 550-53/2.

Area Handbook for Republic of Tunisia. 1970. xvi + 415p. il. $3.25. D 101.22:550-89.

Area Handbook for Republic of Turkey. 1970. 438p. il. $3.50. D 101.22:550-80.

Area Handbook for Uganda. 1969. 456p. il. $3.50. D 101.22: 550-74.

Area Handbook for the United Arab Republic (Egypt). 1970. xx + 555p. il. $3.75. D 101.22:550-43/2.

Area Handbook for North Vietnam. 1967. 494p. il. $2.50. D 101.22:550-57.

Area Handbook for South Vietnam. 1967. 510p. il. $1.75. D 101.22:550-55.

Area Handbook for Zambia. 1969. 482p. il. $3.75. D 101.22: 550-75.

1185. **Pocket Guides.**
These booklets contain information on the size, political and economic structure, history, ethnic background, and customs of the countries. They include many photographs and illustrations, a long glossary of commonly used words and phrases, and tips on courtesy and conduct to be followed. Designed as a guide for U.S. servicemen stationed in these countries, these

pocket guides will also interest civilians planning travel or those who wish to learn about these countries.

> **Pocket Guide to the Caribbean.** 1966. 78p. il. $0.35. D 2.8: C 19.
> **Pocket Guide to France.** 1964. 42p. il. $0.25. D 2.8:F 84/964.
> **Pocket Guide to Germany.** 1965. 54p. il. $0.45. D 2.8:G 31/965.
> **Pocket Guide to Great Britain.** 1963. 68p. il. $0.30. D 2.8: G 79b/963.
> **Pocket Guide to Greece.** 1966. 50p. il. $0.30. D 2.8:G 81/966.
> **Pocket Guide to Italy.** 1964. 64p. il. $0.40. D 2.8:It 1/964.
> **Pocket Guide to Japan.** 1970. 116p. il. $1.00. D 2.8:J 27/970.
> **Pocket Guide to Korea.** 1970. 106p. il. $1.00. D 2.8:K 84/970.
> **Low Countries [Netherlands, Belgium, and Luxembourg].** 1970. 127p. il. $1.25. D 2.8:L 95/970.
> **Pocket Guide to the Middle East [Iran, Iraq, Israel, Jordan, Lebanon, Libya, Saudi Arabia, the Syrian Arab Republic, and the United Arab Republic].** 1969. 116p. il. $1.00. D 2.8:M 58/969.
> **Pocket Guide to Okinawa.** 1968. 78p. il. $0.45. D 2.8:Ok 3/968.
> **Pocket Guide to the Philippines.** 1968. 84p. il. $0.55. D 2.3: P 53/969.
> **Pocket Guide to Spain.** 1966. 45p. il. $0.40. D 2.8:Sp 1/966.
> **Pocket Guide to Thailand.** 1970. 50p. il. $0.45. D 2.8:T 32.
> **Pocket Guide to Viet-Nam.** 1970. $0.55. D 2.8:V 67.

TREES

See also—Forestry and Forest Products.

1186. Checklist of Native and Naturalized Trees of the United States (including Alaska). 1963. 472p. $3.00. A 1.76:41.
This work, by E. L. Little, is the official standard for tree names in the U.S. Forest Service. It is the only available reference which lists all species of native and naturalized trees in the United States with their correct scientific names and currently used synonyms, approved common names and other names in use, and ranges or natural distirbution.

1187. Christmas Trees, The Tradition and the Trade. 1967. 31p. il. $0.15. A 1.75:94/4.
Gives an historical sketch of the origin of Christmas trees, popular U.S. trees, identifying the principal Christmas trees, location, harvesting, commercial distribution, USDA grades, and other related information.

1188. Color It Green with Trees, A Calendar of Activities for Home Arborists. 1968. 16p. il. $0.20. A 1.68:791/2.

1189. Eastern White Pine. 1971. 4p. il. $0.10. A 13.31:P 65/7/971.
The Eastern white pine has been in great demand in America for more than three centuries. Until 1895 it led all species in lumber production. Contains description and growth of the Eastern white pine, supply, production, characteristics, properties and principal uses.

1190. Engelmann Spruce. 1970. 8p. il. $0.10. A 13.31:Sp 8/3/970.
This spruce, from the Western United States, has many uses. Among them are home construction, plywood manufacture, food containers, pulp and paper. Pamphlet contains description of the growth of the spruce, supply, production, characteristics and properties, and principal uses.

1191. Giant Sequoias of California. $0.25. I 29.2:Se 6/3.
These great trees, often called "nature's forest masterpieces," have long been a source of wonder and amazement to many visitors. This pamphlet vividly describes these age-old trees.

1192. How a Tree Grows. 1970. 8p. il. $0.10. A 13.72:T 71.

1193. How to Buy a Christmas Tree. 1971. 12p. $0.15. A 1.77:189. S/N 0100-1519.
Gives information on the grades and species of Christmas trees, what to look for when buying a tree, and how to care for the tree to insure freshness throughout the holiday season.

1194. Important Forest Trees of the United States. By E. L. Little. 1949. Yrbk. Sep. No. 2156.
Available from Forest Service, U.S. Department of Agriculture, 12th and Independence Avenue, S.W., Washington, D.C. 20250.

1195. Silvics of Forest Trees of the United States. 1965. 762p. il. $5.50. A 1.76:271.
Comprehensive information is given for the major forest trees in the United States, including life histories of 125 tree species, material on soils, which trees will grow in which soils, and climatic conditions under which each species will grow.

1196. Sixty Trees from Foreign Lands. By E. L. Little. 1961. 28p. AH 212.
Primarily for identification, this bulletin presents descriptions and drawings of 60 species of trees introduced from foreign countries and commonly planted in different parts of the United States. Among these trees are some popular for various purposes, such as wood and lumber, shelterbelts, Christmas trees, shade, ornament, street, highway, and landscape planting. Available from Forest Service, U.S. Department of Agriculture, 12th and Independence Avenue, S.W., Washington, D.C. 20250.

1197. **Subdivisions of the Genus Pinus (Pines).** 1969. 51p. il. $0.70. A 1.38:1144.

1198. **To Know Trees, Important Forest Trees of the United States.** 1950. 41p. il. $0.20. A 1.10/a:2156.

1199. **Tree Preservation Bulletins:**

> **Transplanting Trees and Other Woody Plants.** 1969. 59p. il. $0.35. I 29.26:1.
> Shows how to prepare a tree for moving, ready the soil, dig and wrap the roots, and replant. Also discusses choice of plant materials, big-tree moving, methods, and equipment.
> **Tree Bracing.** 1963. 21p. il. $0.15. I 29.26:3.
> Contains modern methods used in tree preservation such as cabling, rod bracing, lag and eyebolt installation, and other related techniques.
> **Shade Tree Pruning.** 1961. 25p. il. $0.15. I 29.26:4.
> Gives the reasons and suggests the most appropriate time for pruning shade trees. This bulletin also describes the different phases of pruning, types of cuts, wound dressing and shaping, branch selection, and required equipment. Pointers on pruning shrubbery are also included.
> **Spraying and Other Controls for Diseases and Insects That Attack Trees and Shrubs.** 1968. 52p. $0.35. I 29.26:6.
> Lists the diseases and insects which attack trees particularly in the eastern United States. Also discusses the precautions to be taken in spraying to avoid injury to plants, harmful effects to wildlife, health hazards to humans, together with spray formulations and preparations.

1200. **Trees for Shade and Beauty, Their Selection and Care.** 1970. 8p. il. $0.10. A 1.77:117/2.
Gives information on selection of trees for beautification of homes and streets. Tells how to plant trees and care for them, and also includes suggestions to civic groups regarding community action in replacing lost shade trees.

1201. **Trees of the Forest, Their Beauty and Use.** 1967. 24p. il. $0.25. A 1.68:613/2.
The story of growing trees and timber in National Forests is presented in this pamphlet. It briefly describes and illustrates the growth and geographic locations of American trees, e.g., Douglas fir, Ponderosa pine, Southern pine, Sugar maple, and White oak. Ten National Forests open to visitor exploration are described in detail.

1202. Useful Trees of the United States Tree Description Sheets.
A series of popular four-page leaflets on 28 common forest trees (Eastern, Southern, and Western). Each has a description with illustrations of the tree, bark, insect enemies, and diseases.

EASTERN

> **Eastern White Pine.** 1-FS-71.
> **Shortleaf Pine.** 5-FS-75.
> **Red Spruce.** 8-FS-78.
> **Eastern Hemlock.** 10-FS-80.
> **Eastern Redcedar.** 13-FS-83.
> **White Ash.** 18-FS-88.
> **American Elm.** 19-FS-89.
> **White Oak.** 20-FS-90.
> **Black Walnut.** 21-FS-91.
> **Yellow Birch.** 22-FS-92.
> **American Beech.** 23-FS-93.
> **Sugar Maple.** 24-FS-94.
> **American Basswood.** 25-FS-95.
> **Black Locust.** 26-FS-96.
> **Yellowpoplar.** 27-FS-97.
> **Sweetgum.** 28-FS-98.

SOUTHERN

> **Eastern White Pine.** 1-FS-71.
> **Longleaf Pine.** 3-FS-73.
> **Shortleaf Pine.** 5-FS-75.
> **Eastern Hemlock.** 10-FS-80.
> **Eastern Redcedar.** 13-FS-83.
> **Baldcypress.** 15-FS-85.
> **White Ash.** 18-FS-88.
> **American Elm.** 19-FS-89.
> **White Oak.** 20-FS-90.
> **Black Walnut.** 21-FS-91.
> **American Beech.** 23-FS-93.
> **Sugar Maple.** 24-FS-94.
> **American Basswood.** 25-FS-95.
> **Black Locust.** 26-FS-96.
> **Yellowpoplar.** 27-FS-97.
> **Sweetgum.** 28-FS-98.

WESTERN

> **Western White Pine.** 2-FS-72.
> **Sugar Pine.** 4-FS-74.

Sub Alpine Fir. 7-FS-77.
Ponderosa Pine. 6-FS-76.
Sitka Spruce. 9-FS-79.
Western Hemlock. 11-FS-81.
Douglas Fir. 12-FS-82.
Western Redcedar. 14-FS-84.
Giant Sequoia. 16-FS-86.
Redwood. 17-FS-87.

TREES—PESTS AND DISEASES

1203. **Cone and Seed Insects of Western Forest Trees.** By F. P. Keen, F.S. 1958. 168p. Tech. Bull. No. 1169.
Available from Forest Service, U.S. Department of Agriculture, 12th and Independence Avenue, S.W., Washington, D.C. 20250.

1204. **Diseases of Shade and Ornamental Maples.** By C. May. 1961. 22p. AH 211.
Available from Forest Service, U.S. Department of Agriculture, 12th and Independence Avenue, S.W., Washington, D.C. 20250.

1205. **Douglas-Fir Beetle.** By J. C. Evenden and K. H. Wright, F.S. 1955. 4p. For. Pest. Lf. 5.
Available from Forest Service, U.S. Department of Agriculture, 12th and Independence Avenue, S.W., Washington, D.C. 20250.

1206. **Dutch Elm Disease and Its Control.** By R. R. Whitten and R. N. Swingle. 1964. 12p. il. $0.10. A 1.75:193.
Discusses Dutch Elm disease, which was unknown in America before the 1930s, and the methods of controlling the spread of the beetle which causes it.

1207. **Internationally Dangerous Forest Tree Diseases.** 1963. 122p. Misc. Pub. No. 939.
Available from Forest Service, U.S. Department of Agriculture, 12th and Independence Avenue, S.W., Washington, D.C. 20250.

1208. **Maple Diseases and Their Control, A Guide for Homeowners.** 1970. 8p. il. $0.10. A 1.77:81/4.

UNITED STATES—GENERAL

1209. **America the Beautiful [colored posters].** 1966. $5.00/set of 52. A 57.8/2:set.
A U.S. Department of Agriculture Soil Conservation Service series of 52 full-color lithographs (20 x 24 in.) representing each state plus Puerto Rico and the Virgin Islands.

1210. Facts about the United States. 1964. 35p. il. $0.25. D 2.14:GEN-13.
An up-to-date source of information on the land and the people, the government, natural resources, the arts, living standards, foods and housing, health
and medical care, education, social security, labor and labor unions, American women, youth, recreation, religion, and fields of activity—agriculture,
electric power, manufacturing, industries, communications, transportation,
foreign trade, and science.

**1211. Our American Government, What Is It? How Does It Function?
185 Questions and Answers, A Comprehensive Story of the History and
Functions of Our American Government Interestingly and Accurately
Portrayed.** 1971. xvi + 45p. $0.35. 92-1:H.Doc. 31.

1212. Our Flag. 1970. 33p. il. $0.50. 91-2:H.doc. 209.
Full-color pictures of early American flags and full-color reproductions of
the 50 states and the District of Columbia flags highlight this booklet.
Brief notes on various early American flags, the complete story of the
stars and stripes, instructions on displaying the flag, and approved flag
customs are included.

1213. Territorial Areas Administered by the United States. 1971. 25p. il.
$0.20. I 35.2:T 27/2/971.
Gives a brief description of the offshore areas which are administered by the
Department of the Interior. Also included are references to other outlying
areas under U.S. control which are under the administration of other departments, and islands of disputed ownership.

1214. United States Government Organization Manual 1971/72. 1971.
809p. il. $3.00. GS 4.109:971. S/N 2203-0887.
This official organization handbook of the federal government describes the
creation and authority, organization, and functions of the agencies in the
legislative, judicial, and executive branches; provides supplemental information including brief descriptions of quasi-official agencies and selected
international organizations. Included in most agency statements are new
"Sources of Information" listings which tell the public what offices to
contact for information on such matters as consumer activities, environmental programs, government contracts, services to small businesses, employment, and the availability of speakers and films for educational and civic
groups. Also included are approximately 45 charts showing the organization
of the government, the Senate, the House of Representatives, the departments,
and the major independent agencies; a literal print of the Constitution of the
United States, its signers, and amendments to date; an alphabetical listing
of names mentioned in the Manual; and a comprehensive index.

**1215. Where to Write for Birth and Death Records, United States and Out-
lying Areas.** 1970. 9p. $0.15. HE 20.2002:B 53/970.
Gives complete details on how to obtain birth or death certificates or other
records which may prove birth facts. Information includes chart, by states,

showing cost of full copy, cost of short form or birth card, address of vital statistics office, and date of original records.

1216. Where to Write for Marriage Records, United States and Outlying Areas. 1971. 6p. $0.15. HE 20.2002:M 34/970.
Provides addresses of vital statistics offices where marriage records can be obtained. This booklet also includes information on the cost of records, data on how far back the records go in the offices, and other general facts helpful in obtaining these records.

UNITED STATES—ARMED FORCES

1217. American Military History. 1969. 701p. il. $8.00. D 114.2:M 59.
This one-volume history of the United States Army in peace and war from its beginnings in 1775 through its operations in Vietnam in 1967 is the latest work to be published by the Army's Office of the Chief of Military History. In addition to its 28 chapters, the volume contains numerous maps and photographs, a bibliography, and a comprehensive index designed to satisfy both the casual reader and the dedicated Army history buff.

1218. American Ships of the Line. 1970. 44p. il. $0.50. D 207.10/2:Sh 6/4.
This publication provides a historical narrative on the development of these ships and contains the authorizing acts in chronological order, followed by individual ship historical sketches.

1219. Armed Forces Insignia. 1969. 37 x 26 in. $0.25. D 2.9:2B.
A poster displaying the insignia for the commissioned officers and enlisted men of the U.S. Army, Navy, Air Force, and Marine Corps.

1220. The Battleship in the United States Navy. 1970. 64p. il. $0.65. D 207.10/2:B 32.

1221. Before You Enter the Army. 1971. 39p. il. $0.25. D 101.22:608-32.
This pocket-sized pamphlet is designed to answer the questions a soldier and his family may have about beginning Army service. A special tear-off sheet is included to be kept for reference by the family.

1222. Civil War Naval Chronology, 1861-65:

> **Pt. 1, 1861.** 1961. 41p. il. $0.25. D 207.2:C 49/pt. 1.
> **Pt. 2, 1862.** 1962. 117p. il. $0.60. D 207.2:C 49/pt. 2.
> **Pt. 4, 1864.** 1964. 151p. il. $0.75. D 207.2:C 49/pt. 4.
> **Pt. 5, 1865.** 1965. 149p. il. $0.75. D 207.2:C 49/pt. 5.
> **Pt. 6, Special Studies and Cumulative Index.** 1966. 477p. il. $2.50. D 207.2:C 49/pt. 6.

1223. A Concise History of the United States Marine Corps, 1775-1969. 1971. x + 143p. il. $1.25. D 214.13:M 34/2/775-969. S/N 0855-0050.
Presents in concise form the full sweep of the history of the Marine Corps

through narrative, art, and photographs. It highlights significant events and provides an extensive guide for further and more detailed reading.

1224. Dictionary of American Naval Fighting Ships:
An alphabetical arrangement of the ships of the Continental and U.S. Navies, with an historical sketch containing pertinent information on each one.

> **Vol. 1, A-B.** 1970. 351p. il. $5.00. D 207.10:1.
> **Vol. 2, C-F.** 1969. 591p. il. $6.50. D 207.10:2/rep.
> **Vol. 3, G-K.** 1968. 876p. il. $6.00. D 207.10:3.
> **Vol. 4, L-M.** 1969. 745p. il. $7.50. D 207.10:4.

1225. Marine Corps Combat Art Collection.
These reproductions, suitable for framing, were made from original paintings in the U.S. Marine Corps Combat Art Program.

> **Marine Corps Combat Lithographs.** 1968. 16 color prints /set, each 16 x 20 in. or 20 x 16 in. $2.75/set. D 214.16:C 73.
> **Marine Corps Combat Art:**
> **Series III A.** 1970. 8 color prints/set, each 16 x 20 in. or 20 x 16 in. $2.25/set. D 214.16:C 73/no. 3A.
> **Series III B.** 1970. 8 color prints/set, each 16 x 20 in. $2.25/set. D 214.16:C 73/no. 3B.

1226. Marine Corps Reserve, A History. 1966. 311p. $3.50. D 214.13: R 31/2.

1227. Marine Troop Leaders Guide. 1971. 410p. il. $2.25. D 214.9/4: 1-2/2. S/N 0855-0058.
Presents a checklist of basic duties for troop leaders at the platoon, section, squad, and fire team level in combat operations.

1228. Medal of Honor, The Navy, 1861-1949, "Above and Beyond the Call of Duty." 1950. 327p. il. pl. $4.00. D 201.2:M 46/861-949.

1229. Naval Aviation in World War I. 1969. 90p. il. $1.25. D 207.10/2: Av 5/2.

1230. Our Navy in Action.
A series of color lithographs depicting some of the highlights of U.S. Naval history from the Revolutionary War through the Korean Conflict. These pictures, which are suitable for framing, include a famous quotation related to the specific action pictured as well as a descriptive caption placing each event in our nation's history. The name of the artist, the medium, and the location of the original painting also appear on the fact of each print.

> **Series 1.** 1968. Portfolio of 12 color lithographs, each 16 x 20 in. or 20 x 16 in. $2.50. D 207.10/2:N 22.
> **Series 2.** 1969. 12 color lithographs, each 16 x 20 in. $3.00. D 207.10/2:N 22/no. 2.

1231. **The Pentagon.** 1968. 16p. il. $0.10. D 101.55:2/4.
Virtually a city in itself, the Pentagon, headquarters of the Department of
Defense, is the world's largest office building. Contains photographs and
many interesting facts about the Pentagon.

1232. **Report of the President's Commission on an All-Volunteer Armed
Force.** 1970. 211p. $1.25. Pr 37.8:Ar 5/R 29/970.

1233. **Space and the United States Navy.** 1970. 80p. il. $1.75. D 207.2:
Sp 1. S/N 0846-0042.
Prepared by the editors of *Naval Aviation News*, this publication contains a
number of illustrated articles depicting the U.S. Navy and its role in space.

1234. **Submarine in the United States Navy.** 1969. 25p. il. $0.40. D 207.
10/2:Su 1/969.

1235. **Uniforms of the United States Navy.**
A series of color lithographs, 16 x 20 in., depicting the history of naval
uniforms, both officer and enlisted man, from 1776-1967. These pictures,
which are suitable for framing, are enclosed in a portfolio along with a
booklet that provides the historical background of the uniforms presented
in each picture.

>   **1776-1898.** 1966. Text of 13 leaves, issued in portfolio with
>   12 lithographs. $3.50. D 207.10/2:Un 3.
>   **1900-1967.** 1967. Text of 14 leaves, issued in portfolio with
>   12 lithographs. $3.50. D 207.10/2:Un 3/900-967.

1236. **United States Army Installations and Major Activities in the Continental United States.** 1970. 17p. $0.30. D 101.22:210-1/25.
Contains a list of Army installations and major activities, limited to depots,
hospitals and industrial activities. One listing is alphabetical showing the
post office address of each installation or activity; the other is an alphabetical
listing within each U.S. Army Area and the Military District of Washington,
U.S. Army, showing the location of each installation or activity at that
installation.

1237. **United States Naval Aviation, 1910-1970.** 1971. 440p. il. $4.00.
D 202.2:Av 5/2/910-70. S/N 0841-0059.
Gives a chronological record of significant events in Naval Aviation's
growth and development from its beginning in 1910 through December 1970.

1238. **United States Naval History, A Bibliography.** 1969. 33p. il. $0.35.
D 207.11:H 62/969.
This brief bibliography is designed to assist students and researchers in the
selection of titles on naval history. It covers Naval history by periods;
Marine Corps history; Coast Guard history; and special subjects such as civil
affairs and military government, diplomacy and foreign relations, ships,
aircraft and armament, and strategy and tactics.

1239. U.S. Naval History Sources in the Washington Area and Suggested Research Subjects. 1970. v + 82p. il. $1.00. D 207.6/2:H 62/970. S/N 0846-0044.
This publication identifies archival, manuscript, and other special collections in the Washington area. Specific information on individual collections is given, as well as descriptions of the repositories.

1240. U.S. Navy Diving Manual. 1970. 687p. il. $7.25. D 211.6/2:D 64/970.
Reflecting new developments and current procedures in the diving field, this manual includes information on the general principles of diving, surface-supplied diving, self-contained diving, first aid and emergency procedures, and diving accessories.

UNITED STATES—CENSUS BUREAU

1241. Do You Know Your Economic ABC's? Uncle Sam Counts, The Story of the Census '70. 1969. 48p. il. $0.35. C 1.2:Un 1.

1242. Fact Finder for the Nation. 1970. 62p. il. $1.25. C 3.2:C 33/13/970.
This booklet describes the development of the Bureau of the Census, the methods the Bureau uses, the facts it collects, the way the data are used, the special facilities and services available, and the organization of the Bureau.

UNITED STATES—CIVIL SERVICE

1243. Career in the Foreign Service of the United States. 1969. 24p. il. $0.50. S 1.69:132/3.

1244. Careers in Psychiatry in the U.S. Public Health Service. $0.30. FS 2.22:P 95/8/968.

1245. Careers in the U.S. Department of Commerce, An Equal Opportunity Employer. 1970. 100p. il. $1.00. C 1.2:C 18/970.
Lists the wide variety of employment opportunities within the Department. Economists, patent examiners, statisticians, engineers, oceanographers and meteorologists are among the almost 1,000 college-trained people employed annually. Career fields are described briefly; also describes what this Department does, explains the role of offices and bureaus, and indicates where and how the Department uses specific degree majors.

1246. Careers in the U.S. Department of the Interior, A Directory for College Students. 1970. 71p. il. $0.50. I 1.73/2:3/2.

1247. Civil Service Retirement System. 1970. 8p. il. $0.10. CS 1.59:3/11.

1248. Employment Outlook:
Reprints from the 1970-71 *Occupational Outlook Handbook.*

> Government (except Post Office). $0.15. L 2.3:1650-127.
> Includes civilian employment in federal government, state
> and local governments, and the Armed Forces.
> Post Office Occupations, Mail Carriers, Postal Clerks. $0.15.
> L 2.3:1650-128.

1249. Engineering Career for You in the Soil Conservation Service. 1965.
12p. il. $0.10. A 1.38:715/3.

1250. Federal Career Service at Your Service, An Introduction to the
Federal Personnel System, 1969. 1968. 24p. il. $0.30. CS 1.2:C 18/4/969.

1251. Federal Careers for Women. 1967. 14p. il. $0.10. CS 1.48:35/7.

1252. Federal Jobs Overseas. 1970. 12p. il. $0.10. CS 1.48:BRE-18/2.
This pamphlet explains how jobs are filled, discusses conditions of employment, indicates the kinds of skills agencies use, and lists addresses to which
inquiries may be sent.

1253. The Foreign Service of the Seventies. 1970. 36p. il. $0.60. S 1.69:
142. S/N 4400-1311.
The Foreign Service is broadening its recruitment base in the 1970s in
response to the needs for increasingly specialized competence in our foreign
relations at all levels. This pamphlet presents some appealing career profiles
in administration, economics, political, and public affairs within the Foreign
Service.

1254. Guide to Federal Career Literature. 1969. 32p. $0.55. CS 1.61:C 18.

1255. In Public Practice, Lawyers in the Federal Government. 1970. 15p.
il. $0.20. CS 1.48:69/3.
Describes opportunities for lawyers and law students in the federal government. Also, positions which require legal background but not bar membership are discussed. Information on how to apply and a list of federal agencies
are included.

1256. A Job with the Forest Service, A Guide to Non-Professional Employment. 1970. 18p. il. $0.15. A 1.38:843/9.
Discusses what the Forest Service does; professional and nonprofessional
jobs in the Forest Service; the types of programs that train you for these
positions; salaries; and eligibility.

1257. Key People, Careers in Education with Your Federal Government.
1969. 20p. il. $0.25. CS 1.48:73/2.
Tells how working for the federal government offers the opportunity to follow
a particular interest within a broad framework of programs and locations at
home and abroad.

1258. Prepare Yourself for Postal Examination, Mail Handler, Distribution
Clerk, Mail Carrier. 1969. 129p. il. $1.25. CS 1.28:2450-R.

1259. **Preparing for the Federal Service Entrance Examination, Sample Questions and Suggestions on How to Do Your Best When You Take the Test.** 1966. 16p. il. $0.20. CS 1.7/4:F 31.

1260. **Profiles, Careers in the U.S. Department of Agriculture.** 1968. 196p. il. $3.25. A 1.38:1071.

1261. **Public Service Careers, Jobs and Advancement in Public Agencies.** 1969. 8p. il. $0.10. L 1.2:P 96/5.

1262. **Science and Engineering Careers in Government, Descriptions of Beginning Jobs for Young People.** 1967. 21p. $0.30. CS 1.2:Sci 2/5/967.

1263. **Scientific Careers in the Agricultural Research Service.** 1969. 35p. il. $0.55. A 1.38:798/5.

1264. **These Are Yours.** 1970. 16p. il. $0.15. VA 1.19:05-27/2.
Provides a description of employment benefits for government employees, including salary, cash for ideas, vacations, financial protection against sickness and unemployment, life and health insurance, retirement, and survivor benefits. For more specific information on retirement, see:
>   **What's New in Retirement, Questions and Answers About**
>   **Recent Changes in the Civil Service Retirement System.**
>   1971. 15p. $0.10. CS 1.2:R 31/7. S/N 0600-0500.

1265. **Working for the Bureau of Outdoor Recreation.** 1971. 8p. il. $0.25. I 66.2:W 80.
This booklet discusses the career opportunities with the Bureau and the requirements necessary for such careers, explains the training opportunities and benefits available, and lists the location of the headquarters and regional offices.

1266. **Working for the U.S.A., Applying for a Civil Service Job, What the Government Expects of Federal Workers.** 1970. 37p. il. $0.20. CS 1.48: 4/18.

UNITED STATES—COMMERCE DEPARTMENT

1267. **The United States Department of Commerce, Serving a Growing Economy and a Growing People.** 1970. 36p. il. $0.70. C 1.2:C 73/ 10:970. S/N 0300-0297.
This booklet describes the services provided by the Department to the economy and to the general public.

UNITED STATES—CONGRESS AND THE PRESIDENT

1268. **Congress, the President, and the War Powers.** 1970. vi + 601p. $2.50. Y 4.F 76/1:C 76/9.
Presents hearings concerning the proper roles of Congress and the President in exercising the war-making powers of our national government.

1269. **Congressional District Atlas (Districts of the 92d Congress).** 1970. 220p. il. $1.75. C 3.62/5:970. S/N 0301-0142.
This atlas presents maps showing boundaries of the congressional districts for the 92d Congress of the United States. The maps are arranged in alphabetical order by states. In addition, this atlas includes listings of the congressional district or districts in which counties and specified cities are located and provides an alphabetical list of the counties in each congressional district.

1270. **Congressional Pictorial Directory, January 1971, 92nd Congress.** 1971. 202p. il. $2.75. Y 4.P 93/1:1P/92. S/N 5270-0568.
Contains photographs of President Richard M. Nixon, Vice President Spiro T. Agnew, officials of the Senate, House, and Capital, and Members of Congress, by states. Also includes a list of the state delegations, and alphabetical lists of the Senators, Representatives, and Resident Commissioner, showing home post office and political alignment.

1271. **Congressional Record.** (Daily while Congress is in session.) Subscription price: $1.50/month (for subscription purposes, 20 daily issues constitute a month). X/a:(Cong.)
Contains a verbatim official report of the debates and other proceedings of the open sessions of Congress. Subscriptions are accepted for one or more months, at any time during the session. Discounts are not allowed on this subscription.

1272. **Documents Relating to the War Power of Congress, the President's Authority as Commander-in-Chief and the War in Indochina.** 1970. 252p. $1.00. Y 4.F 76/2:In 2/6.
The Senate Committee on Foreign Relations has initiated an inquiry into the division of constitutional authority between the Congress and the President respecting military operations amounting to an exercise of the power of the United States to make war. These documents have been compiled to facilitate the discussion of matters relating to the war power.

1273. **Enactment of a Law, Procedural Steps in the Legislative Process.** 1967. 29p. $0.20. 90-1:S.doc. 34.
Describes the steps necessary to pass a bill from its introduction through its final enactment into law.

1274. **Franklin D. Roosevelt and Hyde Park, Personal Recollections of Eleanor Roosevelt.** 1969. 18p. il. $0.20. I 29.2:R 67/2.

1275. **Inaugural Addresses of the Presidents of the United States.** 1969. 279p. il. $1.50. 91-1:H.doc. 142.
This volume contains a collection of the Presidential inaugural addresses, from President George Washington's first inaugural address, April 30, 1789, to President Richard Milhous Nixon's address on January 20, 1969. A small picture of each of the Presidents is presented, including the four Presidents who did not make inaugural addresses.

1276. Majority and Minority Leaders of the Senate, History and Development of the Offices of the Floor Leaders. 1970. 19p. $0.15. 91-2:S.doc. 53.

1277. Presidential Inaugurations, A Selected List of References. 1969. 230p. il. $2.00. LC 2.2:P 92/3/969.

UNITED STATES—CONSTITUTION AND RELATED DOCUMENTS

1278. Bill of Rights. 1958. 33 x 31 in. $0.45. GS 4.11/2:B 49.
This is a facsimile of the enrolled original of the Bill of Rights, which is now in the National Archives in Washington.

1279. Constitution of the United States of America, Analytical Index, Unratified Amendments. 1967. 72p. $0.25. 90-1:H.doc. 124.
Contains the text of the Constitution and all 25 amendments, together with the dates of ratification, information regarding the proposed amendments that were never ratified by the states, and a detailed analytical index of the Constitution and the 25 amendments with references to articles, sections, and clauses.

1280. The Declaration of Independence. 1958. 35 x 29 in. $0.45. GS 4.11/2:D 37.
The original Declaration of Independence is now on permanent display in the National Archives. This facsimile is reproduced in the yellowish tint and faded brown ink of the original document.

1281. Documents Illustrative of the Formation of the Union of the American States. 1927, repr. 1965. 1115p. il. $7.50. 69-1:H.doc. 398.
This collection of documents on the origin and development of our constitutional history presents, under one cover, the most significant documents relative to the formation of the American Federal States. Among these documents are the Declaration of Independence, the Articles of Confederation, the Constitution of the United States, the first 19 amendments to the Constitution, notes and papers of such well-known figures in American history as Alexander Hamilton, James Madison, and others.

1282. Passage and Ratification of the Twenty-Sixth Amendment, Report of Constitutional Amendments Subcommittee. 1971. 29p. $0.20. Y 4.J 89/2: T 91.
The twenty-sixth amendment lowering the voting age to 18 became a part of the Constitution on July 1, 1971. This document provides a concise history of the legislative development, the passage by Congress, and the ratification by the states of this important Constitutional amendment.

UNITED STATES—COURTS

1283. The Supreme Court of the United States. 1961. 8p. il. $0.05. Ju 6.2:Su 7/2/961.

Tells about the U.S. Supreme Court and its work and describes the U.S. Supreme Court Building. Photos of the Justices are inserted.

1284. **The United States Courts, Their Jurisdiction and Work.** 1971. v + 15p. il. $0.15. Y 4.J 89/1:C 83/6/971. S/N 5270-1019.
This handbook explains in concise form just what the judicial branch is, and describes the system of courts clearly and briefly.

UNITED STATES—HISTORY

See also—Indochina War; Korean War; United States—Armed Forces; World War II.

1285. **The American Civil War; A Selected Reading List.** 1960. 24p. $0.25. LC 2.2:C 49/5.

1286. **The American Revolution, A Selected Reading List.** 1968. 38p. $0.50. LC 1.12/2:R 32.

1287. **America's Oldest Legislative Assembly and Its Jamestown State-houses.** 1956. 46p. il. $0.30. I 29.52:2/2.

1288. **Appomattox Court House National Historical Park, Virginia.** $0.10. I 29.21:Ap 6/2.

1289. **Bureau of Engraving and Printing, A Centennial History 1862-1962.** 1964. 199p. il. $7.00. T 18.2:H 62/2/862-962.
Recounts the background of getting the Bureau firmly established, of the almost half-century span of opposition to the Bureau's very existence, and of the numerous investigations it has undergone. Includes some 70 illustrations of other products, printing and processing activities, and production equip-ment—both old and new.

1290. **The Capitol, Symbol of Freedom, A Pictorial Story of the Capitol in General and the House of Representatives in Particular [Omnibus of the Capitol].** 1966. 120p. il. $0.50. 89-1:H.doc. 260.
This book provides a view of American tradition. Includes scenes from various Presidential inaugurations; State of the Union addresses; portraits or photographs of those elected Speaker of the House of Representatives since 1789; scenes of various Presidents and foreign notables addressing the Congress; photographs of other government buildings in the Capital City, and a wide range of interesting, timely information and pictures con-cerning the operation of Congress.

1291. **Colonials and Patriots.** 1964. 320p. il. $2.75. I 29.2:H 62/9/v. 6.
This volume deals with great "outdoor archives" of American history as found in historic sites and structures. *Colonials and Patriots* has two parts. The first offers a brief historical background for the period 1700-1783 in Ameri-can history. The second represents the major contribution made in this

work. It consists of classified, carefully evaluated descriptions of historic places that should be visited by anyone who wishes to become acquainted with American history. Photographs are included, as well as the locations of many of the historic sites mentioned.

1292. **Custer Battlefield National Monument, Montana.** 1969. 93p. il. $1.25. I 29.58:1/3.
This handbook provides photographs, illustrations, and historical information on Custer's Last Stand and the monument which now commemorates that event.

1293. **Explorers and Settlers.** 1968. 506p. il. $3.50. I 29.2:H 62/9/v. 5.
This illustrated volume describes our European heritage and traces the extension of the Old World into the New. During the era of discovery, exploration, and settlement, a colorful procession of explorers, conquistadors, missionaries, and other settlers came to these shores. In the course of time, they amalgamated their diverse cultures and nationalities into a distinctive American civilization. The volume also describes 256 historic sites in 38 states, Puerto Rico, and the Virgin Islands.

1294. **Fort Sumter National Monument, South Carolina.** 1962. 47p. il. $0.35. I 29.58:12/2.

1295. **Founders and Frontiersmen.** 1967. 410p. il. $3.00. I 29.2:H 62/9/ v. 7.
This book recounts the struggles and achievements of the Founding Fathers and early frontiersmen during the critical, formative years between 1783 and 1828. A brief background narrative outlines the major historical events. The volume also describes 134 historic sites in 28 states and the District of Columbia—extending from the Atlantic coast to the first tier of states in the trans-Mississippi West.

1296. **George Washington Carver.** 1970. 12p. il. $0.10. SI 3.2:C 25. S/N 4701-0104.
Briefly describes the life of George Washington Carver and how he strove to ease the burdens of the poor in America.

1297. **Gettysburg National Military Park, Pennsylvania.** 1962. 50p. il. 13 pl. $0.40. I 29.58:9/2.

1298. **Golden Spike.** 1969. 62p. il. $0.60. I 29.58:40.
This centennial edition of the *Golden Spike*, which includes a number of interesting photographs, discusses the origin and building of the Pacific Railroad and describes the Great Railroad Race—the dash to Promontory— and the driving of the last spike.

1299. **A Guide to the Study of the United States of America.** 1960. 1193p. il. $7.00. LC 2.2:Un 3/4.
This is one of the most comprehensive bibliographies on the subject. Material is arranged in 32 chapters describing approximately 10,000 books that

reflect the historical development of the United States. All entries have long annotations, and the work is well indexed.

1300. **James Towne in the Words of Contemporaries.** 1955. 36p. il. $0.20. I 29.50:5/2.
A presentation of excerpts and selections from records, laws, accounts, and descriptions made by men who lived in or were associated with "James Towne."

1301. **The Louisiana Purchase.** 1967. 21p. il. $0.15. I 53.2:L 93/967.
An historical sketch from the files of the old General Land Office, a predecessor of the Bureau of Land Management.

1302. **National Register of Historic Places, 1969.** 1969. xiv + 352p. il. $5.25. I 29.76:969.
The National Register is a current listing of over 1,100 historic properties owned, preserved, and managed by city, county, state, federal, and private agencies and individuals throughout the United States and its territories as of June 30, 1969. Each entry provides name, address, date, and an historical description, including present condition.

1303. **Our Flag.** 1970. 33p. il. $0.50. 91-2:H.doc. 209.
Filled with many historical facts, this pamphlet relates the story of the flag, includes notes on various early American flags, full-color pictures of these flags, and gives instructions on displaying the flag. A colorful reproduction of our present 50-star flag graces the cover of this pamphlet. It also includes full-color reproductions of each flag for the 50 states and the District of Columbia.

1304. **Periodical Literature on the American Revolution, Historical Research and Changing Interpretations, 1895-1970.** 1970. iv + 93p. $1.00. LC 2.2: Am 3/3/895-970. S/N 3001-0040.
A representative list of studies that have appeared during the past 75 years in historical journals, festschriften, and collections of lectures or essays.

1305. **Popular Names of U.S. Government Reports, A Catalog.** 1970. v + 43p. $0.55. LC 6.2:G 74/970. S/N 3005-0004.
Contains a selection of significant reports published as early as 1821 and reports appearing after 1965. Many of the 753 reports of U.S. executive, legislative, and judicial bodies cited here are important documents in U.S. history and are primary sources for research. The reports in the catalog are arranged alphabetically by popular name.

1306. **Prospector, Cowhand, and Sodbuster.** 1967. 320p. il. $3.00. I 29.2: H 62/9/v. 11.
This work describes more than 200 sites and buildings in 18 western states that illustrate or commemorate our western heritage and also provides a background narrative. The site descriptions include information on location, ownership and administration, historical significance, and present appearance.

1307. **Statue of Liberty National Monument, N.Y., Liberty Island, N.Y.**
1961. 40p. il. $0.35. I 29.58:11/2.

1308. **Where a Hundred Thousand Fell, The Battles of Fredericksburg, Chancellorsville, the Wilderness, and Spotsylvania Court House.** 1966. 56p. il. $0.70. I 29.58:39.

1309. **The White House.** $0.10. I 29.21:W 58/4.
Briefly gives the history of the White House, home of the President of the United States, and describes the main rooms of this famous home.

1310. **Yorktown, Climax of the Revolution.** 1956. 26p. il. $0.20. I 29.50:1.

UNITED STATES—POSTAL SERVICE

1311. **National ZIP Code Directory, 1971-72.** 1971. $10.00. S/N 3900-0233.
This directory enables the user to determine the ZIP Code for every mailing address in the nation. ZIP Code listings are arranged alphabetically by state. Within each state a complete listing is given of all post offices, stations, and branches with the appropriate five-digit ZIP Code for each delivery area. An appendix after each state gives the ZIP Code for each address in the larger cities. Also in this directory are: a ZIP Code area map; a listing of two-letter state abbreviations; a listing of Sectional Center Facilities; ZIP Code prefixes by state; a numerical list of post offices by ZIP Code; and a listing of postal units discontinued.

1312. **Neither Snow, Nor Rain, The Story of the United States Mails.** 1970. 99p. il. $1.25. SI 1.2:M 28.
The story begins with the origins of the postal service in ancient times, about 4,000 years ago. It continues with an account of the methods of postal communication through the early Egyptian, Chinese, and Roman eras, to Medieval Europe and to Colonial America, through the Civil War years, World Wars, and up to the present day. The story of the development of the mail service is part of the story of the development of the nation as a whole, from colonial postrider to steamship and stagecoach, train, and airplane. Illustrations accompany the text.

1313. **State Postal Maps:**
    Alabama, Jan. 1, 1969. Scale 50 mi.=4 in. 1969. 22 x 32 in.
        $0.35. P 1.39/2:Al 1b/969.
        Inset: Birmingham and vicinity.
    Alaska. Being revised. P 1.39/2:Al 1s.
    Arizona. Scale 60 mi.=5 in. 1966. 40 x 33 in. $0.35. P 1.39/2:
        Ar 4i.
    Arkansas, Dec. 1, 1968. Scale 50 mi.=4 in. 1969. 26 x 28 in.
        $0.35. P 1.39/2:Ar 4k/968.

California-Nevada (Northern section), Feb. 1, 1969. Scale
50 mi.=2 in. 1969. 32 x 22 in. $0.35. P 1.39/2:C 12/969.
California-Nevada (Southern section), Feb. 1, 1969. Scale
50 mi.=2 in. 1969. 32 x 22 in. $0.35. P 1.39/2:C 12/2/969.
Insets: San Francisco and vicinity, Los Angeles and vicinity.
Colorado. Scale 30 mi.=3 in. 1966. 36 x 52 in. $0.35. P 1.39/2:
C 71.
Inset: Denver area.
Florida, Mar. 1, 1968. Scale 40 mi.=3 in. 1969. 32 x 23 in. $0.35.
P 1.39/2:F 66/968.
Georgia. $0.35. P 1.39/2:G 29/969.
Hawaii and Islands of the Pacific Ocean. Scale 25 mi.=5 in.
July 1, 1966. 29 x 42 in. $0.35. P 1.39/2:H 31.
Insets: Guam Island, Wake Island, Caroline and Marshall
Islands, and American Samoa.
Idaho. $0.35. P 1.39/2:Id 1/969.
Illinois. July 1, 1969. Scale 40 mi.=3 in. 1969. 32 x 22 in. $0.35.
P 1.39/2:Il 6/969.
Insets: Chicago, East St. Louis and vicinity.
Indiana, Sept. 1, 1969. Scale 30 mi.=3 in. 1969. 32 x 20 in.
$0.35. P 1.39/2:In 2/969.
Iowa. $0.35. P 1.39/2:Io 9/969.
Kansas. $0.35. P 1.39/2:K 13/969.
Kentucky. Scale 30 mi.=4.2 in. 1966. 30 x 59 in. $0.35.
P 1.39/2:K 41.
Inset: New Madrid.
Louisiana, Dec. 1, 1968. Scale 40 mi.=3 in. 1969. 25 x 29 in.
$0.35. P 1.39/2:L 93/968.
Maine. Scale 30 mi.=4.5 in. 1966. 51 x 35 in. $0.35. P 1.39/2:
M 28.
Insets: Portland and vicinity, Bath and vicinity.
Maryland, Delaware and the District of Columbia, Nov. 1, 1968.
Scale 25 mi.=3 in. 1969. 22 x 32 in. $0.35. P 1.39/2:M
36/968.
Insets: District of Columbia and vicinity; Baltimore and
vicinity.
Massachusetts, Rhode Island and Connecticut. Dec. 1, 1969.
Scale 25 mi.=3 in. 1969. 26 x 32 in. $0.35. P 1.39/2:M
38/969.
Inset: Boston and vicinity.
Michigan, June 1, 1969. Scale 40 mi.=3 in. 1969. 32 x 22 in.
$0.35. P 1.39/2:M 58/969.
Inset: Detroit and vicinity.

Minnesota, May 1, 1969. Scale 40 mi.=3 in. 1969. 32 x 26 in. $0.35. P 1.39/2:M 66/969.

Mississippi, June 1, 1969. Scale 40 mi.=3 in. 1969. 32 x 22 in. $0.35. P 1.39/2:M 69 i/969.

Missouri. Scale 40 mi.=4.4 in. 1966. 36 x 46 in. $0.35. P 1.39/2:M 69o.
Insets: St. Louis and vicinity, Kansas City and vicinity.

Montana. Scale 70 mi.=5.8 in. 1966. 34 x 52 in. $0.35. P 1.39/2:M 76.

Nebraska, Jan. 1, 1969. Scale 40 mi.=3 in. 1969. 18 x 32 in. $0.35. P 1.39/2:N 27/969.
Inset: Omaha and vicinity.

New Hampshire and Vermont. $0.35. P 1.39/2:N 42h/969.

New Jersey, Nov. 1, 1968. Scale 15 mi.=3 in. 1968. 32 x 21 in. $0.35. P 1.39/2:N 42j/968.
Insets: Newark, Jersey City area.

New Mexico. Oct. 1, 1969. Scale 60 mi.=4 in. 1969. 31 x 26 in. $0.35. P 1.39/2:N 42m/969.

New York (Eastern section). $0.35. P 1.39/2:N 42y/969.

New York (Western section). $0.35. P 1.39/2:N 42y/2/969.
Insets: Greater New York and adjoining counties, New York City.

North Carolina, Mar. 1, 1968. Scale 50 mi.=4 in. 1969. 21 x 32 in. $0.35. P 1.39/2:N 81c/968.

North Dakota. $0.35. P 1.39/2:N 81d/969.

Ohio, July 1, 1969. Scale 40 mi:=4 in. 1969. 32 x 25 in. $0.35. P 1.39/2:Oh 3/969.
Insets: Cincinnati and vicinity, Cleveland and vicinity.

Oklahoma. Scale 50 mi.=5 in. 1966. 41 x 36 in. $0.35. P 1.39/2:Ok 4.

Oregon, May 1, 1969. Scale 40 mi.=3 in. 1969. 32 x 25 in. $0.35. P 1.39/2:Or 3/969.
Inset: Portland and vicinity.

Pennsylvania (Eastern section), Aug. 1, 1969. Scale 20 mi.=3 in. 1969. 29 x 25 in. $0.35. P 1.39/2:P 38/969.
Insets: Philadelphia and vicinity and Pittsburgh and vicinity.

Pennsylvania (Western section), Aug. 1, 1969. Scale 20 mi.=3 in. 1969. 29 x 25 in. $0.35. P 1.39/2:P 38/2/969.

South Carolina. Scale 50 mi.=6.4 in. 1966. 33 x 41 in. $0.35. P 1.39/2:So 8c.

South Dakota, Mar. 1, 1969. Scale 50 mi.=4 in. 1969. 32 x 24 in. $0.35. P 1.39/2:So 8d/969.

Tennessee, Mar. 1, 1969. Scale 30 mi.=2 in. 1969. 32 x 12 in. $0.35. P 1.39/2:T 25/969.

Texas (Eastern section), Apr. 1, 1969. Scale 50 mi.=3 in. 1969.
32 x 22 in. $0.35. P 1.39/2:T 31/969.

Texas (Western section), Apr. 1, 1969. Scale 40 mi.=2 in. 1969.
32 x 22 in. $0.35. P 1.39/2:T 31/2/969.

Utah. $0.35. P 1.39/2:Ut 1/969.

Virginia. Sept. 1, 1969. Scale 30 mi.=3 in. 1969. 32 x 20 in.
$0.35. P 1.39/2:V 81/969.

Washington. $0.35. P 1.39/2:W 27/969.
Inset: Seattle and vicinity.

West Virginia. $0.35. P 1.39/2:W 52v/969.

UNITED STATES—SELECTIVE SERVICE SYSTEM

1314. **The Draft Lottery and How It Works.** By Betty M. Vetter, Executive
Director, Scientific Manpower Commission. 1970. p. 18-22. Free.
This is a reprint of an article in *Occupational Outlook Quarterly*, Summer
1970. The bill amending the draft law was signed by President Nixon on
November 26, 1969. This publication describes the new regulations to
govern the selection method and explains the new system and its implications for young men planning their education and careers. Available from
U.S. Department of Labor, Bureau of Labor Statistics, Washington, D.C.
20212.

1315. **Legal Aspects of Selective Service.** 1969. 90p. $1.00. Y 3.Se 4:
2L 52/969.

1316. **Selection Service System, Its Concept, History and Operation.** 1967.
37p. $0.30. Y 3.Se 4:2Se 4/3.

1317. **Selective Service News.** (Monthly.) Subscription price: $1.00/yr.
Y 3.Se 4:20/vols.
A medium of information between National Headquarters and other com-
ponents of the Selective Service System.

1318. **You . . . and the Draft.** 1967. 6p. $0.05. Y 3.Se 4:2D 78.
The law under which the Selective Service System operates requires that
every young American man, within five days after his eighteenth birthday,
register with his local Selective Service Board; be aware of his responsibilities
under the law; and perform these responsibilities as ordered by his local board.

UNITED STATES—STATE DEPARTMENT

1319. **Your Department of State.** 1970. 16p. il. $0.15. S 1.69:124/5.
Presents information on how the Department of State works, what it does,
and other miscellaneous facts about the Department. Foreign policy goals
are also briefly listed.

UNITED STATES—STATISTICS

1320.   **Directory of Federal Statistics for States, 1967.** 1968. 380p. $2.25.
C 3.6/2:St 2/3.
This directory is a tabular guide to sources of current (1960 and later) socioeconomic data for individual states published by federal agencies. It contains
detailed summaries of types of information to be found in more than 700
publications.

1321.   **Historical Statistics of the United States, Colonial Times to 1957.**
1960. 789p. il. $6.00. C 3.134/2:H 62/957. **—Continuation to 1962 and
Revisions.** 1965. 154p. $1.00. C 3.134/2:H 62/957/cont. 962.

1322.   **Pocket Data Book USA, 1971.** $1.75. C 3.134/3:971. S/N 0301-
1731.
This is the third edition of this popular reference book issued by the U.S.
Department of Commerce, Bureau of the Census. Over 300 pages of tables
presenting current, authoritative statistics on all major facets of the economic
and social structure of the United States—population, education, health,
government, prices, labor, income, welfare, defense, recreation, agriculture,
industry, science, etc.

1323.   **Population Trends in the United States, 1900 to 1960.** 1965. 416p.
il. $2.25. C 3.212:10.

1324.   **Statistical Abstract of the United States, National Data Book and
Guide to Sources:**

> **1967.** 1050p. il. $4.00. C 3.134:967.
> **1968.** 1034p. il. $4.75. C 3.134:968.
> **1969.** 1032p. il. $5.75. C 3.134:969.
> **1970.** 1018p. il. $5.75. C 3.134:970.
> **1971.** $5.50. C 3.134:971.

The Statistical Abstract is traditionally the most authoritative, comprehensive
one-volume collection of the latest facts and figures on the economic, political, and social structure of the United States. From more than 200 different sources—federal agencies, private research groups and individuals, and
international organizations—come the "figures" that go into this unique
reference book. Some of the major subjects covered in compact summary
form through the more than 1,300 tables, charts, and maps are: agriculture,
business, education, employment, foreign trade, geography, health, military
services, population, recreation, veterans' affairs, world economy, and many
others. There are also sections on Historical trends, Explanatory text for
each section, A guide to statistics sources (including state statistical abstracts),
A description of other major Census Bureau publications, Weights and
measures, and a detailed index.

1325. **Statistical Services of the United States Government.** 1968. 156p.
pl. in pocket. $1.50. PrEx 2.2:St 2/968.
Designed to serve as a basic reference document on the statistical programs of
the U.S. government, this booklet describes the statistical system of the
federal government; presents brief descriptions of the principal economic and
social statistical series collected by the government agencies; and contains a
brief statement of the statistical responsibilities of each agency and a list
of its principal publications.

UNITED STATES—VETERANS

1326. **Federal Benefits for Veterans and Dependents.** 1970. 66p. il. $0.30.
VA 1.34:IS-1/13.

1327. **Reemployment Rights of Federal Employees Who Perform Duty in
the Armed Forces.** 1970. 7p. $0.10. CS 1.48:51/9.

1328. **Veterans' Reemployment Rights Handbook.** 1970. 196p. $1.00.
L 25.6/2:V 64/970.
Designed to assist those who are concerned with the reemployment rights of
veterans, this handbook covers such subjects as an explanation of just who is
eligible for reemployment rights; applying for reemployment; applicant's
qualifications; change in employer's circumstances; position to be offered
and rate of pay to be provided; seniority rights, and duration of rights;
vacations, and disabled applicants. At the conclusion of the text of each
subject, several examples are given which clearly explain the subject matter.

URBAN LIFE

1329. **Beauty in the Urban Environment, How Federal Urban and Housing
Aids Can Make Cities and Suburbs More Attractive.** 1965. 8p. il. $0.20.
HH 1.2:B 38.

1330. **Book About Space.** 1968. 52p. il. $0.75. TD 2.102:Sp 1.
This publication pictorially traces the evolution of highway development—its
origins, its role as an early answer to urban America's growth, and its new
potential as a basic tool for shaping our cities to be as useful and comfortable
as their citizens demand and deserve.

1331. **Changes in Urban America 1969.** 44p. Rpt. 353.
Available from the Bureau of Labor Statistics, U.S. Department of Labor,
Washington, D.C. 20212.

1332. **Cities in Crisis, The Challenge of Change.** 1967. 47p. il. $0.55. FS
14.2:C 49/2.

1333.   **The Model Cities Program, A Comparative Analysis of the Planning Process in Eleven Cities.** 1970. 72p. il. $0.65. HH 1.2:M 72/6. S/N 2300-0171.
Presents a detailed comparative analysis of the initial Model Cities planning period for Atlanta, Georgia; Cambridge, Massachusetts; Dayton, Ohio; Denver, Colorado; Detroit, Michigan; Gary, Indiana; Pittsburgh, Pennsylvania; Richmond, California; Rochester, New York; San Antonio, Texas. The publication illustrates the difficulties the cities had in responding to the program's planning requirements, and defines the reasons for these difficulties; and offers an initial and tentative frame of reference wherein choices can be made and the results predicted by HUD and cities concerning alternate Model Cities planning and action strategies.

1334.   **The Quality of Urban Life.** 1970. 773p. il. 16 pl. $5.00. Y 4.B 22/1: Ur 1/4/pt. 2.
Presents hearings to examine the environmental and sociological quality of urban living in the United States.

1335.   **60 Books on Housing and Urban Planning.** 1966. 19p. $0.20. HH 1.28:2.

1336.   **A Time to Listen, A Time to Act, Voices from the Ghettos of the Nation's Cities.** 1967. 133p. il. $0.45. CR 1.2:T 48.
Provides insights into what slum residents think and feel about the conditions in which they live.

1337.   **Urban Outlook, Selected Bibliography of Films, Filmstrips, Slides, and Audiotapes.** 1969. 38p. $0.45. HH 1.28:95.

1338.   **Urban Public Transportation, Selected References.** 1966. 20p. $0.20. HH 1.28:3.

1339.   **Urban Renewal: One Tool Among Many, The Report of the President's Task Force on Urban Renewal.** 1970. 15p. $0.20. Pr 37.8:Ur 1/R 29.
This report discusses problems affecting a successful urban renewal program, such as its low rating for federal attention. It also discusses the objectives of urban renewal, specific recommendations for the Urban Renewal Program, and recommendations covering other matters closely related to the Urban Renewal Program.

VEGETABLES

See—Fruits and Vegetables.

VIETNAM WAR

See—Indochina War.

WATER

1340. **Directory of Information Resources in the United States, Water.**
1966. 248p. $1.50. LC 1.31:D 62/3.

1341. **Has the United States Enough Water?** 27p. il. $2.25. I 19.13:1797.
Estimates total natural water supply and amount available in 19 major
drainage basins; projects current water demand to 2000 A.D.; suggests
possible courses of action for optional use. Includes three water-supply maps.

1342. **Manual for Evaluating Public Drinking Water Supplies.** 1969. 62p. il.
$0.40. FS 2.6/2:W 29/6.

1343. **New Water.** 1970. 36p. il. $0.60. I 1.2:W 29/4/970.
Provides general information concerning the history, activities, and objectives
of the Department of the Interior's program to develop economical processes
for the conversion of sea or brackish waters to fresh for the purpose of
conserving and increasing the water resources of the nation.

1344. **A Practical Guide to Water Quality Studies of Streams.** 1970. 135p.
il. $0.70. I 67.8:St 8.

1345. **A Primer on Ground Water.** 26p. il. $0.25. I 19.2:W 29/6.
Popularized, yet authoritative, booklet on nature of ground water, occurrence
throughout the United States, and importance in the water cycle.

1346. **A Primer on Water Quality.** 28p. il. $0.30. I 19.2:W 29/9.
Guide to understanding what constitutes water purity, unusual properties of
water, and how water is affected by nature and man.

1347. **Reservoirs in the United States.** 1966. 115p. $1.00. I 19.13:1838.

1348. **River of Life, Water: The Environmental Challenge.** 1970. 96p. il.
$2.00. I 1.95:6.
This full-color book presents the story of water and its hydrologic cycle,
the environmental challenge and how we have mismanaged water. It shows
water-rich and water-poor areas of America, discusses the creation of more
fresh water, fish, wildlife and people, water for recreational purposes, and
how water works for man.

1349. **Your Water Supply and Forests.** 1971. 17p. il. $0.15. A 1.75:305/3.
S/N 0100-0646.
Discusses water and watersheds, how watersheds work, some benefits we get
from them, what we must guard against, and what we can do to insure safe
and dependable water supplies.

WATER SAFETY

See also—Boating

1350. Drownproofing Can Save Your Life. 1966. 4p. il. $0.05. A 1.68:777.
Illustrates drownproofing, a method of keeping yourself afloat for hours even if you can't swim. Also illustrated is a combined drownproofing and travel stroke which enables an individual to move several miles through water without tiring.

1351. Overboard with Chest Waders, Hip Boots, or Rain Gear. 1970. 5p. il. $0.10. C 55.314:635. S/N 0320-0005.
Neither chest waders, hip boots, nor rain gear will cause you to drown if you don't panic. Waders, the most dreaded of the three, can actually be the safest. These facts should be of particular interest to sportsmen, commercial fishermen, and biologists.

1352. Pool Drownings and Their Prevention. 1967. 14p. Free. 7700-009.
Principal causes of pool fatalities, selection and construction of barriers against trespass, and safety in pool design and operation are investigated. Available from Consumer Product Information, Washington, D.C. 20407.

1353. Safety Tips In, On, and Around Water. 1967. 4p. il. $0.05. FS 2.6/2:Sa 1.
A wallet-sized illustration of safety tips for swimming and boating enthusiasts plus a drownproofing technique which could save your life.

WEEDS

See also—Poisonous Plants.

1354. Common Aquatic Weeds. 1969. 43p. il. $0.50. A 1.76:352.

1355. Lawn Weed Control with Herbicides. 1968. 24p. il. $0.20. A 1.77: 123/2.

1356. Selected Weeds of the United States. 1970. 463p. il. $4.00. A 1.76: 366.
Illustrates and describes many of the important weeds in the United States and indicates their geographical distribution in this country. The 224 species of weeds included in this handbook are some of the prevalent weeds in croplands, grazing lands, noncroplands, and aquatic sites.

1357. Suggested Guide for Weed Control, 1969. 1969. 70p. $0.70. A 1.76: 332/969.

1358. Wild Hemp (Marijuana), How to Control It. 1970. 8p. il. $0.10. A 1.68:959.
This leaflet describes what wild hemp looks like, how it can be controlled and precautionary measures to be taken in the use of chemicals for its control. Illustrations show the plant in various stages of growth.

WEIGHTS AND MEASURES

1359. **Brief History and Use of the English and Metric Systems of Measurement, With a Chart of the Modernized Metric System.** 1969. 4p. il. $0.20. C 13.10:304A/2.

1360. **Do You Know Your Economic ABC's? Measurement, Pacemaker of American Economic Growth, A Simplified Explanation of the Role Measurement Plays in our National Economy.** 1967. 31p. il. $0.25. C 1.2:M 46.

1361. **Household Weights and Measures.** 1960. 11 x 8.5 in. [Wall card, printed on both sides.] $0.10. C 13.10:234.
The purpose of this card is to present in convenient form the weights and measures tables most useful for household purposes, together with associated weights and measures information of general household interest.

1362. **The International System of Units (SI).** 1971. v + 39p. $0.50. C 13. 10:330. S/N 0303-0756.
This publication contains resolutions and recommendations of the General Conference of Weights and Measures on the International System of Units.

WOMEN

Included in this section are general works about women, women's rights, and women in the work force. For further information on women in the labor force, write Women's Bureau, Department of Labor, Washington, D.C. Information about women as homemakers is available from the Department of Agriculture and the Children's Bureau of the Department of Health, Education and Welfare.

For related information, *see also—Labor* and *Occupations.*

1363. **Background Facts on Women Workers in the United States.** 1970. 20p. $0.30. L 13.2:W 89/12.
Discusses number, age, marital and family status, occupation and industry, and earnings of women workers.

1364. **Changing Patterns of Women's Lives.** 1970. 6p. il. $0.05. L 13.2: W 84/43/970.
A girl today can anticipate a very different way of life from that of her grandmother or even her mother. This brochure gives a brief description of a revolution that has taken place in the life patterns of women and girls.

1365. **Handbook on Women Workers, 1969.** 1969. 384p. il. $1.50. L 13.3:294.
This handbook assembles factual information covering the participation and characteristics of women in the labor force, the patterns of their employment, their occupations, income, and earnings, education and training, and the federal and state laws affecting civil and political status and employment.

1366. **Job Training Suggestions for Women and Girls.** 1970. 15p. il. $0.15. L 13.11:40/3.
Gives a brief summary of job training opportunities available to women and girls and indicates various kinds of facilities offering such training.

1367. **Labor Legislation for Women Workers: 50 Years of Progress.** 1970. Available from Women's Bureau, U.S. Department of Labor, Washington, D.C.

1368. **Laws on Sex Discrimination in Employment, Federal Civil Rights Act, Title VII, State Fair Employment Practices Laws, Executive Orders.** 1970. 20p. $0.30. L 13.2:Em 7/10/970.
This publication is a compilation of legislation, executive orders, and state provisions which have been issued with regard to job equality for women.

1369. **A Matter of Simple Justice, The Report of the President's Task Force on Women's Rights and Responsibilities.** 1970. 33p. $0.30. Pr 37.8:W 84/R 29.

1370. **Underutilization of Women Workers.** 1971. 25p. il. $0.35. L 13.2: W/89/11/971.
Briefly describes the statements and charts documentary aspects of the underutilization of women workers. It is hoped that these highlights on the economic position of women workers may prove helpful in efforts to assure more effective use of our national resource of womanpower.

1371. **Who Are the Working Mothers?** 1970. 4p. il. $0.10. L 13.11:37/9.
Provides information on the status of working mothers and on the factors that motivate them to seek paid employment.

1372. **Women College Graduates: Will They Find Jobs?** *Occupational Outlook Quarterly*, Fall 1970. 11p. Free.
Two of every five women in professional jobs are teachers. However, the changing supply-demand situations in individual professional occupations during the 1970s suggests that unless women enlarge the range of occupations for which they prepare, outlook for women college graduates may be less favorable than in recent years. Available from Bureau of Labor Statistics, U.S. Department of Labor, Washington, D.C. 20212.

1373. **Women in 1970, Citizens' Advisory Council on the Status of Women.** 1971. 23p. $0.40. Y 3.In 8/21.2W 84.
Discusses many subjects of concern to improve the status of women, including equal legal rights, maternity leave for employed women, equal employment opportunity, part-time employment, child development programs, and occupational counseling of young girls and mature women seeking to return to the labor market. Also endorses and discusses the proposed equal rights amendments to the Constitution.

1374. **Women Workers Today.** 1970.
Discusses personal and employment characteristics. Available from Women's Bureau, U.S. Department of Labor, Washington, D.C.

1375. **Women—Their Social and Economic Status; Selected References.**
41p. Free.
Available from The Library, U.S. Department of Labor, Washington, D.C.

WORLD WAR II

1376. **The Ardennes: Battle of the Bulge.** By H. M. Cole. 1965 720p. maps.
$7.50. D 114.7:Eu 7/v. 8.
The German winter counteroffensive from jump-off on 16 December 1944
until Allied armies were ready to eliminate the bulge in their lines in early
January 1945 is here related. German plans and Allied reaction are described
in detail.

1377. **At Close Quarters.** 1962. 579p. il. $4.75. D 207.10/2:Q 2.
This volume covers the origin and development of the PT boat. It describes
the main operations of these craft. A complete list of all PT boats and
appendices listing PT personnel wounded, killed, and receiving awards are
included.

1378. **Chronology: 1941-1945.** Comp. by Mary H. Williams. 1960. 660p.
$4.75. D 114.7:C 46.
The chronology is primarily one of tactical events from the attack on Pearl
Harbor on 7 December 1941 to the signing of the instrument of surrender on
the *Missouri* on 2 September 1945, with emphasis on ground action of U.S.
armed forces. Air and naval cooperation, combat actions of foreign units—
both Allied and enemy—and general events of world-wide interest are
detailed within the scope of space limitations. Well indexed.

1379. **Combat Squadrons of the Air Force World War II.** 1969. 841p. il.
$8.25. D 301.26/6:C 73/2.
This collection of squadron histories has been prepared by the USAF Historical Division. Each squadron is traced from its beginning through March 5,
1963, the fiftieth anniversary of the organization to the First Aero (later
Bombardment) Squadron, the first Army unit to be equipped with aircraft
for tactical operations. For each squadron there is a statement of the official
lineage and date on the unit's assignments, stations, aircraft and missiles,
operations, service streamers, campaign participation, decorations, and
emblem.

1380. **The Corps of Engineers: The War Against Japan.** By Karl C. Dod.
1966. 759p. maps. $5.50. D 114.7:En 3/v. 2.
In the Pacific the Engineers had an enormous construction task in areas
ranging from northwest Canada to Australia, and as diverse as primitive
islands and highly industrialized metropolises. Engineer activities in each
major area, with particular emphasis on those in General MacArthur's
Southwest Pacific Area, are described.

1381. **Cross-Channel Attack.** By Gordon A. Harrison. 1951. 519p. maps. $6.75. D 114.7:Eu 7/v. 2.
An introduction to the tactical volumes of the subseries on the European theater, this volume covers (in seven chapters) the prelude to the assault of June 6—the preparations and discussions of strategy on both the Allied and the German sides from 1941 to 1944—and describes (in three chapters) the combat operations of the First U.S. Army in Normandy from D-Day to July 1, 1944.

1382. **The Employment of Negro Troops.** By Ulysses Lee. 1966. 740p. $10.00. D 114.7:N 31.
A Negro scholar and officer tells in detail the story of how the Army employed Negro troops before and during World War II and describes the combat experiences of Negro units in the Mediterranean, European, and Pacific theaters.

1383. **End of the War in the Pacific, Surrender Documents in Facsimile.** 1945. 24p. il. $0.30. AE 1.2:Su 7.

1384. **The Fall of the Philippines.** By Louis Morton. 1953. 626p. maps. $8.50. D 114.7:P 11/v. 4.
The three-month defense of Bataan, the siege of Corregidor, the soldier's life in the crowded intimacy of Malinta Tunnel, MacArthur's evacuation, and the surrender of 78,000 men are all described in detail in this account of the biggest military disaster suffered by U.S. forces in World War II.

1385. **Germany Surrenders Unconditionally, Facsimiles of the Documents.** 1945. 41p. il. $0.30. AE 1.2:Su 7.

1386. **Guadalcanal: The First Offensive.** By John Miller, Jr. 1949. 413p. maps. $4.00. M 103.7:P 11/v. 2.
The story of the first victory on the long road to Tokyo is one of a comparatively small number of units operating in a restricted area; it has thus been possible to carry the narrative down to the level of companies, platoons, and even individuals. This volume shows the contribution of all services to this victory and the relationship between air, ground, and surface forces in modern warfare.

1387. **History of U.S. Marine Corps Operations in World War II:**

> **Central Pacific Drive.** 1967. 685p. il. 8 maps attached to inside of back cover. $7.25. D 214.13:W 89/v. 3.
> **Victory and Occupation.** 1969. 945p. il. 11 maps attached to inside of back cover. $11.75. D 214.13:W 89/v. 5.

1388. **Master Index: Reader's Guide II.** 1960. 145p. $1.50. D 114.7/2:2.
This publication provides a brief analytical description of each of the first 53 volumes published in the series "United States Army in World War II." An interim revision of the Reader's Guide is planned for 1971. When the entire series is complete, a Master Index will be prepared, covering every volume.

1389. **Okinawa: The Last Battle.** By Roy E. Appleman, James M. Burns, Russell A. Gugeler, and John Stevens. 1948. 529p. maps. $8.50. D 114.7: P 11/v. 1.

The price paid for Okinawa was dear. The final toll of American casualties was the highest experienced in any campaign against the Japanese. The cost of the battle to the Japanese was even higher. The story of the last battle of World War II is vividly told by U.S. Army historians who accompanied American forces to the Ryukyus.

1390. **Pearl Harbor, Why, How, Fleet Salvage, and Final Appraisal.** 1968. 377p. il. $4.00. D 207.10/2:P 31/2.

1391. **Salerno to Cassino.** By Martin Blumenson. 1969. 491p. maps. $9.50. D 114.7:M 46/2/v. 3.

The story of operations in Italy is carried from the invasion of the Italian mainland near Salerno through the winter fighting and up to the stalemate in the battles for Monte Cassino (including the Rapido River crossing) and in the Anzio beachhead.

1392. **The War Against Germany: Europe and Adjacent Areas.** 1951. 448p. $6.00. D 114.7:P 58/v. 2.

The build-up in the United Kingdom and the Normandy, Northern France, Rhineland, Ardennes-Alsace, and Central Europe campaigns are illustrated.

1393. **The War Against Germany and Italy: Mediterranean and Adjacent Areas.** 1951. 465p. $6.25. D 114.7:P 58/v. 1.

Some 450 pages of photographs with explanatory text graphically portray various aspects of the war in North Africa and the Middle East, Sicily, Corsica, and Sardinia; and Italy and southern France.

1394. **The War Against Japan.** 1952. 471p. $6.25. D 114.7:P 58/v. 3.
The conflict in the Pacific, from pre-Pearl Harbor training in Hawaii to Allied landings in the Japanese home islands, is depicted. Included is a section of the China-Burma-India theater.

INDEX

Entries in this index are primarily to subjects, both specific and general. For those works which may be popularly known by the title, however, title entries are also made. Please note that the numbers in the index refer to entry numbers in the text. But, since all titles in a series are assigned only one entry number, a page reference is also provided for individual works listed under a series—e.g., Artists, commercial, 960 (p. 129).